PRAISE

"The only way to become a customer-centric company of the future is to change old practices and mindsets. In *Journey to Centricity*, Ilenia shares valuable insights and best practices for any company wanting to put their customers at the centre while also making a positive economic, social and environmental impact."
—MASSIMILIANO POGLIANI, CEO at illycaffè

"In *Journey to Centricity*, Ilenia Vidili not only outlines why it is so important to become more customer-centric, she also provides practical ways to create a customer-centric organisation. Her lucid explanations and examples bring the new age of customer capitalism to life."
—ROB MARKEY, Senior Partner at Bain & Company and co-creator of the Net Promoter System®

"Ilenia Vidili points out important and urgent tasks for all business leaders to act in the interests of their stakeholders. Her fresh approach to customer centricity is a clear movement towards the necessary focus on sustainable business and customers' increasing demand for it. Every business leader should read this book!"
—MARCO GAZZINO, Head of Innovability® at Enel X

"All leaders are ultimately responsible for achieving results. This book shares practical examples and best practices, helping leaders across the world to become better. *Journey to Centricity* is full of insights into how to inspire and engage employees, retain customers and increase revenue."
—VICTORIA ROOS OLSSON, Senior Leadership Consultant at FranklinCovey

"*Journey to Centricity* gives a fresh and powerful message for timeless topics of this business era. By combining best practice from the world's top organisations with extensive research, this book will help you better understand how to be the disrupters of the future."
—TIM HELDMANN, Former CMO at Polestar

"As a customer experience leader, I've learned the hard way how difficult it can be to drive customer experience initiatives within an organisation without the right mindset. In her book, Ilenia Vidili proposes a significant transformation of the way business gets done. A transformation that is not only about the strategy but more about changing mindsets, behaviours, structures, culture and old practices that don't favour a customer-centric environment."

—SUSANNA BAQUÉ, Senior Director Global Customer Experience at SCIEX

"The world is ever changing, and customers continuously demand that businesses change with it. This book can help you understand how the world of business is changing, why it's changing, and what you need to do about it. A must-read!"

—ANDREA ISOLA, General Manager at N26 Italy and Southeast Europe

"In her book, customer centricity fellow Ilenia Vidili delivers a new lens for leaders to view their customers with empathy – the foundation for sustainable customer-centric approach."

—ALEX ALLWOOD, customer experience authority and author of *Customer Empathy*

"*Journey to Centricity* isn't just a book – it's a blueprint to become the customer-centric company of the future. It's impossible to read this book and not creating value for all stakeholders. A must-read!"

—STEVE SPIRO, CEO at Halotherapy Solutions

"In *Journey to Centricity*, Ilenia Vidili offers a visionary perspective on this new phase in stakeholder capitalism. Her book explains why the old and stale capitalism has not been working and why we need a better understanding of the technology-driven social economics that is now taking root – one that creates value for all stakeholders."

—DANIEL ARAYA, Senior Fellow at the Centre for International Governance Innovation (CIGI)

"In *Journey to Centricity*, Ilenia Vidili clearly and concisely uses real-life examples to illustrate how organisations of all sizes can successfully move from their theoretical understanding of what it means to be customer-centric to actually being customer-centric. Readers will understand the importance of having and living an organisational purpose, leading with empathy, adopting positive and considerate mindsets, elevating the experiences people have, and, ultimately, becoming a force for good in a world that desperately needs more care."
—LARA KHOURI, Founder of There Is No Spoon CX, EX & Change Leadership Training and Consulting

"As new generations of consumers, employees and businesses enter the scene, making their mark on the world and shaping how people want to be treated, Ilenia Vidili's *Journey to Centricity* is more relevant than ever. This book is a must-read in a landscape that never stays the same and where businesses are undergoing massive disruptions."
—LISA DANCER, customer experience expert

"Thorough and thought-provoking, *Journey to Centricity* packs all key concepts to either be introduced or re-inspired by customer centricity. If all this is new to you, it will feel like drinking from a fountain on a hot day. If you already know your way around, you're still in for a discovery of new value models, stakeholder capitalism, innovation and sustainability. Bottom line is that by the time you reach The Bottom Line chapter, Ilenia will have guided you on an eye-opening journey to customer centricity, and you'll be happy you went along."
—ANA LUISA ROMERO, Organizational Design Manager at Univercells

JOURNEY TO CENTRICITY

A CUSTOMER-CENTRIC FRAMEWORK FOR THE ERA OF STAKEHOLDER CAPITALISM

ILENIA VIDILI

TABLE OF CONTENTS

YOU MUST READ THIS BEFORE STARTING YOUR JOURNEY

"Oh, come on. You've got to be joking. It's clearly a duck!"
"What do you mean it's a duck? It's a cute rabbit! Can't you see the long ears?"
"There is no way that's a cute rabbit. It's an old duck with a long bill!"
"Are you guys blind?"

The argument went back and forth. I first saw the iconic duck-rabbit image during a university lecture. Our lecturer used psychologist Joseph Jastrow's illusion image to demonstrate that one's perception does not represent a full picture of reality.[1] Most students who looked at the left side of the image saw a duck, while those looking at the right side saw a rabbit; others saw both.

Our perception is the lens from which we view people, experiences and things. The lessons from the duck-rabbit illusion can also apply to the business world. Businesses suffer from the clash between *how they think they do business* and *what the rest of the world thinks of them;* that is to say, the *inside world perspective* versus the *outside world perspective.* In other words, most customers see a duck, while businesses see a rabbit.

Customer experience (CX) is a widely discussed topic around the globe. It has been said that the term *customer experience* was mentioned over a million times across social media channels in 2020. Every business talks about it, but not everyone agrees about which components are the most crucial. Some think that customer experience involves simply customer service, or optimising the customer journey, while others think that they can just plug in flashy software and miraculously provide a good customer experience.

For the purposes of this book, I will define customer experience as *the subjective perception that every individual customer has of your brand across all stages of their interaction – pre-purchase, during purchase and post-purchase.* It is what customers feel, think and perceive while trying to satisfy their needs or wants through your brand. The sum of these emotions, sensations and impressions determines whether they want to engage as a customer with your brand – to potentially become a repeat customer. If their experience is positive, they'll be left with a good, long-lasting impression, whereas a negative experience could leave them running from your brand forever.

The customer journey, on the other hand, is a series of interactions that occur as the customer tries to reach a specific goal. For years, businesses have focussed on mapping customer journeys, creating voice of the customers programmes, and providing positive customer experiences – which continue to be essential elements of the customer experience toolbox. Customer experience initiatives, when executed correctly, can indeed result in great outcomes.

But too many companies narrowly define themselves as customer-centric as a result of optimising a set of touchpoints and/or delivering one positive experience. Likewise, many CEOs around the world say that they care about their customers. In fact, I dare you to find a CEO who doesn't.

These acts are rarely enough to build a truly strong and consistent customer-centric company that fosters ongoing loyalty and brand evangelism. Why? Because these leaders are still stuck in their product mentalities, siloed procedures and excessive focus on short-term results, distracted from the need to become customer-centric. The events within boardrooms are so far from the frontline – and from the customer. Running a company from the perspective of revenue, costs and sales performance clouds the view of customer relationships – and makes it very hard to maximise their health and value.

Delivering a good, positive experience once, twice or even occasionally also doesn't make you a customer-centric business. There are many companies that provide outstanding experiences, but they are not customer-centric. Why? Because they don't sustain those great customer experiences. They don't have a customer-centric approach and culture embedded into their overall strategy.

Today, customer centricity is the driving force that most organisations have yet to embrace. The opportunity for these leaders lies in realigning the future of their businesses to effectively engage with customers throughout their life cycle.

With this book, I want to take you on a journey where you'll not only be inspired as a leader to improve your *customer experiences*, but also to incrementally improve their *human experiences.* Human experiences consider customers not as mere users but as human beings with values and beliefs, with emotions and purpose.

There is not one model for how customer-centric companies will operate in the future. Every company is different, so some aspects of this book may apply to your business, and others may not. I will help you consider both *the duck* and *the rabbit*, as you explore the topic. In other words, I will help you set aside preconceived perception biases or reactive impressions, and focus on what research, best practices, generational mindsets and a futurist's perspective can tell us about how to optimise customer centricity. I will approach the topic from a holistic view, providing a complete picture of all components that, in my view, comprise customer centricity. It will be up to you which ones to prioritise in your own transformation.

Keep in mind that becoming customer-centric is not an overnight fix. But it is my hope that your journey to centricity, as I will call it, becomes as easy as reading this book; I have done my best to structure it clearly. The road to customer centricity it's hard, but the results for your business will be worthy.

HOW THIS BOOK WILL BENEFIT YOU

To help you see your business from the perspective of your customers, I want to share with you a framework that you can use in your journey to centricity. You'll be inspired to follow this path to become truly customer-centric. This journey will help you abandon old processes and thinking, and adopt the necessary approaches to succeed.

In every chapter, you'll be encouraged to leverage the single most valuable assets you have: your people and your customers. You'll understand how consumer behaviour and expectations, especially those of Millennials and Generation Z, are shaping the very fabric of society and business. As a Millennial myself, and the sister of a Gen Z, I want to help you explore how these two generations are disrupting the world of business. I want to share what you can do to engage with that disruption in a productive and powerful way.

I also want to inspire you to combat inefficient processes, product mentalities and lack of customer focus. My biggest ambition is to make your business relevant in the era of stakeholder capitalism. *Journey to Centricity* will challenge you to start asking uncomfortable questions such as *why*, *how* and *who*. It will help you craft a more human brand – one that customers want to engage with and include as their life partner.

The book is powered by three main pillars: *humanity, technology,* and *culture.* Each pillar dives deeply into three elements, where I share experiences, knowledge and viewpoints.

Humanity. This pillar explains the "why". It is the pillar by which your brand finds its mission and reason for being alive. It's also the pillar by which your brand becomes more human with its customers, through using an empathic human touch and sustainable corporate responsibility. Ensuring that your company *does what it says* will earn trust, build a strong purpose, foster authenticity, and therefore ensure relevance.

Technology. This pillar reasons the "how"–specifically how customer-centric companies use the necessary technologies as enablers for delivering their customer experiences. This pillar will explore how you can use product innovation, ease of use and hyper-personalisation to improve the buying experience and the lives of your consumers.

Culture. This pillar discusses the "who", and dives into how your company must transform its culture to become a customer-centric business of the future. Investing in this process fortifies your brand, and creates a place where employees feel motivated, valued and appreciated. To achieve this transformation, leaders must invest time and effort in changing the old-style mindset and silo structures.

Perhaps you're wondering why I'm so passionate about customer centricity. Before quitting corporate life, I worked as a marketer for various multinationals, in both business-to-consumer (B2C) and business-to-business (B2B) worlds. Every day, I would notice that the gaps between customers and companies, employees and customers, and employees and their leaders were far too wide. These gaps form naturally, because when we start working for organisations, we have to adhere to rules, processes and targets that force us to forget how human we are.

Over the past few years of my entrepreneurial journey, when talking to business leaders and C-level executives, I've noticed that the gaps don't seem to get any narrower. The more I travel, visit clients and speak at conferences packed with executives of all levels of seniority, the more I see where businesses actually stand in society today. The gaps remain, and solutions are needed to close them.

In my role as an international advisor, I am typically hired as an outsider by companies who want to see both internal and external perspectives, and to become *truly* customer-centric. This book is driven by a huge need to share my ideas with you, to prompt change in how companies do business, and consequently to prompt change in the world.

By the way, you'll read the word "change" quite a lot, because this is where any journey should start - with the desire to transform.

WHY AND HOW I WROTE THIS BOOK

Writing my first book felt like the hardest challenge ever. The amount of perseverance, discipline and focus required over the last year has been incredible. Not to mention the butterflies in my tummy and the emotions I feel by presenting to you the proudest piece of my professional and personal life so far.

What pushed me to finish the book is my passion for customer centricity, which ties into my strong mission. My mission is to see a better future, where companies:

- embrace a higher purpose;
- create value to all stakeholders;
- contribute to society by taking their social responsibility seriously; and
- show us all a better business world.

I started the research long before COVID-19, while on trains around Europe, in conference centres in London, in boardrooms in Singapore, and in various coworking spaces around Southeast Asia. I have been inspired in Bali, enlightened in New York, and, finally, saddened in Italy seeing the world crumbling due to an apparently innocuous virus. I am now writing this book in my lovely homeland, Sardinia where as a child, my deepest wish was to write a book, and where I have rarely spent time over the last 18 years.

Throughout this book, I have tried to remain balanced when presenting issues that we face in the business world, their consequences, and the solutions I see for creating a better way of doing business. The views that I present are my own, based on my working experience, opinions as a customer, and my advisory role in the customer centricity field. They are inevitably coloured by my childhood memories, travel experiences and professional life as a young adult.

The main research in this book is qualitative and supplemented by desk research. I have included studies of academic excellence associated with internationally renowned university professors. I have been honoured to interview senior executives from world-class organisations, which I share with pleasure with you. Anything wise in these pages, you should credit to the experts I have interviewed and to those that I have mentioned. Anything foolish, assume it's my error.

All the examples that I have covered are of business-to-consumer (B2C) companies, because I wanted to delve deep into this category. I plan to provide you with a business-to-business (B2B) version of *Journey to Centricity* in the future. This doesn't mean that the principles of this book are not also applicable for the B2B world. The fundamentals of customer relationships are the same, because B2B companies consist of people – and sell to other companies also consisting of people.

I hope I've achieved my aim to cover enough material to make the topic useful, insightful and interesting for you.

The interviewees of this book, listed alphabetically below by first name, have made it much richer than it would otherwise have been. Thank you for your time, insights and contributions.

Alan Zorfas
Co-founder and Chief Intelligence Officer at Motista

Alex Allwood
Customer experience authority and author of *Customer Empathy: A Radical Intervention in Customer Experience Management and Design*

Andrea Isola
General Manager at N26 Italy & Southeast Europe

Daniel Araya
Senior Fellow at the Centre for International Governance Innovation (CIGI)

Denise Lee Yohn
Brand leadership expert and author of *Fusion: How Integrating Brand and Culture Powers the World's Greatest Companies*

Don Peppers
Customer centricity authority and author of *Customer Experience: What, How and Why Now*

Joana de Quintanilha
Vice President and Principal Analyst at Forrester

Marco Gazzino
Head of Innovability® at Enel X

Massimiliano Pogliani
CEO at illycaffè

Peter Fader
Professor of Marketing at The Wharton School of the University of Pennsylvania and co-founder of Theta

Rob Markey
Senior partner at Bain & Company and co-creator of the Net Promoter System®

Steven Van Belleghem
Customer-centricity expert and author of *The Offer You Can't Refuse: What If Customers Ask for More Than an Excellent Service?*

Steve Spiro
Chief Executive Officer at Halotherapy Solutions and Chairman of the Global Wellness Institute

Thimon De Jong

Lecturer on Social Influence at Utrecht University and Founder of Whetston

Tim Heldmann

Former Chief Marketing Officer at Polestar

Victoria Roos Olsson

Senior Leadership Consultant at FranklinCovey

Zachery Anderson

Chief Data and Analytics Officer at NatWest

At the end of this book, you'll be encouraged to take a temperature check on how customer-centric your business actually is. I recommend you do this quick survey after you finish the book, but feel free to do it at any time. You can find the customer-centric barometer at www.ileniavidili.com/barometer.

As with anything, I'd love to hear your thoughts. Please feel free to send me your feedback, comments and questions at ilenia@ileniavidili.com.

I hope that this book will spark ideas, cover potential solutions, inspire you to think differently, and ultimately, to become more *customer-centric*.

Are you ready to follow me on this journey? If so, read on!

CHAPTER 1

WHEN THE LAND CHANGES

"Change is the law of life, and those who look only to the past or present are certain to miss the future." – John F. Kennedy[1]

On August 5, 2018, I was having dinner with a friend at a terrace restaurant in the "Island of Gods", Bali, when the lights went out, the walls started cracking, plates and glasses smashed on the floor, tables and chairs collided, electricity poles swayed and people screamed, cried and ran, desperately trying to hold onto something. I ran as fast as I could to get myself to a safe place; and then, after about 40 seconds, the ground gradually stopped moving. The longest 40 seconds of my life had caused no deaths that I could see, just fear – a lot of it.

A magnitude 7.0 earthquake had just triggered a deadly tsunami in Bali's neighbouring island of Lombok, Indonesia. While I hadn't witnessed any deaths, it had killed more than 560 people, injured more than 1,000 and displaced nearly half a million.[2] Indonesia sits on the Ring of Fire, the string of frequent tremors and volcanic eruptions that circles virtually the entire Pacific Ocean,[3] making it one of the most disaster-prone countries in the world. Entire buildings were flattened; schools and hospitals were completely demolished. Many homes collapsed, and many others were seriously damaged; locals were forced to stay in tents for months. Lombok needed to be rebuilt from the ground up.

The neighbouring island of Bali is not just a popular tourist destination, as we know it; it is also home to thousands of expats and location-independent workers. Remote freelancers, employees and entrepreneurs who live and work outside of traditional corporate infrastructure consider it their home. These individuals are typically Millennials and Gen Z workers who are part of this story. This was also the case for me for many months. Why am I telling you this?

In 1934, a British historian by the name of Arnold Toynbee, in his book, *A Study of History,* analysed the genesis, growth and fall of every human civilisation. He found that these change events followed a simple pattern or formula: *challenge* and *response*. The challenge was presented by a major force, say a tsunami; and the response was generated by the people – individuals and institutions. The quality of the response dictated whether the civilisations would grow or die.[4]

While Toynbee used this formula to explain the rise and fall of 28 great civilisations, this model can also be applied to the same extent to organisations and the challenges they face from the "digital tsunami" – the major force released by digital technologies. The digital revolution is the adoption and the proliferation of digital technologies, which began in the latter half of the 20th century, and is still affecting many different markets today.[5] It behaves like a tsunami, retracting and gathering strength out on the ocean, before hitting again. For decades, the digital revolution presented both an opportunity and a dilemma for many businesses. Some ignored the alerts and threats, while others embraced them and thrived. Although a major force, such as that of a digital tsunami, provided the opportunity for transformation, many businesses are still operating with practices that may not longer work in the 21st century.

Over the course of the last 10 years (2010–2020), the increasing challenges of our global society and the use of new digital applications have seen the arrival of new consumer behaviour. The collision of the physical and digital worlds has affected every dimension of business, individuals and society as a whole. The hyper-connectivity of our daily lives has shaped entire generations that are transforming the way businesses operate.

Additionally, multi-generational behaviour plays a more important role in businesses than it did in the past. The following generations are currently in the workplace and/or consumers in society:

- Baby Boomers were born post World War II. They saw previous generations sacrificing everything for the war, so they worked very hard for their livelihood. They grew up fighting to compete for resources.[6]
- Generation X followed and started to introduce the idea of a solid work-life balance into the workforce.[7]
- Millennials came of age in the new millennium and during a time of rapid technological change, forcing companies to examine how they do business for decades to come.[8] Anyone born between 1981 and 1996 is a Millennial.[9]
- Generation Z has come on the scene as the generation of influencers. Born after 1997, they have been exposed to the internet, social networks and mobile systems since their very early youth.[10] To put this into perspective, Gen Z comprises 32 per cent of the global population (2.47 billion of the 7.7 billion people on Earth),[11] surpassing Millennials, who account for 23 per cent.[12]

What younger generations – Millennials and Gen Z – have in common is the strong belief in their individual power to drive change. They direct their time and energies towards actions that can drive the change that they want to see in the world, but they expect businesses and governments to do more to achieve a better future. According to Deloitte these actions involve "increasing political involvement, aligning spending and career choices with their values, and driving change on societal issues."[13]

FULL CIRCLE

During the 1990s, I didn't have a smartphone or an iPad to keep myself entertained in the school summer holidays, so I used to spend my time helping my aunty, Marta, in her little newsstand shop for a couple of hours a day. I helped her open the shop, clipped the front pages of the daily newspapers to the metal covers, and prepared locally made biscuits and coffee for breakfast. One of my favourite things to do was to sit behind the counter, surrounded by piles of out-of-date magazines, and shadow my aunty as she served. Her shop was in the main street of our small town in the heart of Sardinia, where thousands of tourists passed to reach the beach, or stopped for a quick break. Besides the tourists, her daily customers included everyone from parents taking their children to the nearby school, to grandmothers going to daily mass, and children looking for the latest edition of "Topolino" (an Italian comic series of Disney cartoons). Regardless of who they were, they would spend a good 30 to 40 minutes chatting with aunty Marta. Many shared war memories; some the best way to make a lasagna; others football results.

I loved seeing my aunty connecting with people from all walks of life. When tourists came along to buy a map of Sardinia, she would venture a conversation in her broken English, as she tried to make them feel welcome. She was able to pivot the conversation with any customer, and she offered coffee and biscuits to make them feel comfortable enough to share their stories.

I loved watching her not only serve these people as customers, but as human beings. She remembered every customer's name, their most-read newspaper, their birthday, how much they had spent, how much they could afford to spend. She kept their tabs, and she'd bring up their previous conversations so that their stories were validated.

How did she remember all that? She used to keep a little journal next to the till, and when she saw a customer approaching, she would have a little sneak peek. This is what we call a *customer relationship management*

(CRM) software in today's business world, and that information about her customers is what, today, we call *data*. With customers she had never met, such as tourists, she wouldn't keep them for too long or spend much time and effort taking notes about them, but she still loved serving them – occasionally offering handmade biscuits and telling them the best route to the beach.

I watched this woman with little education caring so much about her customers, putting aside her stories to serve others and make them feel they belonged. My aunty was a very humble shopkeeper who taught me the very basics of customer relationships. She used to say to me, "If you want to do this job one day, you need to know every customer personally like I do, and you need to understand their needs almost implicitly and viscerally." She didn't just sell newspapers and magazines; she acted as an advisor. Her customers preferred to buy from her, because she connected with them.

If my aunty could create that sort of customer intimacy with very little budget and no tech resources, why can't businesses of the 21st century – which have all the tools – do the same? To help answer this, I interviewed Peter Fader, Professor of Marketing at The Wharton School of the University of Pennsylvania and co-founder of Theta. Peter told me, "The very basic idea of customer centricity goes all the way back from a small shop, where the owners run it day to day. They know the customers walking in, they understand what makes them different. They have a sense of which ones are going to stay with them through good times, as well as bad. The problem is that as you open up the second store, and more stores, you give up on all that, because it becomes all about scale, and it becomes about getting things moving as quickly and as cheaply as possible. You lose that intimacy."

The concept of customer centricity is very attractive in its elegance, but it hasn't been easy for companies to implement and stick to it. Many have tried to be customer-centric, failed, and remained sceptical about it. If, originally, a shop owner or business leader knew every customer personally, how and why have businesses lost this customer-centric touch? The reason is because the culture, systems, people and values aren't aligned to put the customers first.

There are three major eras that explain why and how customer centricity is being lost. In this chapter, I'd like to give you a brief understanding of the context and reason for being customer-centric, while providing you with the foundation for the concepts that I will share in the chapters ahead.

THE SHAREHOLDER PRIMACY ERA | 1970–1989

In this era, companies existed primarily to make profit for their shareholders. This perspective was popularised by Nobel Prize laureate and economist Milton Friedman in his ferocious article, 'The Social Responsibility of Business Is to Increase Its Profits.'[14] What Friedman was effectively stating was that companies must focus on pursuing self-interest. To pursue this goal, they had to sell as many products or services as possible, to as many people as possible, in order to make as much profit as possible. The sole focus was on the product that needed to be sold, with the philosophy of mass production at scale and the faster the better. This created a hyper-focus on short-term results – which was a problem, because these companies were seen as pursuing profit at the expense of employees and consumers.

How did this happen? When companies hit a downturn, they faced a dramatic need to cut back spending on areas such as marketing, initiatives to create customer intimacy and then employees, whether in the contact centre or on the retail floor. On top of the cuts, they created other sources of revenue, such as new fees. These factors could balance the books in the near term and create greater profit, but at the expense of the relationship with customers and employees.

This was also the era of "command and control". Companies would physically disrupt other companies through innovations like cheaper, newer and more convenient products. But companies formed in this era had limitations. They had early technologies as their foundations, which quickly became obsolete. The world wide web was not yet widespread. With information only available on paper, companies needed a sufficient product and an advertising campaign a few times a year to gain attention. They communicated with their customers in a very linear way and had a level of control in terms of what their customers bought, read and listened to.

Over this era, companies built up a somewhat arrogant position in their market. The aforementioned strategy worked for centuries and, in many, many cases, companies continue to operate in this way, even in the 21st century. But cracks are starting to show. Today, businesses are under a lot of pressure for many different reasons, such as commoditisation of products, more empowered consumers and lack of relevance in highly saturated marketplaces.[15]

Senior executives worry whether they have the right business model and the right technologies to give their company a future, but they still put functional and financial priorities ahead of customer needs.

If your company was formed in this era, or operates like companies of this era, then you may be stuck in a time warp of product mindset, a hierarchical manner of managing people and obsolete ways of interacting with your customers. Your mission statement may still be something overly vague and inane like "Our mission is to continue to provide access to diverse services to stay relevant in tomorrow's world." Nonsense!

BUSINESS-AS-A-MACHINE ERA | 1990–2021

In 1995, when the internet started to be consumerised, entire households used it at scale to buy things. Most companies of the previous era were curious about digital technologies, but not curious enough to quickly adopt a digital mindset. They lacked an understanding of how emerging technologies could help both internal processes and their customer interactions.

But customers weren't as slow to adapt as companies. The birth of the internet and mobile technologies started influencing customers who had pervasive access to information and multiple channels to choose from.

Media also needed to adapt. Up to the early 2000s was the golden era for media, television, print and radio, as they dominated brand communication. Then the internet started controlling our attention, so consumer behaviour changed. Marketers started to fear the advent of social media, because they had a lot of control over the way they portrayed their business to the world. The dynamics of the market changed in this era. New technologies and new business models disrupted many of those companies born in the shareholder primacy era – those that thought they were untouchable. Kodak, Blockbuster, Maplin, Toys "R" Us, Debenhams and many others felt the challenge for years and eventually filed for bankruptcy.

Harvard Business School professor Clayton Christensen popularised the concept of *disruptive innovation* to thousands of business leaders with his book *The Innovator's Dilemma*. Incumbents born in the shareholder primacy era spotted, adopted and in some cases developed these technologies, but considered snubbing investing in them. Many thought new digital technologies were too weak for the mature and advanced way in which these companies operated.[16]

This increasing dominance of online channels combined with hesitancy by incumbents to adopt the necessary technology led to the rise of new disrupters, or *new entrants*. These companies were (and are) often led by Millennials – and in some cases Gen Z – who better understand the needs, frustrations and preferences of their own generations. New entrants are smaller, more agile, more digital, and bring products and services that offer better customer experiences. In short, they have a more customer-focussed business model and are often set up by frustrated ex-employees of incumbents. Automation and artificial intelligence are largely part of these companies.[17] An example of these new entrants is

N26, a completely virtual neo bank headquartered in Berlin. We will explore more on N26 later in this book.

Who's responsible for all this disruption? The digitalisation of things? Or business leaders who have fallen behind the evolution of technology and that of the consumer? If you lead a company that was formed in this era and operate by its premises, then it may appear that you are heading in the right direction. But the problem with business-as-a-machine companies is that they tend to focus too much on the brightest piece of technology, and their employees are taught to think and act pretty much like their algorithms. Often this leads to a shift in focus from the customer. Employing a team of data scientists and using the latest software is *not* enough.

THE CUSTOMER-CENTRIC COMPANY OF THE FUTURE | 2022 AND BEYOND

Today there are very few companies that are truly customer-centric. Most companies focus on volume – both volume of customers and of profits. The number of customers means nothing if the relationship with them is flat, and profit means nothing if it is not sustainable in the long term.

Peter Fader believes in *customer heterogeneity* – that not all customers are equal. They are all unique, and some customers are more valuable than others. Instead of focussing merely on the quantity of customers, he suggests finding the most valuable customers and creating a more meaningful relationship with them. This begs the question: how?

The technologies available today cannot, of course, exactly replicate that small-shop customer intimacy, but they can do a pretty good job at collecting a huge amount of information about customers and differentiating them. The use of customer insights can lead to strengthening customer relationships, if used wisely. For example, firms that are able to use digital technologies to enhance the customer experience can understand customers with information such as who's buying what and when, what they do, what they say, what their acquisition funnel is. This information basically allows companies to treat customers differently based on their individual needs – just like my aunty did, but at scale.

Even companies born in the business-as-a-machine era that have the tech capabilities to be customer-centric are only doing it to a small degree. Most of the time, this is because they lack the customer-centric mindset and culture, which ends up being a big weakness that is reflected in everything they do.

Another trend that I see among companies is that they still focus too much on the newest version of their product and its performance, rather than the relationship with their customers. When it comes to product focus, Peter shared with me that "most companies are born around a product that they can sell, a product that creates all the enthusiasm and earnings needed for customer-centric initiatives. But the problem is that too many companies lose touch with their customers as their growth plateaus. Of course, selling products remains extremely important because, let's be honest, you can't figure out who your best customers are before you know what you're selling them. So, you have to start with a product or service."

If companies want to move back to customer centricity after their growth plateaus, is it too late? Peter tells me that it's never too late, but "it's very important to start developing the infrastructure, collecting the data, getting the mindset, and even developing the customer-centric culture as early as possible". Too often the product-centric approach gets prioritised over the customer-centric approach, because it is short-term and brings return on investment (ROI) immediately.

In a product-centric world, the research and development (R&D) department would come up with a better version of an existing product, or a completely new one, and sell it in big retail stores without fully understanding who would buy that product. This strategy can work with great success – until the growth stalls.

Peter tells me the story of how Electronic Arts (EA), an American video game company, moved from product-centric to customer-centric with the help of Zachery Anderson, the former senior vice president and chief analytics officer, who led the transformation at that time (more of Zachery in Chapter 7). Peter uses Zachery's strategy at EA as a great example of the difference between product-centric and customer-centric companies.

Peter asked me, "Have you ever watched those cooking shows where they bring a bunch of chefs in?"

"Yes," I answered.

"So, instead of going to the chefs and saying, 'We want every one of you to come up with a great meal of your choice', the show gives each of them a fixed set of items to cook with – often some unusual ones – and says to each chef, 'Now come up with a delightful meal.' Providing the ingredients is a great way to inspire thinking in an 'outside-in' manner, which is key to customer centricity." A product-centric business creates a product or a service with the hope to sell that product to as many people as possible – like creating a meal with no clear parameters on what it should be or who it is for. A customer-centric business instead creates a product (meal) based on customers' needs (ingredients), and focusses on satisfying as many of those customers as possible over the course of an ongoing relationship.

By understanding customer behaviour, needs and expectations on an individual level, we can shape better products – and customer experiences – around them. This is how we can build deeper, long-term customer relationships and elevate the *customer lifetime value* (CLV). CLV is basically how much money a customer will bring your company throughout their entire time as a paying customer of your brand.

For decades, marketing departments used to look at past customer data: how much was spent, when, what was purchased, etc. Peter Fader has been working on predicting the lifetime value of every individual customer. This not only helps in making better business decisions and allocating resources but it also provides a clear picture of buy-in and ROI for customer-centric initiatives.

How do you elevate your CLV? By being customer-centric – which is what this book is all about. If the importance of customer relationships is your top business priority, the quality of your customers will improve tremendously and, consequently, the quality of their purchases will increase.

Peter ended our conversation by saying, "It's not just about the data, the models and the tech; it's more about the organisational transformation." Today there are very few companies that have fully shifted their focus from product to customer. To successfully transition requires a fundamentally different operating model and organisational design.

To give you a more technical definition of customer centricity, I also interviewed Rob Markey, senior partner at Bain & Company and co-creator of the Net Promoter System®. In Rob's view, a customer-centric company has a systematic way of developing insight and empathy so that it can identify unmet and under-met needs of customers, and design solutions and value propositions that address those needs better than anyone else in the world. Rob tells me that there are three dimensions of a customer-centric value proposition:

1. **Rational value:** This value derives from a product or service that you offer which meets some fundamental need of your customers at a reasonable price relative to your competition. Typically, rational value derives from characteristics like product features, benefits, pricing and functionality.

2. **Experiential value:** The value derived from the way a product or service is delivered. This is not only of the difference between the actual delivery of your products and services versus the promises you have made, but is also shaped by the expectations your customers have developed based on analogous experiences from competitors or even other industries.

3. **Emotional value:** The connection that the customer has with the brand and what their purchasing of that brand suggests about their values.

Rob continues that a customer-centric company attracts and acquires new customers largely by earning their trust. This is possible by delivering these three values in such a remarkable way that it not only transforms customers into promoters but provides experiences that are compelling enough to foster loyalty and receptivity to future offerings.

The operating model of this company places the needs of the customers ahead of the functionality of the products, and is built around the customer view rather than functional processes and operations. A customer-centric company is able to understand a longitudinal view of every individual customer, as they pass through the different functions, processes and experiences of the company. This view gives companies the ability to manage and measure the CLV. Rob says that "we are coming full circle" when it comes to customer centricity. We started as customer-centric small shops and, if we invest the time, effort and resources, we will slowly get back to that point with the help of the technology available today. We'll get back to Peter Fader and Rob Markey later in Chapter 13.

Over the past 50 years, companies have been viewed as a major cause of social, environmental and economic problems. This is because they continue to operate with a short-term mindset driven by financial performance in which customers, employees' needs and societal issues remain at the periphery, rather than at the core. Today shareholder primacy is under pressure in many different ways. Research has shown that, since 2000, 52 per cent of companies in the Fortune 500 of the command-and-control era no longer exist.[18] Everything has been changing very rapidly – from technologies to markets to customer expectations – and the speed of change is a very important driver.

The future will be different. The company of the future will be the one that delivers value to its people, whether inside or outside the organisation. With this book, I'd like to expand on what makes a customer-centric company of the future. I believe that companies are ready to enter a new era of business thinking – adopting practices based on human experiences and taking their social responsibility seriously. This is the era where why businesses do it, how they do it and who they do it for are intrinsically linked.

If you are an executive, you don't need charts and numbers to tell you that a new era is birthing; you naturally know and feel it.

Society has been driven by the capitalist system. Capitalism is a vehicle for meeting human needs, improving efficiency, creating jobs and building wealth – but this narrow view prevents companies from also looking at societal challenges.[19] Some 56 per cent of people say that capitalism as it exists today is doing more harm than good, and that democracy is losing its effectiveness.[20] We need a different version of capitalism – a newer version that involves companies playing a positive role in global governance, with a focus on stakeholder return.

Since 1997, Business Roundtable, a non-profit association that represents CEOs of leading US companies, has issued principles of corporate governance, which endorse those of the shareholder primacy era. In 2019, they announced the adoption of a new statement on the purpose of a corporation which moves away from shareholder primacy and includes commitment to all stakeholders.[21] Last year, the World Economic Forum released its 2020 Davos Manifesto, which, according to Klaus Schwab, the Forum's Founder and Executive Chairman, is a set of ethical principles to guide companies to a universal purpose towards its stakeholders.[22] Schwab mentions "stakeholder capitalism", a model that positions private corporations as trustees of society, which are better equipped for today's social and environmental challenges.[23]

In his book *Stakeholder Capitalism*, Schwab explains that stakeholder capitalism takes on board the interest of all stakeholders; companies optimise for more than short-term profits and governments are the guardians of equality and inclusivity of the system.[24]

If you are an executive, you may say, "Wait a minute. Why shouldn't I have the dual goal of putting customers first while ensuring that the business earns an acceptable return on investment?" This is an absolutely fair assessment – and the objective of this book. Focussing on your customers also means that you'll be forced to improve every aspect of your business, from the quality of your decisions, to your operations and the product and service that you provide. This doesn't mean that the profit objective will vanish.[25]

Customer-centric companies of the future are those that are able to unlearn and relearn – and those that have a vision that propels their impact on their customers and the world as a whole.

If this describes your company, my congratulations to you! You seem to have the right components to be a customer-centric company of the future. The future is about having a higher purpose, it's about having an empathic human touch, and it's about creating shared value to improve the lives of your customers, employees, and the broader communities. But this era is still uncertain.

Some elements of previous eras will remain in place, while others will evolve. No matter how different, difficult, easy, digital and robotic it will be, one simple thing is certain: customer relationships will be crucial. Consumers want a relationship with companies that care about them, both as customers and as human beings.

As we have seen earlier in this chapter, companies tend to be resistant to change. The more technology that is out there, the more the market changes, the more consumer behaviour changes, and the more society changes. Those companies that are still in the mindsets of the shareholder primacy and business-as-a-machine eras will fall short because they lack customer focus, which becomes more visible as customer primacy becomes more and more evident.

You may be thinking that you are already customer-centric, and this is where most companies get it wrong – by assuming that change is not needed, when the walls may be slowly cracking, just like the walls of the houses in Lombok. Would you want to live in a tent after a tsunami, or would you want to rebuild a better house?

My mission with this book is to inspire you to take action. The business of businesses is changing again, and those that can't change with it are less likely to survive the next generation of disrupters. Being customer-centric in the 21st century requires change – operationally, yes, but mostly in mindset. As the world continues to rapidly evolve, it feels harder than ever to execute a strategy effectively and sustainably. My aim is to guide your future path on your *journey to centricity.*

PILLAR OF HUMANITY

.

CHAPTER 2

THE HUMANITY OF BUSINESS

"Man is by nature a social animal; an individual who is unsocial naturally and not accidentally is either beneath our notice or more than human." – Aristotle[1]

I lived in a small town in the heart of Sardinia until I was 18 years old, when I then first left for Spain and then the United Kingdom for my studies, and then to quench my thirst by discovering the world. Sardinia is recognised for its beautiful, crystal-clear waters and white-sand beaches – but it's less known for our strong sense of community, respect for tradition and way of life.

Sardinia's economy is mainly powered by tourism, agriculture and farming.[2] To Sardinians, farming has been not only an economic resource but also a passion, for centuries. For as long as I can remember, Sardinia has been an island of solidarity. To give a practical example, when a shepherd loses his flock for whatever reason – whether it's been stolen, or killed by predators, disease or natural disaster – most of the other shepherds on the island will donate a sheep to regroup the flock so that the unlucky shepherd can restart their activity. 'Sa paradura' is an ancient gesture that has existed since the dawn of time to help another farmer in trouble. Although this is a Sardinian tradition, on some occasions

Sardinian shepherds have extended the gesture to other Italian regions, especially in circumstances where the climate has caused disasters. No one keeps the beneficiary accountable to return the gift, but citizens retain a moral obligation to contribute when another shepherd is in trouble.[3]

Although farming can be an isolating occupation, researchers and scientists have identified the sense of connecting to a community as one of the reasons for human beings' quest for longevity. Unsurprisingly, Sardinia holds second place among the world's Blue Zones. The Blue Zones are the five regions across the world where a higher than usual number of people live longer than average.[4] These regions are identified by Dan Buettner in his book *The Blue Zones:*

1. Okinawa, Japan
2. Sardinia, Italy
3. Nicoya, Costa Rica
4. Icaria, Greece
5. Loma Linda, California

According to scientists and researchers, the secret to longevity in these five places is: diet, exercise, finding a purpose in life and belonging to a community – that is, having strong social ties with friends, families and beyond.[5]

The need for connecting with others during the depths of COVID-19 isolation was very apparent. This also played out in businesses. In fact, the positive side of this pandemic showed that the *business of businesses* can be good. When the world stopped as the virus spread, hundreds of companies repurposed their production lines and R&D capabilities to join the fight against COVID-19. Luxury brands and distilleries switched production lines from producing perfume and gin to making hand sanitiser; industrial companies made face masks; luxury hotels temporarily became quarantine centres; and automotive companies quickly switched to producing much-needed medical equipment.[6] We tend to have a negative view of businesses, but if there is one thing that this pandemic has taught us, it is that when organisations of any kind and size work towards something, the world can get fixed.

Traumatic events like natural disasters, wars and pandemics can damage people's mental health, but it is the power of human connection and solidarity that changes the bad. As life returns to normal, the distance between people is likely to expand again. Tragedy often brings us together, but how brief is that connection?

Among the list of global issues that the United Nations is trying to address, we see big data, climate change, gender equality and poverty.[7] Around 60 years ago, it was believed that eliminating poverty was unachievable. In 2018, the percentage of the world population living with less than $1.90 a day was 8 per cent. That is a much better number than the 36 per cent in 1990.[8] Considering the many wrong decisions that we have made in society, it's amazing to see that, in some areas, we are doing better than we think. However, we are doing less well in other areas.

Many of you would see poverty as not having enough income for our basic needs. I see poverty beyond material things and associate it with social isolation, loneliness and lack of human fulfilment, across the age spectrum. I believe that climate change, poverty beyond money, and technology ethics are the three central rising challenges of our era. These challenges cannot be solved by a single government alone. They require collaborative actions among institutions, big and small businesses, and us as individuals around the world. Is there a guarantee that the next century and beyond will work out well? No, nothing is guaranteed. But what we know is that when people, governments and businesses understand that it's possible to address the world's challenges, then we are set for success.

CONNECTED BUT ALONE

We are living in a world where technology is making our lives easier by giving us convenience, information, connectivity and efficiency. We're able to get tasks done more quickly, and thousands of tech apps are bypassing geographical borders and broadening communities across the entire world. We seem to be more connected than ever before.

But how connected are we really? The point I am making here isn't dichotomous – whether technology is good or bad. But too much focus on tech can replace our human connection. We will dive into blending technology into your customer-centric strategy in greater detail in the Pillar of Technology.

The irony is that while these technologies are great at giving us the perception of connectedness in an increasingly populous world, many people are experiencing loneliness in their everyday lives. British historian Fay Bound Alberti defines loneliness as "a conscious, cognitive feeling of estrangement or social separation from meaningful others".[9] It is an unpleasant emotional discrepancy between actual and desired social relationships.[10]

Thousands of newspaper articles[11] describe this social pain as the "loneliness epidemic". It sounds scary to even just read the word 'epidemic' while we grapple with a global health crisis.

Historian, economist and demographer Neil Howe says that loneliness rates differ by age and generation, and, in most societies, loneliness resembles a U-shaped curve: high in adolescence and young adulthood, declining through middle age, and rising again in old age.[12]

As a Millennial myself, and the friend of many Millennials, loneliness is something that troubles us quite a lot, and is, in fact, the number one fear for young people of my generation.[13] As the sister of a young girl, I know that loneliness is something that bothers them too; in fact, 40 per cent of Gen Z adolescents often, or very often, feel lonely.[14] This feeling of isolation is something experienced around the world. In the United States, 46 per cent of Americans feel lonely.[15] Around 30 million European adults frequently feel lonely,[16] and one third of British people also feel lonely.[17] In 2018, the United Kingdom was the first nation to appoint a minister of loneliness,[18] and Japan followed in 2021.[19]

What are the consequences for this painful, universal phenomenon? Scientists have discovered that loneliness shortens lifespans similar to smoking 15 cigarettes[20] a day, and it's associated with a greater risk of cardiovascular disease, dementia, depression and anxiety.[21] The annual cost of loneliness to British employers is \$3.5 (€2.99) billion[22] as it reduces task performance, limits creativity and diminishes reasoning and decision-making.[23] How is it that have we come so far, yet this feeling of loneliness has increased during recent decades?

There are a few different factors. People make more cross-country moves, and therefore are more likely to be living apart from loved ones. People are increasingly divorcing, extending their single status and living alone more than any time in history. In addition, in-person interactions and relationships have been reduced due to uptake in digital nomadism, the on-demand gig economy and more people starting their own business.[24] And, of course, social media and tech play their roles. Not long ago, Netflix released a highly watched documentary called *The Social Dilemma*, which focusses on how social media companies' business models are based on using algorithms that encourage users' addiction to their platforms.[25] I was astonished to see how this documentary reflected our current society and the dangerous human impact of social networking.

Dr Elias Aboujaoude, a Stanford University psychiatrist, says that technology apps and social networking sites distract us by occupying our mental bandwidth and prevent us from recognising our lack of relationships,[26] therefore increasing loneliness. There is no doubt that the social distancing brought by COVID-19 has supercharged this feeling.

People who have frequent, meaningful, in-person interactions are less lonely and healthier than those who rarely have face-to-face interactions.[27] This reinforces the social nature of humans and the importance of having communities. We human beings are inherently cooperative social creatures. We need to belong to small groups that have a clear purpose, and we need human interaction as much as we need screens. We have social needs, and we want to be part of something bigger.

Fay Bound Alberti argues that the chronic form of loneliness is the result of individualism. She says: "Many of the divisions and hierarchies that have developed since the eighteenth century – between self and world, individual and community, public and private – have been naturalized through the politics and philosophy of individualism."[28] In my view, individualism is the child of a capitalistic society. Capitalism is a good enough system, but it needs to have its moral norms, and it needs to serve a larger social good.

So, whose responsibility is it to tackle this problem? Many people point fingers at governments and healthcare systems. I believe that while they play important roles, especially in identifying who's affected by the problem, to truly combat loneliness and isolation, we need the engagement of institutions such as schools, organisations and workplaces. Schools and institutions can help by changing the fundamentals of business education around the world – teaching pupils the benefits of human fulfilment and long-term public good instead of short-term profit. Companies hold tremendous power to drive vast change by strengthening relationships among employees and customers – and by running mentorship programmes and innovation hubs that inspire new entrepreneurs to create communities around a brand. We will look at this in greater detail in Chapter 9.

HOW TO FILL THE VOID?

What does all this have to do with customer centricity? Being a successful customer-centric company of the future means focussing on adding long-term, lifetime value to your customers, rather than just bringing in short-term temporary sales. In Chapter 1, we discussed how most companies operating in the old days threw money into marketing campaigns to push customers down the sales funnel, take market share away from the competition and become more powerful. The Business Roundtable was not only a sign that something was changing, but also that people – in the broad sense – wanted to see change! People nowadays want to buy from, work for and invest in companies that serve a higher purpose to society at large. They want to see companies go beyond words and take action to upend the self-defeating doctrine of the shareholder primacy era.[29]

Technology has been absolutely fundamental in shifting our world to be as efficient as it is today. While automated processes offer incredible benefits for a business, they have disrupted the way we create customer relationships. Technology has accelerated the pace of change, without erasing the need for building customer relationships. As much as we could automate customer interactions, doing business is about creating strong ties with customers, which can never be automated.

Futurist and humanist Gerd Leonhard, in his book *Technology vs. Humanity,* writes: "Apart from being able to simulate human interactions increasingly well, technology does not know nor does it care for happiness, self-realization, fulfillment, emotion, or values and beliefs. It only understands logic, rational action, (in)completion, efficiency, and yes/no answers."[30]

Today's consumers, however, want deeper interactions with the company and its fellow buyers. Customer support and a weekly newsletter is just not enough any more. Investing in the latest technology allows you to reach customers where they are, which is great; but to win in the next generation of customer centricity, you'll need to invert the priority ladder so that people are at the top, not technologies that are seen to improve efficiencies.

Improving business operations is the holy grail in management science. However, an excessive focus on efficiency creates negative effects in other areas of the business, consequently rewarding competitors. In most cases, the functionality of business is highly efficient, but the human experience gets forgotten: mobile apps are optimised for data collection rather than privacy; employee management is optimised for performance rather than mentorship; and products are optimised for margins rather than customer wellbeing.

Amazon, for example, is known for providing the perfect e-commerce experience; but, by prioritising efficiency, it has killed the emotional and human side of shopping through a lack of human connection and interaction. Such technology at scale is playing a key role in increasing loneliness, as we replace deep in-person relationships with weak social connections brought to us by tech apps that brutalise our human spirit. It's no wonder that, in 2019, nearly 80 per cent of startup founders declared that building a community of people was of utmost importance for their business, and 28 per cent said that it was critical for the company.[31]

We can finally say that the business-as-a-machine era is not working well either, and we need to create a system that serves human beings rather than machines.

What is your business actually optimising today? Corporate efficiency over customer happiness and fulfilment? To become customer-centric and solve the issues at the heart of being human, businesses should be addressing loneliness as much as any other need. Reweaving the social fabric and tackling community health are endeavours of critical importance to us as individuals and as a society.

The commercial opportunity is right there too because people are experiencing a crisis of belonging, and companies of the future have an opportunity to step into the void for a deeper, real-world human connection. The brands that help customers and individuals to create meaningful connections will win their loyalty for the long term. These companies can create spaces, experiences, products and services that deliberately foster engaged communities and real connections.

Creating positive experiences across all stages of the customer journey, with the goal of bringing returning customers for the long term, will continue to be an essential element. But the concept of differentiating your business through improving a set of touchpoints may be insufficient for a company of the future to survive the next generation of disrupters. As we are entering a new business era, you'll need to know what the customer of tomorrow wants and expects.

In this age of hyper-digitalisation, the answer lies in shifting your focus to your consumers. This means going beyond providing great customer experiences and involves creating deeper connections that make up human experiences.

Yes, we need brands to be more human, but we are also in the middle of a digital revolution, so we have to be able to find an equilibrium between humanity and the technology that we have available. Consumers want to converse with brands and among one another; not only through social media, but through human interaction too.

Battling loneliness isn't impossible. As a brand, you should take your customers' loneliness seriously to be their companion and become relevant in their lives. Steven Van Belleghem – customer-centricity fellow expert and author of *The Offer You Can't Refuse: What If Customers Ask for More Than an Excellent Service?* – and I share the same view on brands, believing that they should step out and make a concrete contribution to customers' lives. To win the customer relationship of tomorrow, Steven created an efficient model[32] made up of the combination of four specific strategies:

- Good, quality products and services for a good price: the offering of your product and service must be first-class.
- Transactional convenience: use technology in a smart way to make customer interactions easier and more convenient.
- Partner in life: smart brands will succeed in helping customers cope more easily with key concerns in their lives.
- Save the world: every company has the strength to create a social added value, as they take responsibility to do good for society.

To better understand Steven's theory, I interviewed him. He told me, "The first two elements of the model are the new minimum today, but the areas where a business can differentiate right now are in the last two elements [*partner in life* and *save the world*]. This is about the human behind the customer, where you go beyond the product and actually add value in people's lives, rather than just selling them stuff – while also adding value to society at large."

Over the course of this pillar and its elements (the next three chapters), we will look into how to be a *partner in life* of your consumers and how to *save the world* with your consumers. The Pillar of Technology will explore what Steven calls today's "new minimum". I wanted to go a bit deeper and so I asked Steven his opinion on where businesses stand in combatting loneliness around the world. He mentioned how Peloton built communities during the COVID-19 confinement: "People are working out at home in front of a screen. They have access to motivational instructors and spinning classes, live or on-demand, with virtual classmates. So, you have the life component there, because the company is helping you to feel better every day. You have the social component, because other people are trying to achieve the same things you are. And you also have the competitive component as the game aspect is part of the experience."

Peloton sells spin bikes, treadmills and related accessories. But these products, although they are great, are not what drives people's passion for the Peloton brand. A big part of their brand is built around the community they have created. Of course, Peloton customers are all unique and live in different places, but they are all connected from a behavioural perspective: wanting to achieve fitness at home, with access to a community of support and resources. That's how Peloton was able to tap into the power of this community.

Last year, I was invited to speak at a conference in Amsterdam and got to experience another brand built around a community. After the conference, I joined the happy hour for a bit of networking on a beautiful riverside terrace. Meanwhile, a group of about 30 people parked their bikes right where we were. Moving like a swarm of bees, dressed in the same clothes and branded accessories, it was clear that this group belonged together. It was the Rapha Cycling Club (RCC),[33] a global community of passionate, active cyclists created around Rapha's apparel business.

Rapha shops are much more than retail spaces for cyclists and a social media community. They also provide clubhouses and meeting places for road cyclists and fans of cycling. They serve coffee and food to cyclists looking to refuel, as well as offering an extensive programme of live racing, rides and events. How about the digital side of this community? An easy-to-use mobile app connects a global network of more than 13,000 like-minded and passionate cyclists. The app shows hundreds of rides, routes and group chats every week. Why would a for-profit brand put so much effort, time and resources into all this? Because of the incredibly deep sense of belonging that it creates among its members and customers.

Obviously, not all companies are sport-based, but it doesn't mean that they can't tap into the power of a community. During a crisis of belonging, we need great brands that step into the void created by loneliness. This will sow the seeds for the next generation of customer loyalty. In a recent survey, 71 per cent of consumers said that loyalty programmes don't work as they used to. Customers would rather buy because of how relevant a brand is to them.[34] The loyalty era of marketing is slowly coming to an end.

Do you think that Salesforce is a successful business just because of its innovative software? Think again! The company also created a community of nearly two million members who support one another, organise events, and share and produce content. Oracle organises amazing in-person events all around the world, many of which are completely free of charge. I have attended their customer-experience-related conferences in Singapore, London and New York. Immersive workshops, great inspirational speakers, delicious food and plenty of networking opportunities with other like-minded peers make the list of the day. This is a great way to share their voice, network and exchange ideas with customers, partners, employees and even university students. Of course, they also have the chance to pitch their products, but they hold so much value for customers that, whenever there is an Oracle event, developers, customers, consultants, etc. are first in line to attend. People don't only go to conferences because the speakers have something interesting to say, but because simply being there allows them to share ideas with others, connect and create relationships.

You could say that Oracle and Salesforce have a huge budget for this. Well, yes, but it doesn't mean that a smaller budget can't create a community of like-minded people.

Besides Sardinia, I lived in Cambridge, UK, for nearly a decade. I graduated from university and had all my working experience as an employee there. A nice coffee shop called Stir opened up around the corner from where I used to live. At first, it was like a normal coffee shop, where people would get coffee and cake and stay half an hour. After about two years, the way they differentiated themselves from hundreds of other coffee shops and bakeries around the city was to offer something more: a community-centric café. Stir has a dedicated room for events and activities, which include toddler art, children's dance and movement classes and adult pilates. These are paid events. So, is Stir a bakery or a coffee shop? As they proudly say on their website, "It's the social hub of the community, and a place for people to meet, connect, and recharge – but also a place for them to escape and unwind."[35] To spice it up a bit, Stir also offers all kinds of bread via their online shop and monthly subscription bundles, which include home delivery.

Business strategies like those employed by Stir are effective, because human beings are community-driven and tribal. There are many theories which provide insights into customer motives. Maslow's hierarchy of needs studies how humans stipulate a natural progression from physiological needs to higher, self-actualisation wants. Once we get our basic needs of water, food and shelter, we look for love and belonging – which is a key part of the human form. As we are tribal people in the modern day, we still want to replicate that need for tribes.[36]

Communities deliver great benefits for both the members and a company. Focussing on community thus becomes part of a superior business model. According to the *Harvard Business Review*:[37]

- Members that are devoted to your community bring new members, which means lower customer acquisition costs for your business.
- Engaged members are less likely to leave your community, which means increased retention, resulting in higher lifetime value.
- Active members support one another, resulting in lower cost of customer service and therefore higher margins.

Community is a potent strategy. But how do you tap into that potential? Setting up a digital platform or an event every now and then is not enough. You also need to create a "sticky" environment that brings value to the people involved. A strong community around a brand authenticates brand purpose and builds brand trust.

HOW HUMAN ARE WE?

Product-centric companies are obsessed with beating the competition, so they invest huge amounts of money in R&D to come up with a better version of their products, as we've discussed. However, because innovations are easy to replicate, the competition comes up with a similar version of that product, and the innovative company has to come up with a lower price. This creates an endless competitive cycle that causes commoditisation of products in the eyes of consumers.

This product-centric approach considers only the rational aspect of an experience, because it's believed that customers only look at product features, quality and prices. Although these are very important, we human beings are much more complicated than we think. When making decisions, we are influenced by much more than rational factors like price and quality.

In simple terms, the rational part of our brain (left part) understands processes, logic, numbers and science very simply; basically, it wants to evaluate things. The instinctive part of our brain (right part) instead makes instant decisions, which are based on our emotions, feelings, dreams and intuition. Both parts are extremely important. The left part wants things to be easy to understand and convenient – which is what most companies tend to focus on. But these same companies tend to underestimate how to connect to the right side of the brain.[38]

Emotions are seen as "feelings", which are a bit of a taboo for companies. However, in a study of 228 B2C marketing and customer insights decision-makers in the US, 93 per cent of respondents agreed that emotionally connected consumers are more likely to buy from a brand, and 88 per cent agreed that a better understanding of customer emotions helps win new customers. Understanding customer behaviour through data is essential for winning customers' hearts and minds – the formula that keeps them coming back and turns them into advocates for your brand.[39]

Most of us, and most companies, don't know that our rational behaviour (what we do) is based on what emotion we feel. In other words, we are irrational beings by nature, so our feelings often drive our behaviour and overrule our rational thinking.[40] Research shows that connecting with customers on an emotional level – fulfilling their deep and innermost needs – is a more successful strategy to maximise customer value. Meeting deeper needs turns merely satisfied customers into emotionally connected ones.[41] Focussing solely on the left part of the brain can only create satisfied customers – not emotionally connected ones.

I interviewed Alan Zorfas, Co-founder and Chief Intelligence Officer at Motista, a consumer intelligence firm. Alan told me, "Satisfaction, in a sense, is the experiential quality control baseline. In contrast, customers who connect their deeper, more personal, emotional-based motivators to a brand exhibit longer tenures, concentrate more of their spending with the brand, and become its true advocates."

As a customer-centric company of the future, you should direct your orientation away from "one-upping" the competition on product features or satisfaction and instead connect with customers' emotions – what matters the most in their lives. Alan continued by saying, "Companies should shift more of their resources to connecting on an emotional level, not just trying to move dissatisfied customers to satisfaction. The emotional connection actually occurs when the customer connects their emotions to the brand."

It's much easier for companies to gravitate towards fixing dissatisfaction because, as opposed to emotions, satisfaction can be measured in waiting time, ease of purchasing, problem resolution, etc. Of course, it's still very important to fix these issues. According to Alan, customers aren't likely to connect their emotions to a brand if the customer experience is terribly inferior. Yet, emotionally connected customers are also less likely to complain about, and more likely to tolerate, miscues in service.

Emotional connection with a brand or company occurs when people connect their own desires, values and aspirations to the brand. But how do you determine which of those matter? Alan and his team at Motista have created a lexicon of about 300 motivations that can drive customers' behaviour. These include wanting to "stand out from the crowd", "feel a sense of belonging", "protect the environment" and "feel secure".[42] Every business is different: the emotional motivators that work for one business may not work for others, and this means that you'd have to find out your true emotional motivators. Customers become more valuable to a company as they move up the "emotional connection pathway" from being unconnected to being fully connected. On average, customers that are fully emotionally connected are 52 per cent more valuable than those who are just highly satisfied.[43]

So, how does this emotional connection actually happen? Alan says: "While customers will wax rich on the rational reasons they chose a brand, they aren't very good at reporting their emotional-based motivations. By collecting large volumes of data over years, with millions of customers and hundreds of brands across nearly every B2C and B2B category tying emotional motivations directly to behavioural data, Motista can zero in on the emotions that matter. With this new predictive layer of intelligence, we can then identify the emotional 'white space' [customers' needs gaps] that a single brand can – and should – own with its customers."

This can provide a drive for growing the customer lifetime value (CLV), which, as you'll remember, is the metric that indicates the total revenue that you can reasonably expect from a single customer throughout their relationship with your brand.

Emotions don't have to be a taboo for companies, they can be a source of competitive advantage.[44]

In this chapter, we have explored Steven Van Belleghem's partner in life strategy. In Chapter 3, we will look at how creating value for all stakeholders can be associated with Steven's save the world strategy. Over the next three chapters, we'll discover what makes a brand more human based on today's and tomorrow's customer expectations.

Spoiler alert: *purpose, empathy and trust* are the key elements of the Pillar of Humanity for making a customer-centric brand of the future.

PONDER AND ACT

1. How can you shift your focus to bring more humanity into your business?
2. How can you create spaces, experiences, products and services that foster engaged communities?
3. How can you add value to your customers beyond your product?
4. What emotional motivators connect your most valued customers to different categories of your business?
5. How else can you connect emotionally with your customers?

CHAPTER 3: PURPOSE

WHY ARE WE HERE?

*"Give a bowl of rice to a man and you will feed him for a day.
Teach him how to grow his own rice and you will save his life."*
– Confucius[1]

A few years ago, I was in a tumultuous relationship with my corporate job. So, I decided to take a gap year and travel around Southeast Asia as I wanted to discover the beautiful things that existed beyond my desk.

While I was travelling to many stunning places, I decided to join a short travel-work programme, where I could immerse myself in the culture with a couple of hours per week of teaching English as a foreign language to children in the north of Thailand. This was a very short experience and very different from what I had left in my corporate career.

One day, I was teaching the concept of work to children aged 10. I asked them to draw what they wanted to be when they grew up. One kid drew an astronaut, one kid drew a doctor, and another drew a vet. But there was a child at the back who wasn't drawing, so I walked over to help. I showed him pictures of different jobs, like doctors and teachers. After five minutes, the little boy surprisingly drew a farmer.

When his mother came to pick him up, I handed her his drawing and, to satisfy my curiosity, asked her about the connection with it.

She mentioned that the little boy possibly drew that because "his dad is dead, his uncle is in jail, and the one man that often shows him some sort of care is the farmer who works in the rice field next to us". In Asian countries, rice is the equivalent to pasta for Italians. She went on to explain, "Since I'd lost my job, I asked the farm owner to offer me work as a farmer in his field as I needed to provide food for my son. The owner said that he didn't have a vacancy, but he promised to send us food whenever possible. He often brings rice over, and when he comes around, he shows interest in my son, plays with him for five minutes, and has a little chat with him."

I went back to my *ruean* (typical Thai house) thinking about that little boy for the rest of the day – and what it would have meant for him to see the farmer bring rice to him and his mum.

Teaching the concept of work got me reflecting on my corporate career in Europe. I left it because most companies' purpose and values clashed with mine. As a member of the management team, I wanted to work towards a purpose that went beyond profit and numbers. I wanted to promote that purpose outside the company and make sure that it was part of the fabric of the business. We didn't have a purpose, or even a plan to have one. This made it difficult for me to engage.

Today, when I specifically ask company CEOs what their brand purpose is, I often get told, "We donate part of our earnings to ABC charity." This is where most companies get it wrong. If your company is giving away money to random causes or building a volunteer programme because you think that's what you are *supposed* to do in building your brand reputation, you are missing an opportunity to tap into purpose. Those actions don't define your reason for existing in a way that your employees or customers can get behind. And they are clearly not enough for the ever-growing societal problems that we face today.

Let's back up a bit. I believe that companies should exist for three reasons: to advance a higher purpose, to add value in people's lives, and to make a profit – in that order. Profit is an important and essential piece of the equation, but it shouldn't be acquired at the expense of customers, employees or society. Your purpose should be to offer value, and that means creating a product or service that in some way makes the lives of consumers easier and better. We keep creating products and services that are pretty much the same as our competitors', so we end up eroding margins, while losing relevance and competitive advantage, as these products become quickly commoditised.

A better way to make economic profit would be to build customer relationships, while helping the environment and meeting societal needs. Larry Fink, CEO of BlackRock, an asset management multinational, in his 2018 letter to CEOs of companies he had invested in wrote, "Society is demanding that companies, both public and private, serve a social purpose. To prosper over time, every company must not only deliver financial performance, but also show how it makes a positive contribution to society. Companies must benefit all of their stakeholders, including shareholders, employees, customers, and the communities in which they operate."[2]

Customer-centric companies of the future are those that think more deeply about the human needs that are related to the products and services they create.

LIVE HAPP-ILLY

Today, as a customer-centricity advisor, I have the pleasure of encountering many companies. Some are leading the way with a strong and authentic purpose; however, many are struggling to define, much less live, their purpose. Very often, as I've hinted at earlier, I see meaningless purpose statements such as "improving people's lives every day", which mean nothing if they are not executed.

A purpose needs to initiate a movement internally, and it must be woven into your company's operational fabric; otherwise, it holds no value.

In 2011, Michael Porter and Mark Kramer, professors at Harvard Business School, came up with the concept of *shared value*, which they popularised in their *Harvard Business Review* article 'Creating Shared Value'. Professors Porter and Kramer define this concept as the "operating practices that enhance the competitiveness of a company while simultaneously advancing the economic and social conditions in the communities in which it operates. Shared value creation focusses on identifying and expanding the connections between societal and economic progress."[3]

Creating shared value (CSV) is a shift from the traditional mindset that a company can either do good or make a profit, to a business model that can generate sustainable profit by also adding value to the world. CSV is about creating societal value while creating new business opportunities and strengthening competitive positioning, and therefore improving profitability. On the other hand, corporate social responsibility (CSR) is more about donating some of your business resources to charity. While giving is still an important part of being a responsible business, it is also perceived as a cost that does not directly contribute to a company's growth, which is why many companies stop being donors.[4]

A great example of a company that creates shared value is illycaffè, an Italian coffee company known and admired in five continents – and one of my favourite brands out there. The multi-billion-dollar coffee industry helps several tropical countries survive, with approximately 100 million farmers dependent on it.[5] illycaffè believes that in order to have long-term prosperity, the whole company ecosystem must prosper as well. In 1976, illycaffè's founder, Ernesto Illy, said, "The function of an industrial enterprise is fundamental and indispensable, but economic considerations alone cannot be enough to legitimise the work; they need to be integrated with respect for people, the community, and the environment."[6]

I interviewed the company's Chief Executive Officer, Massimiliano Pogliani. When I asked him what illycaffè's purpose was, he told me that it was "to offer the greatest coffee to the world", and this purpose had been passed on across four generations of this family business. But that is not all. Massimiliano dug a bit deeper and told me that illycaffè's purpose goes beyond providing us all with a great shot of coffee. In fact, illycaffè is a company that aims to improve the quality of life of all its stakeholders by creating long-term value through ethics and excellence. He said, "Our ethics involve wanting to provide transparency, sustainability and personal growth; not only to employees, but also to our coffee producers and, more broadly, to the world. Our obsession and passion for the quality of our coffee, for the technology that helps us achieve this excellence, and also for the beauty of our products creates a nice blend between the good and a beautiful, artistic touch – both in our products and in our store experiences."

Professors Porter and Kramer mentioned that companies can create shared value in three ways: by developing new products and markets, by redefining productivity in the value chain and by building supportive industry clusters at their company locations.[7] Each of these activities creates a virtuous circle, which benefits the others.

1. Developing new products and markets

Professors Porter and Kramer argue that, today, companies should develop products and services that fulfil society's needs – healthier products for healthier nutrition, better housing, less environmental damage, help for the ageing, etc. In this way, shared value is created. Companies that still operate in the shareholder primacy era concentrate their product development in a way that drives more and more consumption without posing the basic question: is this product/service actually good for the customer? These days, the demand for products and services that meet broader societal needs is rapidly growing. For example, Millennials and Gen Z are the largest generations of consumers who naturally favour organic food and beverages or natural foods when they shop.[8]

If you are *really* serious about tapping into creating a shared value strategy, start by asking the question: is our product and service good for the lives of our customers? illycaffè has been rethinking its main product – coffee – and working on a project of enriching farmland soils with organic carbon. This helps to sequester atmospheric carbon from the air and boost biodiversity, which in turn produces natural defences against major negative factors impacting agriculture. This leads to a series of cascading effects – including more resilient crops, thanks to better hydration. Reducing the presence of agrochemical residues leaves a healthier product.[9] This is not only an agricultural practice for the coffee sector, but for all farming sectors.

Why don't governments have the power to create initiatives like these? Because governments don't produce products per se; companies do – and they can find new ways to shape better products, while tapping into people's greater needs and sense of purpose.

2. Redefining productivity in the value chain

Opportunities to create shared value also arise while redefining the value chain. Manufacturing products means that a company's value chain inevitably affects the environment in which we live, i.e. water consumption, excess packaging, greenhouse emissions. In our conversation, Massimiliano and I talked in depth about the very essence of what it means to create value for all stakeholders while making profit. Massimiliano was very clear in specifying that illycaffè is not a charity, and that it is interested in growth and profit pursued together, in harmony with social and environmental goals. illycaffè wants to advance a business model in which growth and profit are not seen as anti-ethical, rather in which profit and ethics can go hand in hand while making a positive impact on society. The synergy between today's societal and environmental issues and shared value is created by illycaffè's innovative approach to addressing these issues.

Massimiliano tells me that illycaffè is inspired by eco-sustainability principles across all of its activities and is committed to minimising the impact of everything they do. For example, they have installed solar panels on top of their warehouse in Trieste, Italy; and in their facilities, all electricity used comes from renewable sources, helping to reduce CO_2 emissions. The roasting of the coffee takes place in an ultra-low emissions facility, where smoke discharge stands at one tenth of the legally permitted limit. The heat produced by the roasting is recovered and transformed into hot water, which is used throughout the plants. And they are showing improvement over time in their sustainability practices. In 2019, their water consumption was 25.5 per cent less than in 2018.

Waste management is a primary issue in facing the challenge of climate change. illycaffè recovers 99.4 per cent of total waste produced – for example, plastic from capsules – through innovative solutions that make disposal and disassembly as efficient as possible.[10] Massimiliano proudly shared with me that the company was honoured to be named by the Ethisphere Institute among the world's most ethical companies for nine years in a row,[11] and they are ambitiously committed to being carbon neutral by the time of their centenary anniversary in 2033.

This shared value focus has led illycaffè to achieve many other acknowledgements, including the first company in the world to obtain "Responsible Supply Chain Process" certification for the sustainability of its entire supply chain. Finally, in 2021, illycaffè became the first Italian company in the coffee sector to obtain the international B-Corp certification as a result of its commitment to comply with the highest standards of social and environmental performance.[12] A B-Corp is a non-profit certification that legally requires a business to balance purpose and profit by considering the impact of their decisions on their stakeholders, the environment, and their community.[13]

illycaffè has a responsible supply chain because it actively listens to its customers. Consumers around the world are demanding more supply chain transparency. In fact, a study by the MIT Sloan School of Management found that consumers are willing to pay up to 10 per cent more for products that show more transparency in their supply chain.[14]

illycaffè applies a shared value perspective in everything it does. The company believes that developing a fully sustainable value chain requires commitment throughout the supply chain. For example, illycaffè's passion for offering an excellent product involves working closely to support the growth of its coffee producers that are based in developing economies such as South and Central America, India and Africa. This includes four steps:

- Identifying and selecting the best producers.
- Training the producers by passing on 80 years of knowledge and experience in the coffee business.
- Recognising high-quality standards to farmers by rewarding them with generous financial premiums and long-term contracts.
- Building a community of training institutes, associations, awards and digital communities all over the world.

This sustainable supply chain is not only improving growing techniques and increasing farmers' efficiency, knowledge, product quality and sustainability, but is also strengthening their relationship with them through providing the right financial backing (salaries) to apply for mortgages, pay for their children's education and have a better quality of life. This is a win-win situation that leads to a bigger pie of profit, benefitting both the coffee growers and the company.

3. Enabling local cluster development

Clusters are institutions, trade associations and the broader community such as schools and universities. Porter's shared value strategy teaches us that companies that intend to create shared value should involve their clusters to improve their productivity, and support the development of the clusters in which they operate.

Ernesto Illy Foundation is a non-profit organisation founded by illycaffè that actively supports the development of educational programmes and activities for the communities in which the company operates. The goal of the foundation is to lift as many young people as possible out of poverty and child labour by providing access to education. In Hindiro, Rwanda, the foundation purchased around 2,500 certified-quality coffee trees and used the land as a farmer field school for a cooperative of 40 female coffee producers. The foundation has created a master's degree in coffee economics and science in Italy, which is promoted and organised by a number of Italian universities. The aim is to create a new generation of farmers by offering in-depth training in the coffee industry and in the agro-food sector, which spans from the entire production chain to catering and retail. Ernesto Illy Foundation funds these master's degrees for students of different nationalities, mostly from underdeveloped countries where coffee is planted.[15] I encourage you to take a look at the foundation's extensive website for more information as it's incredibly inspirational.[16,17]

I really hope that these examples help you to understand the importance of creating shared value for your stakeholders. Has this all happened overnight for illycaffè? Of course not! illycaffè has been working for decades on its shared value strategy, which led it to grow revenue, diversify its competitive advantage, expand in new markets and, finally, help its stakeholders grow with them. It's not for me to say that this has taken a lot of energy, commitment and leadership. illycaffè, every day, strengthens its commitment to pursuing a sustainable business model. The B-Corp certification reaffirms its corporate philosophy of operating as a stakeholder company. In addition, illycaffè's sustainability values are committed to creating a shared blueprint for prosperity for people and the planet. They align with the United Nations' 17 sustainable development goals (SDGs), which are an urgent call to action to collectively achieve a better future for the world.[18] The transformation of illycaffè's entire ecosystem generated an economic value of 491 million euros in 2019, which represents an increase of 11.9 per cent since 2018. Net revenue grew by 7.7 per cent and adjusted Earnings Before Interest, Taxes, Depreciation and Amortization (EBITDA) increased by 2.7 per cent, reflecting profitable growth.[19]

As you can see, it is more than possible to make a profit while being ethically, environmentally and socially responsible.

BRAND ACTIVISM, SCOOP BY SCOOP

In Chapter 2, we saw how humans need to belong to a community that aligns with the values and beliefs that run deeply in their DNA. This is not satisfied through a simple social media community, but is based on shared interests and the human need for true connection and belonging.

As the pace of technological advancement accelerates rapidly, and other changes occur across the globe, our human values and expectations change as well. The erosion of faith in institutions has created a societal vacuum; consumers today are more aware and demand more from the companies they use. For example, today, almost two thirds of consumers – especially young generations – make purchasing decisions based on where a brand stands on social or political issues.[20]

What does this mean? It means that customers expect companies to take a position. In the past, companies were rarely seen as agents of change. In fact, hundreds of thousands of companies existed and prospered in the shareholder primacy era without a societal purpose. However, both Millennials and Gen Z have grown up with very distinct priorities and expectations compared with previous generations. They look beyond tangible products and want to know what makes a company tick. They really want to see brands with a strong purpose, breathing new life into their corporate responsibility. These same consumers are willing to walk away from those that don't have such a purpose.

This revolution-based behaviour is amplified by the Swedish teenage climate activist Greta Thunberg. Greta's powerful speeches and ability to mobilise young people brought to light the widening gap that exists between the stagnant establishment mindset and that of her own generation (Gen Z).[21] Greta continuously challenges world leaders at the United Nations. She has received numerous honours and awards, has been included in *Time* magazine's '100 Most Influential People' and in *Forbes'* list of 'The World's 100 Most Powerful Women', and she gained three consecutive nominations for the Nobel Peace Prize during just over four years of her activism campaigns.[22]

In short, today's new generation of consumers are experiencing a world that is falling apart, with constant challenges – climate crisis, income inequality, political polarisation, lack of trust, MeToo, Black-LivesMatter, human rights and many others – and they expect companies to stand for solutions. As Greta Thunberg teaches, we are seeing a revolution that has contributed to anti-establishment, populist politics and a backlash against globalisation. Purchasing products today goes beyond the simple transaction. It's an extension of customers' views, beliefs and lifestyles; it's about making a statement and having a voice; it's a clear political act.[23]

Most marketers (like me before I quit) consider segmenting a customer base by demographics – such as gender, location, age – and craft their communication on product features, price, benefits and quality in the hope this resonates with the customer. But customer demographics are just too broad a way of understanding customers' needs, behaviour and values.

Why do customers' values matter to a company? If the gap between customers' values and business values is too large, companies will inevitably suffer. Customers and employees can sniff out companies that "greenwash" their products and don't actually execute ways to change their practices to protect society and the environment. This is a "cheeky" way of selling that makes the conscious consumer and employee run away and never come back. If we target customers by what they value instead, we align our brand values to their values, and we are able to create a more meaningful, human, authentic and empathic connection. Why is that? Our values inform our feelings and therefore our actions.[24] This creates a relationship based on trust, which is something that we will explore in further detail in Chapter 5.

As marketers, we are taught that everything we put out there must be "perfect", but customers want companies to be real rather than a bad version of perfect. Authenticity is not about sharing the latest product features with a press release, but standing for something bigger than ourselves. Many companies say that they are authentic because that's what they are supposed to say, and not because they want to be. If companies really want to be authentic and to be taken seriously, they need to start to show their true selves, without filters or contradictions, and make major adjustments in the way they do business.

How does all of this play into having a customer-centric business? Most companies have a myopic view. They look at the world from the inside-out rather than looking at it from the outside-in. Yet, serving customers (on the outside) is a better foundation of human economic activity than the mere sale of goods and services (from the inside). By serving customers with products and services to meet their deeper needs, the sales will happen.

I am looking forward to the days when marketers stop pouring huge amounts of cash into marketing the latest product performance and instead focus on the difference they are making. While many companies struggle to convince consumers that their product is better than the competition's, and stamp their feet on the ground when consumers ignore their marketing, other companies have changed their approach. Ben & Jerry's has taken a stance on nearly every major social issue over the last three decades, and it was one of the first companies in the world to give social missions the same importance as economic ones, whether that is racial justice, LGBTQ+ rights, climate change, voting rights, refugee rights, etc. The for-profit ice cream brand has a business model that serves its product as a means to create progressive change, not just generate profit.[25]

Many companies think that becoming political means losing customers. That might be true, but have you ever thought about how many customers you'd lose as a result of launching a product that's not well perceived or as a result of providing a bad service? In a hyper-competitive marketplace, you'd have the chance to stand out through having a voice for what you really believe in.

The market is saturated with advertisements for products promoting their latest features. At a certain point, who cares? Yes, you need a solid product, but it's not enough to sell to your customers. If you are an ice cream company, consumers expect you to make delicious ice cream. But what else are you doing to set yourself apart?

Today, you should be making a difference not only with your product but also with your actions. Ben & Jerry's has seen an increase in people who want to buy its ice cream after its move on many different social and humanitarian issues.[26] Of course, there is a price to be paid if you are courageous enough to share your opinions with the world. But the price of being vanilla is far higher!

Nike, the footwear manufacturer, saw an increase in sales of $6 (€5.12) billion after the company featured an American football player who took a knee against racial inequality while the national anthem played at a football game. The day the campaign launched, the company saw a drop in stocks but quickly rebounded to show a 4 per cent increase. Of course, Nike lost some of its customer base, but it quickly regained a new customer base, which was double what it had lost.[27]

As human beings, we need to identify and self-express our values and concerns; but many people can't do it alone, so they prefer to join a tribe and community that expresses their opinions and gives them a sense of belonging. As a brand, we should ask:

- How can we help our customers to express themselves?
- Can we do it through our voice?
- Or through our brand's values and beliefs?

If you can support customers' values and beliefs, they will let you step into their space. But if you are trying to fake your purpose just to compete, you will fail. *If there is alignment, there is connection.*

Human desire for self-expression and socialisation often pushes customers to become emotionally attached to a brand. In fact, 64 per cent of consumers worldwide make purchasing decisions based on a brand's social or political position.[28]

Patagonia, the American-based outdoor clothing company, created a platform called Patagonia Action Works, which works a bit like a dating site for activists. The platform connects individuals to organisations working on environmental issues in the same community.[29] Companies like Patagonia and Nike are willing to sacrifice sales if it means taking a stance for something they truly believe in.

During the COVID-19 crisis, hundreds of companies stepped up to give a hand in whatever way they could. This doesn't mean that all of these companies consistently do "good". However, in a study carried out by Deloitte, 79 per cent of customers around the world strongly agreed that these actions positively shifted their brand perceptions, while negative brand actions led 66 per cent to walk away from the brand.[30] This is simply to say that if a company creates social value, it aligns its brand integrity with sustained commitment to all stakeholders.

COVID-19 also showed everyone that a single government or individuals alone cannot address the world's social, economic, technological and environmental challenges. The younger generations of customers and employees understand this very well and are asking companies to step up, because they recognise that businesses are often more efficient in solving global issues than governments are. They have the capabilities, the means and the ecosystems to create social benefits.

How does this impact your company? Your company's purpose is your reason for existing, as we've discussed. And the way to tap into that purpose is by looking at the internal DNA of your brand. When moving your purpose from the "add-on feature" to part of the core strategy, the organisational benefits are very rewarding:

- A more unified and more motivated workforce
- Stronger ties with customers and stakeholders
- A broader positive impact on society
- Sustainable, profitable growth
- Relevance in a rapidly changing and commoditised world[31]

Would the little boy ever have drawn a rice farmer if he hadn't been empathic in caring for him and his mother? Probably not. Did the little boy know that the rice wasn't paid for? Of course not! Eventually the farmer went from giving sacks of rice to the little boy's mum (CSR) to teaching her how to plant her back garden (CSV) and harvest her rice. This may not seem like a lot for them to possess, but it allowed the mother to find a vacant position in another rice field.

You don't have to have big budgets to create shared value, but you have to have a big heart. In the next chapter, we will see empathy as part of being a customer-centric company of the future, why consumers are craving it, and what you should do to satiate the empathy hunger.

PONDER AND ACT

1. How can you leverage customers' need for belonging as an expression of their identity?
2. Are there any benefits and societal needs that could be fulfilled by your product or service?
3. Can you get rid of any potential harm by redesigning your product?
4. What values are you giving to your customers and stakeholders? How is your company uniquely capable of providing this value?
5. And, most importantly, how can you change the company mindset from *volume* to *value*?

CHAPTER 4: EMPATHY

CHIEF EMPATHY OFFICER

"The world doesn't just revolve around you." – Barack Obama[1]

During my gap year, I travelled around various places in Southeast Asia. Before heading to Bali, Indonesia, I spent about a month in Malaysia – specifically in the Sabah state, the northern part of the world's third largest island, Borneo. I loved my nomadic life. It allowed me to freely move from country to country, without any urge to get back to my desk.

As someone who grew up in the countryside of a Mediterranean island in a farming-based economy, I have been exposed to nature since childhood. I have also watched thousands of hours of nature documentaries, so, for me, seeing animals in nature is exhilarating. I got to experience a lot of this on my journey!

Nothing beats seeing a wild elephant moving across the Asian forest; going to a sanctuary for a full day of elephant watching was super exciting! There I was, in the Borneo jungle, holding my binoculars, exploring these majestic animals before they would make the list of extinct species. About two kilometres from our Jeep, I was watching a herd of elephants moving together. We spotted a couple of calves in a group, then one of them leaned forward to drink some water, tumbled into a well, and couldn't get out. The calf was too little to use its strength and looked like it didn't know what to do. Mama elephant pushed out dirt to help it climb out, but to no avail; although the hole didn't seem huge, the baby was too little.

We thought of going over there and trying to lift it out, but our tour guide thought it was too dangerous, since Mama and the rest of the herd would get upset at us. As Mama started to get worried, she called the rest of the herd for help, and they all gathered around the well. It didn't seem easy, because although more experienced elephants lent their trunk to the little calf, it kept rolling back in. Mama looked and sounded very stressed, bobbing her head, straightening her tail, and trumpeting a lot. It was heartbreaking, and we felt completely powerless.

The incredible thing was that as Mama looked worried, a couple of herd mates got close to her – looking like they wanted to console her. Our tour guide explained that the mama's mates recognised that she was upset and offered gentle caresses and chirps of sympathy. I was shocked and sceptical – and couldn't believe my eyes! After about two hours of desperation, the herd finally managed to jointly rescue the calf. Witnessing the reunion was a beautiful, emotional moment.

Why am I telling you this story? Elephants are not only considered one of the world's most intelligent species but they also have something akin to humans – *empathic understanding.* Their empathic behaviours include retrieving and "babysitting" calves,[2] recognising one another's pain and responding by making heroic efforts to assist. They rumble with vocal offerings that suggest reassurance. They form a sort of protective circle around a single elephant in pain.[3] This was the day that I actually experienced one of those heroic acts, which saved the baby calf.

And, according to scientists, herd mates experience *emotional contagion* when they recognise distress. In other words, seeing a "friend" in distress, as in the case I witnessed, is distressing to the observers.[4]

Like elephants, we can understand others' emotions, and our empathy grows as a result. We share food with people across the street and help strangers beyond borders, who we will never meet, via donations.

But what actually is empathy? It derives from the Greek words *em* (in) and *pathos* (feeling). It is the ability to step into someone's shoes and to understand their experiences and emotions.[5]

Yes, empathy makes us more human. Adam Smith, the Scottish economist, philosopher and pioneer of political economy, saw us as human beings driven by passions with the ability to reason and sympathise.[6]

In Chapter 2, we explored how different aspects of modern society make us more interconnected than ever – yet also lonelier, shaping what many call the "loneliness epidemic". I'd like to give you better news in this chapter, but the truth about empathy is that the modern world has made kindness and empathy harder. The 2019 edition of the Global Risks Report issued by the World Economic Forum stated that the digital tsunami has marked a blurring of the line between humans and technology. The consequence of this has been an increase in loneliness, extreme political polarisation and a sharp decline in empathy. The report highlights that while online connections can be empathic, empathy in individuals increases six times during in-person interactions.[7] Without that in-person connection, we are at risk of a deficit.

Given the increase in technology, which limits in-person interactions, among other factors, it may come as no surprise that levels of empathy among Americans decreased by 48 per cent between 1979 and 2009, according to a study.[8] British people also feel that empathy is on the wane.[9] In 2006, at Northwestern University, Barack Obama said, "We should talk more about our empathy deficit... We live in a culture that discourages empathy. A culture that too often tells us our principal goal in life is to be rich, thin, young, famous, safe and entertained. A culture where those in power too often encourage these selfish impulses."[10]

I got really curious about the specifics behind why and how empathy is decreasing in our societies. According to social psychologists in the field, technology and social media are to blame, but only partially. Other societal factors come into play, such as self-promotion, personal branding and self-interest.[11] The common denominator is that Western societies are becoming more individualistic.[12,13]

In fact, empathy is the antithesis of individualism and of disconnection. Customs and routines of food shopping, gathering for team sports and even attending religious events can now be carried out in digital form. Increasing misinformation online is fuelling our hate, and anger seems to lower our empathic impulse.

Yet, despite the deficit, awareness is building that we need more empathy. In fact, the European Council has recognised empathy as one of the key skills for the future.[14] Thankfully, there is hope!

But how do we go about instituting change? How can we move from isolated and individualistic to empathic and empowered to connect? Simply put, we can be more empathic ourselves so that people around us feel listened to, understood, valued and appreciated. Let's explore what this means in life and business.

Jamil Zaki, Professor of Psychology at Stanford University and author of *The War for Kindness,* suggests that we all have the capacity for empathy as it isn't a fixed human trait. It is about 30 per cent genetically determined, and therefore something that we can train and sharpen over time. Along with several other authors, Professor Zaki, in his book and studies, demonstrates that human beings not only conform to others' bad behaviours but also adhere to kindness norms, because empathy is contagious. People empathise and sympathise with one another, thereby promoting reciprocal care and altruism.[15,16]

Just like the herd of elephants understanding and reassuring Mama elephant, children imitate exactly what their parents do. Whether it is good or bad behaviour, when children watch us expressing high levels of empathy, they are more able to tune into other people's emotions.[17] The same can be said of leaders who model empathy in the workplace. In other words, the capability to be empathic exists in everyone. We have the physical structure in our brains' *mirror neurons*, which are believed to be the building blocks of empathy. These mirrors give us the ability to understand and feel what others are thinking and feeling.[18]

The main question is: do we want to train these neurons?

Within an hour of the tsunami hitting Lombok, thousands of social media donation campaigns were launched. In just three hours, people from all over the world were empathically aiding those impacted. We are not as bad as we think we are; we have the good within us.

Jeremy Rifkin, economic and social theorist, examined the evolution of empathy in his book *The Empathic Civilization*. He posed an important question: "Can we reach global empathy in time to avoid the collapse of civilisation and save the Earth?"[19]

Rifkin mentions that if we want to extend empathy into the biosphere – within our common community – to reduce the level of narcissism, materialism, violence and aggression, we must externalise our *homoem- pathicus* [caring also for others as opposed to just ourselves], which is repressed by business practices, governments and institutions. We need to think of empathy as the invisible hand allowing us to share our sensi- bility with one another so that we can cohere in larger social units.[20]

What does this all mean for businesses? The empathy deficit in society also means a deficit in the way customers feel treated by companies. A further decline in empathy and an increase in anger would spill over into the workplaces and affect the ability to engage customers.

The challenge for business leaders is to create an empathic corpo- rate culture of openness and responsiveness. We will talk about corpo- rate culture in greater detail in the Pillar of Culture. The mantra of "the business of business is business" has pervaded Western economies for decades, but in an increasingly automated world, there is a strong desire for more empathy. Those businesses that can create an empathic presence for both employees and customers will strengthen the bonds for a broader community – and nurture deeper customer engagement and relationships.

You might be saying "we don't do soft skills". Empathy programmes are often seen as wishy-washy or too feminine, and this is one of the reasons why empathy is not seen as a priority in business. While companies believe that empathy is of utmost importance, most are not able to deliver it. Yet, customers and employees want to buy and work from companies that put people before profit. If we want to lead with empathy, we must understand that it's not just a "soft skill", but an elusive yet critical quality: the more empathic the company, the higher its growth and productivity rates.[21]

Our brains tend to find easy excuses or routes to avoid changing our behaviour; we prefer keeping a fixed mindset. In his book *The War for Kindness*, Professor Zamil mentions that we've all been living like "fixists".[22] Fixists were those geologists who once saw the continents and oceans fixed in one position, while mobilists believed that continents were in motion.[23] We can break fixism by acknowledging that our intelligence, personality and empathy are, to some extent, up to us. Just as we train ourselves to run a marathon by increasing our aerobic capacity a mile at a time, our empathy is like a muscle, trained with experiences, habits and practices.

We have three types of empathy, all of which are useful to understand when applying them to a customer-centric mindset.

1. *Cognitive empathy* is the ability to recognise and understand other people's feelings.
2. The capacity to respond to these feelings with the appropriate emotion is called *emotional empathy.*
3. *Compassionate empathy* is the ability to understand how others feel and why, and then do something to help.[24]

Empathy is one of the most important competencies of emotional intelligence, and a critical leadership skill. Many companies see empathy as an intangible quality that is hard to quantify and measure, yet it is both achievable and crucial. And customer empathy, as we've been exploring, is critical to customer centricity.

How then do you ensure your organisation operates empathically? Companies should embed empathy into the entire organisation, from the boardroom to the shop floor. It should be embedded across three channels: internally across all employees, externally to the customers, and finally to society at large.[25]

I interviewed Alex Allwood, customer experience authority and author of *Customer Empathy: A Radical Intervention in Customer Experience Management and Design*. Alex defines customer empathy as "understanding the customer's perspective, feeling their experience – what it's like to be a customer as if you are living their experience – and then using this perspective in your problem-solving and decision-making. This is why customer empathy is so critical in developing a customer-centric culture; empathy enables customer perspective-taking."

Although empathy is a people skill, it is not taught – unlike the professional skills. And in business, it's often taken for granted. For example, we believe that because we can hear, we know how to listen. Listening with empathy, however, is about more than just hearing the words spoken; it involves possessing an open mind which is free from judgement – setting aside assumptions and acknowledging the other person's perspective.

Alex and I talked deeply about the empathy deficit we see in organisations. Alex believes that, because of "the CX score obsession and the siloed mentality prevalent in organisations, the empathy gap is perpetuated through organisational leadership". As leaders rise in the ranks of their organisations, they become increasingly disconnected from customers. Some executive leaders and senior managers have never spoken with their customers, yet they are trying to make decisions in their best interests. How can you possibly understand the customers and their experiences if you're not interacting with them and listening to them?

Alex suggests that, for an organisation's culture to be customer-centric, "Customer empathy needs to be baked into the day-to-day organisational rituals, and this requires leaders to role model empathic behaviour with their teams, such as asking the question, 'What would our customers think about this?' before making decisions."

EMPATHY FOR EMPLOYEES

During my corporate career I noticed how managers, including me, were rewarded for their ability to optimise things, particularly processes. But my working experience as a manager taught me that putting process optimisation before people leads to a deficit in humanity. Many leaders are struggling to make empathy part of their business habit, because process optimisation seems to be a priority. Yet, to become and remain customer-centric, we should invest in empathy as much as we invest in new technologies – making empathy a strategic focus embedded into the business culture.

Today, not only do we need chief operating officers, chief financial officers and chief information officers as part of the board but also *chief empathy officers*. It's been seen time and time again that leaders, especially members of the C-suite, are accustomed to showing only their strong side and hiding their vulnerable side. Paradoxically, by being more emotionally open and vulnerable, they can show high levels of strength. Empathy doesn't mean being weak or too nice; it means understanding others.

Empathy has an upside beyond customers' responses. Several studies show that empathic professionals excel at work,[26] feel less stressed[27] and show greater collaboration.[28]

As a customer-centric advisor and trainer, I am constantly experiencing the empathy deficit among employees – as well as between leaders and their people. About a year ago, I was contacted by a CEO who was willing to rethink her company's strategy to better meet customer demands and thrive financially. In our meeting with the CEO and her executive team, I mentioned that these were going to be major changes affecting every aspect of the business – from the product and services to the structure of her company. We also talked about empathy, and if this was something that they were prepared to develop as part of their cultural transformation. They looked at each other, then looked at me and told me that they "didn't think that soft skills such as empathy were fundamental for the success of a customer-centric strategy". So, I then asked them how long it had been since they had run an employee engagement survey, and their answer was a couple of years.

Before embarking on the whole transformation, we ran an employee survey to gather the level of employee satisfaction and happiness within the company. Some of the answers included:

- "The best people have quit."
- "Collaborations in teams don't function."
- "The culture is toxic."
- "The CEO doesn't care, and I don't either."
- "I am just doing my job."

The CEO and her team were shocked at the survey results and wondered what had happened. I told them, "You simply put results before relationships over and over again, and results before what you call 'soft skills' over and over again." The employees' words evoked their real emotions and the real climate that ran in the company.

The problem is that the way we think we run our business is not the way others think we run it. As I observed more of this company, the mindset of focussing only on oneself was the norm; collaborating and sacrificing for colleagues and customers was seen as a waste of time. Departments that had the same goal were completely disconnected and creating antipathy between one another rather than empathy.

When there is a culture of empathy, and when employees perceive their manager as empathic, they are more creative, more productive, have greater loyalty and do everything to go the extra mile for customers. Remember when I mentioned that empathy is contagious? This is what I meant. Empathy is spread between people.

So, if you are the leader of your team, by being empathic, you set that tone. People will want to join you, because that positivity is contagious. Whoever behaves differently will be regarded as the odd one out, a position no one wants to be in. They will therefore unconsciously shift to training their empathy muscle in order to connect with their peers. Of course, there are exceptions – people who will not join your culture initiative to embed empathy – but most people will at least try to adopt positive changes. They may need your help through coaching and training, though!

In case you still aren't convinced that empathy matters, let's look at the data. Leaders and companies that embed empathy into their customer-centric strategy perform far better than those that don't, and consequently thrive financially.[29] In the 2020 State of the Workplace Empathy Report, it was stated that 83 per cent of Gen Z employees prefer to work for an employer with a strong culture of empathy over an employer offering a slightly higher salary.[30] Being empathic with customers means showing empathy internally first.

So, how can we realistically redesign interactions with employees to shrink the empathy deficit? The first way is mindfulness. Mindfulness means being present without worrying about the past or future.[31] It involves focussing on the person that we have in front of us, then listening calmly and carefully to what they have to say without being obstructed by our intrusive thoughts and to-do lists. When I was travelling in various Buddhist and Hindu countries during my gap year, I learned that mindfulness is a skill developed through meditation. It doesn't just sound trendy; being present helps us to recognise the emotional states in ourselves and others, facilitating our understanding of human emotions.[32] We practise and develop our empathy muscle by being present – by listening and understanding other people's feelings.

I was recently invited to a three-day event organised by *The Economist*. The first 10 minutes after the opening remarks were dedicated to a meditation session led by Headspace, an online company that teaches how to live mindfully through meditation.[33] I was astonished at how more than a hundred executives closed their eyes to meditate. While I can't tell what others felt after the short meditation, I can share that it gave me clarity and calm when listening to heavy business content for the rest of the day. You can't just sit down, meditate once, be mindful and develop empathy. As with anything, it takes time and dedication – to develop the muscle.

In Chapters 11 and 12, tying in with the topic of empathy, we'll see how we can create a safe environment in which people share their true self in the workplace. Here is a sneak peek:

1. Practise *empathic listening* to help employees decide what is better for each customer at that moment.
2. Actively listen to employees' feedback and empower their expertise and capabilities so your people feel valued and trusted. It's not just about listening to feedback but also about creating *active conversation* to transmit trust and confidence.
3. Encourage people to talk about their vulnerabilities and mistakes by creating an environment where *weaknesses are welcome*.

EMPATHY FOR CUSTOMERS

Everyone goes to Starbucks, but not many people know how Howard Schultz grew the business. Howard Schultz is an amazing human being, not just because he built one of the largest organisations in America and came from very humble beginnings, but especially because he created a different way of building a business – by balancing profit with humanity. Starbucks shows that, even if a company was born in the shareholder primacy era, what matters is its mindset, values and purpose. Not every business decision should be an economic one when running a company. Howard led the company with cultural values and guiding principles defined by the success of his partners (employees). He earned trust levels that exceeded the expectations of his people and customers.

In an interview, Howard talks about involving not only the numbers during their experience but also customer intimacy – the empathy, compassion and understanding of who, in a broad sense, they really are. This is basically the empathic human touch. Howard mentioned that the engine that serves and keeps serving Starbucks is empathy – injected in employees and then passed to customers. He says that in 40 years of running the business, during every Monday board meeting, they had two empty chairs as a metaphor for both employee and customer. If there was a decision to be made or new strategy to embrace, they would ask: will this make partners and customers proud? If the answer was yes, of course, they'd pursue it. If it was no, they wouldn't. Starbucks' purpose was about elevating its partners and customers, and the profit followed.[34,35]

I know what you are probably thinking: this requires a huge amount of time and effort that, as a leader, you don't have, right?! Let me tell you a little story.

I am a huge fan of Sir David Attenborough, the English broadcaster and natural world historian. When carrying out the research for this book, I sent him an open-hearted letter asking him for advice about how companies, employees and customers could tackle the climate change issue. After about a week, a handwritten and signed letter from Sir David Attenborough himself came through the post.

Dear Ilenia Vidili,

You raised an important and complex issue. To answer it would take a lot of time and thought, and at the moment I cannot spare this. If I find myself able to respond in the near future, I will do so.

Yours sincerely,
David Attenborough

As you can see, this didn't give me the answer, but it strengthened my compassion and followship for a man who has dedicated most of his life to a complex cause. He dedicated minutes of his precious time to answer me personally, which elevated me to the top of the world.

Just to put this into perspective, Sir David is 94 years old and speaks regularly for the United Nations, in the British Parliament and in highly reputable newspapers, addressing climate change issues. He has won multiple awards for his breathtaking documentaries and recently released his latest Netflix film, *A Life on Our Planet*. He's a busy man; every day, he gets hundreds of letters from people of all ages, nationalities and religions, and guess what? He makes time to read and answer every one of them.

Could he have answered with a standard automated letter? Yes, of course. But you see his willingness to touch people's lives here? This is what I mean by the *human empathic touch*.

As automation becomes even more ingrained in business processes and people's lives, we expect to automate everything. Customers – and likewise leaders – seem to want everything as soon as possible. Well, you may be able to automate customer interactions with some sort of friendliness, but you'll never be able to automate kindness, empathy and humanity.

If you go to your favourite restaurant, for example, regardless of their latest inventory, you'll want to be treated like a human they value. You'll want to be greeted with the same warmth and offered their latest culinary specialty.

Likewise, as a leader, you don't want to replace the warmth of human empathy towards your customers with the cold and greedy automation of artificial intelligence. I don't mean that you have to rule out technology completely, but as we have seen in Chapter 2, the greatest human need is to feel connection. The glue of that connection is the empathy that is only possible between people.

Technology has other amazing capabilities, but it will never have the power of an empathic human connection – where a human being chooses to show compassion to another. That empathy can be passed on from your corporate leaders to your employees and customers as your secret ingredient. An empathic business environment is, in fact, a potent success pill for establishing long-lasting customer relationships. This empathic ambience can increase leadership efficacy while growing understanding and collaboration among employees, which consequently strengthens relationships with customers.

These days, most communication is digital – bots, email, Zoom, social media, smartphones, etc. The other day, I was trying to buy my usual hairstyling products from the company's website: I had a friendly greeting from their chatbot, which was nice:

"Hey Ilenia! How's your day been?"

I replied, "It could be better. My grandmother dyed yesterday." I accidentally misspelled 'died'.

"That's great! In what colour?"

I left the website... You see why you can't really automate empathy, kindness and compassion?

Customer-facing employees have the important role of passing a company's empathy to their end clients. They can express appropriate empathic language and tone of voice to better understand and address the situation. These aspects are key to activating closeness and authenticity with the customer during any communication, whether written or verbal. Empathy helps your employees to see the world in the eyes of the customer and have the right emotional response to satisfy them.

We need to train our employees to walk in our customers' shoes and think more like them. This can be done by spending more time with customers so that employees understand them better. Another effective way of doing this is to physically design the actual experiences so that employees see what the customer feels. We learn much more when we are physically engaged in an activity, not just designing it on the white board.

An American public utility company that provides natural gas and electricity noticed that low-income customers weren't paying their energy bills. So, after analysing the situation, they realised that their billing process presented too many unexpected charges. They brought a number of employees into a physical exercise to get a taste for their everyday customer experience. The team of consultants gave each employee a handful of biscuits and told them that several everyday actions would require them to pay with a number of biscuits. For example, taking the lift rather than the stairs would cost three biscuits when arriving at their destination. The training day went on with actions costing unexpected charges. Some employees couldn't buy lunch or pay for a chair to sit on, because they had unexpectedly run out of biscuits to pay for such necessities. This empathy experience made the group understand that many people with limited resources couldn't afford to pay their bill if unexpected charges were applied. The energy company then created an innovative pilot billing programme which featured bi-weekly billing periods, text updates on usage amounts and personalised home audits for energy efficiency.[36,37]

EMPATHY FOR SOCIETY

Earlier in this chapter, we saw how the increased use of social media and technological development has created a world of polarised opinions, and social isolation is hampering emotional intelligence. Satya Nadella, CEO of Microsoft, once said, "Our core business is connected with the customers' needs, and we will not be able to satisfy them if we don't have a deep sense of empathy."[38] Microsoft Finland decided to go a bit further on building an empathic brand by assigning empathy as one of its social initiatives. This led to several other endeavours. For example, as a leading technology company, Microsoft wanted to contribute to reducing cyberbullying and to do something concrete to prevent it. It joined forces with other organisations and NGOs to reach this common goal.

Along with the Trade Union of Education in Finland (OAJ), The Mannerheim League for Child Welfare and many others, they launched the Empathy Package in 2019. The package offers parents, teachers, children and young people tools, guides and materials for learning and teaching empathy.[39] Jussi Tolvanen, CEO at Microsoft Finland, said, "Parents need more information and better tools to prevent online bullying. As a technology company, it's our responsibility to participate in preventing negative behavior online, as well as creating more empathic communication. I hope that with technology, we can find more ways to reduce online bullying, and increase empathy on the internet."[40] After only six months, the Empathy Package reached more than 33 million people and engaged more than 160,000 users.[41]

I think this example can go beyond Finland. The customer-centric company of the future is not defined by traditional marketing or short-term gain, but by the emotional connection between leaders, employees, customers and society. Empathic communication can humanise brands, when "humanity as the new engagement" needs to take centre stage.[42]

As Howard Schultz advises, "We need to start by trying to help one person each day, touch one person's life every day, and bring love, kindness, and joy to this person."[43]

PONDER AND ACT

1. How can you train the empathy muscle in your organisation?
2. What actions can you take to show your empathic human touch?
3. How can you operationalise empathy and make it a performance metric?
4. How can you design physical experiences to better understand customer needs, emotions and situations?
5. How can your company serve society to lower the empathy deficit?

CHAPTER 5: TRUST

THE CURRENCY OF TRUST

"Trust is like the air we breathe – when it's present, nobody really notices. When it's absent, everyone notices." – Warren Buffett[1]

As an ex-corporate marketer in both B2C and B2B companies, my strategy, like many companies out there, was to be present at major conferences, tradeshows and social gatherings in our industry. This was to increase our brand awareness and generate business opportunities, but also to get inspired by amazing talks.

When I quit my corporate job to become an entrepreneur, I kept this very important aspect of doing business. Today, I spend lots of time at conferences and networking events to get to know people – which is something I love doing and a key part of my job. As an international speaker myself, who travels the world to inspire hundreds of executives to embrace customer centricity, I find those speakers who have the power of communicating complex topics in simple ways inspiring. These also seem to be the talks that I remember the longest.

In 2019, I attended a conference where Rachel Botsman, Trust Fellow at Oxford University's Saïd Business School, was one such speaker. She opened the speech with a little game for the audience, where she presented three different company logos from different industries. We had to clap for the company that we trusted the most. When she mentioned Uber, a good number of people clapped. When she mentioned Facebook, very few people clapped. And when she mentioned Amazon, unsurprisingly, nearly everybody clapped. Rachel then did the game again but replaced the logos for politicians. She then replaced clapping with booing, so instead of clapping for the most trusted company, we would boo for the least trusted politician. A lot of people booed for Putin, nearly everyone booed for Trump, and very few people booed for Theresa May.

The game wasn't really to categorise the audience, but rather to explain that trust is very subjective and contextual. For example, we trust Amazon to deliver our parcels on time, we don't trust Facebook with our data and so on.

When companies want customers to try new technologies, products and services, they require customers to give them their trust. Rachel calls this "the trust leap" – in other words, a jump into the unknown that becomes safer, as more and more people try the new technology or product. She says that trust is "a confident relationship with the unknown".[2]

When trust breaks down, first it triggers emotions; people feel confused and angry. Second, it triggers behaviours; people become defensive and disengaged, which is something extremely hard to repair.[3]

Rachel tells us that in any organisation, we have two types of currency: money and trust. The currency of money, as we know, is measurable. It allows you to exchange your product and services for money that you can then invest in many other things. Every organisation in the world also has another type of currency – trust. If money is the currency of transactions, trust is the currency of interactions, Rachel explains.[4] This currency is equally important and valuable, but far more fragile.

We have trusted institutions, governments and corporations in many ways since the Industrial Revolution, but we have entered this age where "trust is flowing sideways to colleagues rather than CEOs, to peers rather than authorities, to neighbors rather than regulators, to bloggers rather than journalists, and to Facebook 'friends' rather than experts," says

Rachel. "Trust used to flow upwards to institutions like banks, government and the media."[5]

Unfortunately, it is widely seen and talked about that this type of trust has been steadily declining and continues to do so through major violations of the social contract – corporate wrongdoings, government corruption, misinformation. Examples include the credit crunch financial crisis, the Wirecard accounting scandal, the Cambridge Analytica scandal and widespread abuse in the Catholic Church. In 2019, only 17 per cent of Americans trusted their government to do "what is right", while in 1964, the level of trust in America was 77 per cent.[6] In the UK, Brexit was partly a rebellion against an establishment that people felt never listened.[7]

In my chat with Daniel Araya, Senior Fellow at the Centre for International Governance Innovation (CIGI), and a dear friend, I asked him about the reasons for the decline of faith in institutions like the Catholic Church and governments in Western societies. Daniel said, "This decline is related to rising corruption and greed among political and corporate elites. Together, rising social inequality and climate change are adding layers of panic and anxiety, and this is ultimately undermining the credibility of established institutions. In turn, governments are lobbied by the fossil fuel industry to maintain policies that are counter to human survival. That's why people are frustrated. This is creating waves of populism, both in the US and Europe, that will continue to grow – both on the left and the right."

But governments are not the only ones that are affected by the decline in trust; the Catholic Church is another institution that has been dealing with a lot of criticism recently. Daniel continued, "The Church represents a standard for maintaining certain social protocols regarding how people should treat one another. If these spiritual and religious beliefs are eliminated, how do we fill the vacuum? Currently, we are doing it with consumerism, which is driving depression, anxiety and a crisis of belonging."

I asked Daniel what was to blame for all of this.

"The blame is rooted in a market society. When everything is driven by the market and viewed as a commodity, human value is reduced to material wealth, or to beauty, or to what resources we have. A capitalist market allocates resources efficiently. But a market society without human values or community ends up becoming too brittle, too greedy."

This is certainly quite frightening, but this erosion of faith in both governments and religions has created a void that customer-centric companies of the future may be able to help fill. It is also a wake-up call that forces many companies around the world to think about why and how trust can be earned and re-earned with customers, employees and society at large. In fact, according to the 2019 Edelman report In Brands We Trust?, people around the world are disappointed in brands' lack of societal impact. Just under half of those surveyed said that companies can do more to solve social ills than governments; however, 56 per cent said that too many brands are using societal issues as a marketing tool.[8]

One of the shocking indicators that trust in institutions is failing was when the former Italian Prime Minister, Giuseppe Conte, called the Italian top influencers Chiara Ferragni and her rapper husband Fedez in the midst of the COVID-19 pandemic to urge their fans to wear face masks to raise awareness about battling the outbreak. Ferragni alone has nearly 23 million Instagram followers,[9] which is more than one third of the Italian population.

Consumer trust in brands has declined around the world in recent decades. Customers, especially new generations, are less trusting of brands and advertising, and highly likely to turn to friends, family and anonymous social media users for buying recommendations. This means that when trust is low, brand competitiveness gets even fiercer. All the while, for consumers, it is very easy to switch from company A to company B.

The convergence of the mobile, social and big data megatrends has shifted the balance of power away from the companies and shaped more empowered consumers, allowing unprecedented price and choice control.[10]

If you have any connection with your marketing department – and you should – it's no secret that most customers are becoming sceptical about your marketing and advertising campaigns. The same Edelman report states that 74 per cent of people use one or more advertising avoidance strategies, such as ad blockers and opting out, and a study carried out by the American Association of Advertising Agencies reports that only 4 per cent of customers believe brands practise integrity.[11]

Before the internet was part of our lives, people used to share "reviews" about their customer experiences across garden fences. Today, the intention is exactly the same, but the scale is magnified. Trust, therefore, has become a major concern among companies, and it is one of the key factors to consider when improving customer relationships.

ARE YOU A TRUSTWORTHY COMPANY?

For years, companies elbowed to rank their position in "most trusted" lists of the year, which these days mean very little to consumers. Consumers don't trust brands just because they say nice things on social media, but they are constantly evaluating specific outcomes in relation to their expectations.[12] Trust happens between people, and it's what glues relationships together, which is another reason why consumers have a tendency to trust companies that show their humanity.

One of the most common misconceptions that Rachel highlighted in her talk is that brands can *build* trust with their customers. Use of the phrase "building" trust suggests that you are in control, but actually trust works in a way that your brand continuously needs to *earn* it. Trust is not built, but is given once earned. The question is then not "How can we build trust?" but rather "How can we be a trustworthy company?"

Rachel shares that being trustworthy is made up of four different characteristics – two *soft* traits and two *hard* traits – which are some of the ingredients that customers look for in a company today. The two soft traits are:

Integrity, which we discussed in Chapter 3. In short, this is about how the customer's values are aligned with your brand values. In other words, is your company promise aligned with its actions?

Empathy, which we discussed in Chapter 4. This involves walking in someone's shoes and understanding their emotions.[13]

Before looking into the hard traits, let's see how soft traits play in practice.

In Chapter 3, we saw how illycaffè does an amazing job at keeping the bar high for its business ethics and moral code, which affect every stakeholder who interacts with the organisation. Of course, any organisation can put a load of words together in a statement and talk about what their values are, but the difference between these companies and trustworthy ones is that trustworthy companies like illycaffè live and breathe by those standards in everything they do. In fact, in our conversation, Massimiliano Pogliani, the company's Chief Executive Officer, told me, "Brands do not have values as such, but their people do, and therefore the leaders who adhere to a certain way of working, a certain way of doing business, and a certain leadership transfer these values like a waterfall to their people of all levels – including customers, growers, employees, partners and shareholders."

Coffee is one of the most widely consumed beverages in the world, but unfortunately,[14] due to the climate change issue, the land suitable for the cultivation of Arabica coffee could shrink by 50 per cent by 2050,[15] while global demand is expected to almost double by then. Massimiliano shared that a partnership of advanced genetics research led by illycaffè and Lavazza (illycaffè's competitor) had released the sequence of the Coffea arabica genome, which would accelerate the scientific efforts to ensure the future of coffee agriculture as a sustainable crop. This research was made available to coffee producers and coffee companies around the world via the World Coffee Research website,[16] which proved to be a pivotal step in supporting the coffee industry as a whole, as it faces up to the damage caused by climate change.

As mentioned, this project was carried out with a major competitor of illycaffè. When I asked Massimiliano about this, he mentioned that when it comes to the global environment and society as a whole, illycaffè's purpose is not to compete against others but to cooperate for the future of the entire coffee production supply chain and that of the environment.[17] Eventually, Massimiliano ended the conversation by reminding me of the words of Ernesto Illy, who said, "Knowledge must be spread to the world, because by sharing knowledge, the quality of life of the people can be elevated."

Purpose and integrity can be neither faked nor automated, so technology won't be able to help with these. Millennials and Gen Z can smell it from miles away if you are not a brand with an authentic purpose and strong integrity, kept over time.

As I mentioned, Rachel also discussed two hard traits of trust, which explain how individuals and companies operate:

Competence, which answers questions such as: can this company help me? Does it have the skills to do what it says it can do? Does this product satisfy my needs?

Reliability, which depends on two things: responsiveness, which involves how the company shows up on time or answers questions, and consistency of behaviour over time.[18]

The chaos of the 2008 financial crisis instilled lack of trust in banks around the world and brought the rise of what we mentioned in Chapter 1, the new entrants, or "neo banks", which reshaped consumer banking. Neo banks are digital banks that operate virtually, without any branches. Analysts say that one of the key reasons why these fintech companies have been extremely successful is because trust in banks is waning. In recent years, these challenger banks have been specialising in areas and a customer approach that was underserved by the established banks.[19] Monzo, Revolut, N26 and others are the result of the financial crisis of 2008 and other bank scandals.

Millennials are very sceptical about putting their money into traditional banks, because they grew up during the greatest financial recession and saw how their parents lost their savings overnight. Tech companies such as Uber, Amazon and Apple have been setting the rules in which impatient and tech-savvy consumers expect things: quickly, clearly, easily and via all-in-one apps.

Since the launch of the iPhone and mobile apps, consumer behaviour changes and expectations have skyrocketed. Today, traditional banks are trying to regain their lost market share, while trying to adapt to the mobile-first trend and online banking. They are reducing the number of physical branches and, in particular, trying to regain their customers' trust. The question is, will they make changes soon enough to survive?

Today, the way that people can save their finances looks very different from how it was before the 2008 crisis, and trust is a very important component in the banking sector. Trust glues the relationship between a bank – whether a traditional bank or a neo bank – and their customers. We choose our bank on the basis of how safe it is, how convenient it is to use their mobile app, how easily we can make changes to our accounts, the support we receive when we run into problems, the imposition of fees for services and frequency, and the policies around these fees.

Essentially, the principal responsibility of any bank is to earn trust. I interviewed Andrea Isola, General Manager at N26 Italy & Southeast Europe, to learn how the company managed to be *competent* and *reliable* while keeping their *empathy* and *integrity* high through its "no-branch" and "app-only" strategy. N26 has redesigned banking for the 21st century, serving 7 million customers in 25 countries.[20] They have been at the forefront of this revolution, as one of the fastest-growing digital banking platforms in Europe and the US. Andrea tells me that N26's customer value proposition is based on five factors:

Simplicity. This involves giving a simple and quick service by reducing the complexities and frictions of traditional banking processes, to provide an intuitive user experience with easy-to-understand communication. For example, opening an account with N26 takes only eight minutes, and changing a password takes only a couple of seconds from the mobile app. Withdrawing cash can be done from any ATM around the world with a simple and quick enabling touch from the app.

Transparency and fairness. This includes providing a service based on fair prices and zero hidden fees. This is achievable first because of the company's honesty, and second because of their lean infrastructure, which keeps their costs low and helps them remain competitive in the marketplace. But transparency also means using easy and clear communication that everyone can *really* understand.

Security. Being a fully licensed, European digital bank born in the digital era means that N26 has built trusted technologies that are quick and safe. They have several security measures in place, including 3D secure authentication, to verify your purchase; a one-click card-locking feature if you misplace your card; biometric authentication; and a discreet mode to blur the screen when using the N26 app in public – features that help prevent fraud. I love how they speak directly to my worries: "As a digital bank, we have great in-app features such as being able to lock a lost card, and also unlock it again if you then find it down the back of the sofa."[21]

Innovation. N26 is not only safe, transparent and simple, but it is a highly innovative brand as well. They add value to customers' lives in an interactive and cool way. Customers can deposit and withdraw not just from ATMs but also from stores and supermarkets. They can also get customised insights into spending habits. The innovative feature that I love the most about N26 is that I am able to split a dinner bill directly from the bank's mobile app. No more awkward moments of giving or owing your fellow diners change; N26 thought of removing them from the equation.[22]

Global community. N26 is not just a bank, but a global community of 7 million users. Society's mindset is locked in the "money taboo", in which people aren't comfortable talking about money. To tackle this, the company started "The Big Banking Chat" community, in which they answer all customers' questions related to money and finances.[23] These are not FAQs, such as "Where can I find my IBAN number?", but deeper questions so that people can form a better relationship with their money. The main objective is to give confidence by simplifying complex issues and providing a clear path for customers to reach their life goals. It's fascinating to hear from the bank of the future about conversations such as, "What if 'less is more' was held in the same regard as the pursuit of wealth?" and explanations on difficult topics such as why interest rates are higher on loans than on savings.

What else would you add to the list of characteristics of a highly trustworthy digital bank? Empathy, of course. Andrea tells me that Italian customers, more than other European customers, are very chatty and love to ask for recommendations from customer service agents. The company therefore provides specific, ongoing training on improving customer service agents' empathy and listening skills for the Italian market.

Andrea ends the conversation by saying that 65 per cent of N26's customer base are under 40 years old, accounting for Millennials and Gen Z, and 35 per cent are 40 and above, which accounts for Gen X and Baby

Boomers. The latter has increased over the COVID-19 pandemic. Many new customers who had never tried digital banking and e-commerce have said that they are enjoying the ease and speed of it. I experienced N26 while I travelled across Southeast Asia, around different underdeveloped countries, and, yes, I can say that this bank is really worth my time and trust.

These traits can give us a better perspective when looking into our organisation to see where the trust discrepancies are – changing our behaviour to become a more trustworthy brand.

One day I was delivering a talk on customer centricity in London to a small group of senior executives of multinationals. Of course, trust was part of the talk. At the end of my talk, a man asked a question: "Let's take Ryanair as an example. People hate it for delivering very bad experiences. They are not very trusted, yet people keep buying from them, and they keep making lots of money. Why is this?" The man made a good point. Ryanair, the European budget airline, is a good example because, yes, people keep on buying from them. They gain the currency of money, but over time, they lose the currency of trust.[24]

Ryanair experiences short-term rather than long-term success. Their customers are not loyal and not fully engaged with the company. As soon as another budget airline shows up with more or less the same price point but a better customer experience, customers are naturally inclined to take the trust leap.

In my opinion, if there is one good thing that Ryanair does, it is that they provide cheap fares so that everyone is able to travel and experience the world. This is something that 15 years ago was affordable only to affluent travellers.

THE PROMISES WE KEEP – OR DON'T

For years, we have been analysing what makes a customer experience tick, mapping customer journeys and trying to understand the shifts in customer expectations. In my lovely chat about all things customer experience with Joana de Quintanilha, Vice President and Principal Analyst at Forrester, we also discussed the major changes in customer expectations. In her Forrester report carried out across sectors and geographies, she discovered that, yes, customers expect you to deliver their purchases on time – but their expectations go beyond this. They want brands to be more transparent, to actually "walk the talk" rather than putting out a brand promise, to deliver experiences in line with their values. And they want a more human connection. Across this set of customer expectations one thing is certain: if your brand does not deliver on its promises, the gap between *promise* and *delivery* widens, and therefore you lose the currency of trust.

Joana tells me that companies have a lot more control over how those expectations are shifting and how we meet them as brands. A lot of achieving this comes down to holding a more active conversation with customers and staying true to the brand promise. She stated, "We need to go back to our brand promise and ask ourselves: what are the promises we're making? What kind of expectations is our promise setting with our customers? Are we living up to those expectations? Can we do a better job of measuring where we're falling short? How can we fix it?"

She continues by saying, "Customers are much more forgiving than we give them credit for. What they don't like is to be kept in the dark. They lose trust if we don't communicate clearly that we can't meet their expectations. It is much better to avoid doing things or sharing any kind of communication that is not aligned with our promises." In other words, the brand communication should be transparent in its promise and its delivery. Be it an experience, a product or a service, the company and its communication need to be consistently reliable and capable of maintaining the promise.

For example, if your company promises "to improve the individual's quality of life through its natural products", but the people behind picking the raw ingredients work in bad conditions, then you are creating a huge trust gap. This last part of the reliability trait involving consistency is hugely important in customer centricity. In fact, Forrester states that consistent positive customer experience coupled with frequency and intimacy of interaction help a company to earn consumer trust over time.[25]

And what if you break your customer's trust? Good luck with that. Your job is to recover the customer relationship as soon as possible, which is something that we will explore in detail in the Pillar of Technology.

We have seen that companies can earn trust, but earning trust is not only the responsibility of the chief marketing officer (CMO) or marketing department. All members of the C-suite, and all other departments, should work together cohesively to achieve this alignment and meet customers' evolving expectations.

Earlier in this chapter, I mentioned that trust is very subjective and contextual. Saying that "we trust a brand" or "we don't trust it" doesn't mean anything without context or perspective, i.e. trusting a brand to deliver.

The same applies for the people who experience the brand: the C-suite, the rest of the employees and, of course, the customers. Every executive sees trust through their own lens and within the context in which they operate. For example, the chief information officer (CIO) may see trust in terms of data privacy and cybersecurity, while the CMO may see trust through the lenses of customer experience and marketing. For the other company employees, and the customers, trust varies too. But one thing is common: when companies don't keep their promises, trust erodes into something extremely hard to repair – disappointment and disengagement.

In recent years, the C-suite has been expanding with new management positions to reflect the importance of trust and customer centricity. For example, the appearance of the chief trust officer (CTrO) in corporate governance is an indication that a new business climate is on the horizon – driven by a culture of more accountability than in previous eras.[26]

In Chapter 3, we talked about how brand values speak directly to your customer values, which is a more meaningful way of serving their needs. If you are able to connect on a human and empathic level, your customers will be more attuned to trusting your promise and believing that you – as a company – are fully capable of delivering that promise. Also, by understanding your customers' values, you can be sure that your stated brand promise is fully aligned to their values and beliefs.

Your brand values, integrity and societal purpose can be as powerful as a religion. In Chapter 2, we explored how many organisations root their ideology into something they truly believe in and stand for. The vacuum formed by a lack of trust is creating a unique and historic opportunity: you can fill that vacuum and earn people's trust by creating a sense of belonging and human connection. A trust strategy around your business requires not only effort but a different organisational mindset; if you want to strengthen your customer relationship, you must earn their trust.

This chapter wraps up the Pillar of Humanity. As ethical business conduct gains prominence as a means to evaluate the authentic trustworthiness of a brand, profit alone is no longer the sole measure of a company's success. Consequentially, it is important to continually evaluate your business practices and decisions, if you want to grow the trust of your customers.

In the Pillar of Technology, we will explore how successful customer-centric companies of the future use available technology to elevate their human experiences – showing their brand trustworthiness through delivering *capability* and *reliability*.

PONDER AND ACT

1. Is your product, service or experience worthy of your customers' trust?
2. Do a temperature check within your company on trust's soft traits (integrity and empathy) and hard traits (competence and reliability). Is your brand's promise fulfilling your customers' expectations?
3. Can you measure where your brand is falling short?
4. How can you fix it?
5. How are you doing *as a leader* in demonstrating these traits?

PILLAR OF TECHNOLOGY

CHAPTER 6

HUMANISING TECH

"The human spirit must prevail over technology."
– Albert Einstein[1]

In March 2009, a chap called Robert Jones was driving back from his friend's house when the petrol light came on, notifying him that he had only seven miles left in the tank. Robert searched his GPS for the nearest petrol station and followed a suggested shortcut. As he drove down the road, the route got narrower and steeper. Despite it being apparent that a narrow cliffside path is not where you'd normally find a petrol station, Jones trusted the satnav and carried on driving, until his car became stuck, and dangerously close to a 100-foot drop. He was found guilty of driving without due care and attention. Robert Jones told the court that he was driving with care, and that he had followed the device to the letter.[2]

What would you do if you found yourself in a similar situation, with your partner sitting next to you, telling you to turn in the opposite direction to the one the satnav's suggesting? Who would you trust? Well, you don't need to answer that – you would trust the satnav, even though you know you'd have to deal with the repercussions of not listening to your partner.

This is today's reality: we tend to trust technology more than people – at least in some areas.

In previous chapters, we explored the erosion of trust in businesses and institutions. We saw that trust is a complex matter, and that as an organisation, you need to earn it over and over. Yes, because when I said that you *earn* trust by delivering on your promise, I also meant you earn trust via the interactions that your customers have with the company software and artificial intelligence algorithms they engage with.

Algorithms are everywhere today: in hospitals, in our cars, and even in courts. They know what we like and dislike. They suggest what to read and watch, and they even match us with a date. When Netflix recommends a film based on our viewing history, we press play, enjoy the film and trust it for the next time. Same goes for Spotify when it recommends songs based on our playlists; we in turn trust it every single time. Every time the algorithm keeps its promises and delivers on our preferences, it earns our trust.

This doesn't mean that customers don't appreciate the human touch behind companies – or that it's not a crucial component, even when a company relies on algorithms. Rachel Botsman, from the previous chapter, suggests that our trust doesn't lie in the technology, but in the company's culture. "Companies should create the right cultures around the technology, and continuously ask themselves whether their product or service deserves someone's trust."[3] We should therefore introduce empathy, kindness and humanity to machine-human interactions in ways that improve the customer experience, to earn and keep our customers' trust.

Do you have emotionally intelligent people who understand empathy? Are your data scientists, engineers and others being trained in empathy?

Most of the tech applications that companies use today, and that we come across as customers, are powered by artificial intelligence (AI). In short, AI tools simulate human intelligence – they are programmed to think like humans and mimic our actions.[4] Machine learning (ML) is a subset of AI, which automatically learns from patterns of data and then applies that learning without the need for human intervention.[5] These applications have proven to be extremely beneficial for both companies and consumers. For example, they are used in collecting, processing and analysing astronomical amounts of customer data – and in automating repetitive tasks, allowing humans to dedicate more time to customer relationships. At least this is how it should be.

TECH AS AN ENABLER

For decades, corporate decisions about the implementation of technology have been made on the basis of increasing profitability, optimising efficiencies and minimising the costs of human-customer contact. Very often, AI-based tools are adopted because they are easier to manage, faster, cheaper and more efficient than humans. This is not only a very risky approach, but it also focusses on processes rather than customers. It happens when you have a process that you want to deliver consistently at high quality and low cost; in order to make that process work, your customer must do XYZ actions. This also means that your employees strictly adhere to the rules and have limited flexibility to go the extra mile for your customers. If you have a process focus, then you also have silos issues – and that creates another downward spiral of troubles that run counter to creating a customer-centric company of the future.

It's understandable that cost-efficiency is a business imperative, but too few companies consider using these intelligent technologies to *empower* rather than *replace* the human touch that they often neglect. Too often these days, the latest, flashiest technology gets prioritised over authentic customer engagement. Customer centricity is, by contrast, rooted in listening to and fulfilling customers' needs, and consistently solving their problems.

If you are one of these companies valuing processes over people, I warn you that, by automating as many customer interactions as possible, you are making your brand increasingly impersonal.[6] The performance and efficiency mindset is still part of the broken capitalist system that we widely talked about at the beginning of this book, and it will limit your advancement.

In a widely read piece I wrote for *Entrepreneur Media*, I stated: "The belief that these digital tools can improve customer engagement like a miracle is just an illusion, despite offering an effective and efficient way to speak to large audiences. The reality is that these technologies are greatly designed to replicate some sort of friendliness but are simply not able to offer the much-needed level of human connection customers need."[7] I don't mean to belittle algorithms; I simply think that too much of one thing can be bad for the whole. There is nothing wrong with striving for the latest piece of software, but the thing that you should also evaluate is how these technological innovations can solve *real* human problems for both customers and employees. Unfortunately, or fortunately, your success is no longer only about technology – if it ever was.

More often than not, when I advise businesses on customer-centric practices, the main questions leaders ask are about the latest customer experience software to use. A lot of companies focus on using tech software, because it's good for their bottom line or for the way in which they are structured.[8] Tech adoption in the workforce can have many benefits. For example, colleagues can easily communicate across the globe, reducing environmental damage and lowering expenses. Some companies think that using many different business tools to automate and improve processes will skyrocket employee productivity and customer engagement. But, unfortunately, tech tools take as well as give.

Let me give you some bad news. Recent Deloitte research suggests that always-on employees can be affected by negative factors such as lower performance and weaker wellbeing.[9] In addition, switching between too many tech platforms, apps and software systems brings side effects such as higher costs and lack of collaboration in teams.[10] Your workforce may be able to see the increased productivity return in the short term, but too much tech follows the law of diminishing returns.

We must invest as much energy in the health of our people as we do in upgrading our tech. It sends shivers down my spine when I hear companies rushing for easily monetisable, consumer-automated interactions. Gary Hamel and Michele Zanini, two of the world's most influential management thinkers, state in their book, *Humanocracy*, that while there may be many routine tasks that fall into the automation basket, our work environments should be redesigned to draw out the irreplaceable human aspects of every company role; that is, creativity and innovation.[11]

Excessive automation may suppress human skills such as creativity, innovation, problem solving, intuition and empathy. If you want to become a customer-centric company of the future, you still need those human skills, and you should still rely on humans. Who is going to spot innovation opportunities? Who is going to show empathy with your customers?

When Elon Musk wanted to fully automate Tesla's factory in 2018, he fell short. Why? His reason was that "excessive automation was a mistake" and that "humans are underrated".[12] So, what are the options then, to avoid a situation like the one Elon faced? You should automate in a way that does *more good than damage* to your business and customers. You should adapt your technology to fulfil the needs of your customers and employees, not just arbitrarily force a system to work without consideration for whether it will harm your human interactions. If you are using more technology for the sole purpose of optimising costs and efficiencies, you need to be aware of the broader cost that you'd be paying as a result of losing human skills.[13]

With so many machines out there, and the increasing need for human connection, you should consider creating a customer-human-tech relationship that gives your business a distinct competitive edge. Is there a framework that helps structure these interactions? No. There is no model and no framework, but there are a few guidelines that may help you strike a balance between technology and humanity.

Joana de Quintanilha, Vice President and Principal Analyst at Forrester, tells me that this balance is incredibly important. Joana believes that companies today should be using human-centred design (HCD), designing for humans using technology as a way to enable the customer experience and/or employee experience.

"Technology has tons of advantages and is incredibly enabling, but we must use it in such a way that it is human-centred. We need to apply more emotional intelligence when designing the customer experience. Connecting with people on a human level is more important than the technology that we're actually using." When designing human-centred products, customer experiences or even processes, we should immerse ourselves in the lives of our customers and try to understand their needs, motivations and concerns.

I must say that I do come across companies that are adopting human-centred design methods and leaving behind the "checking all potential tech software boxes" kind of approach, but they are few and far between. AI- and ML-based tools are widely used; however, it is wise to remember that it is not about replacing people, but about leveraging these tools and customer insights to better serve your customers. No matter how many tech apps you provide to your employees, if you don't have a customer-centric culture, tech will not be of much help.

Companies using these technologies in balance with humanity have made significant improvements in their customers' lives, while increasing revenue and lowering costs.[14] For example, Starbucks' AI recognises customers who have opted in for shop service through their smartphones, when they go into one of their coffee shops. The technology then informs the barista of the customer's ordering history so they can then offer them something they might enjoy.[15] Other examples include using AI-enabled voice analytics software to help customer service agents better understand customers' emotions, in order to adjust their tone of voice and reflect an appropriate response.[16]

TECH AND TRUST

The digital tsunami consists of multiple technologies, such as e-commerce, blockchain, augmented reality and the internet of things, that are powered by sensors; tiny devices that detect and respond to changes in an environment. These sensors can gather a huge amount of customer data that basically provide the breadcrumbs that your customers leave you with.

But this overload of information comes with a downside. The amount of digital saturation over the last few years, let alone during and after COVID-19, is increasingly causing digital fatigue in such a way that customers have a love–hate relationship with tech. This is another reason why we have to be incredibly mindful of balancing tech and humanity.

For example, tech has led to innumerable benefits to both consumers and businesses, but it is also increasing data breaches and privacy violations. In many ways it has fractured customer trust all over the world – Cambridge Analytica's data privacy scandal in the West,[17] Sina Weibo's leak of millions of users' data onto the dark web in the East,[18] and others. The companies that can achieve a good balance between technology and humanity, coupled with addressing customers' concerns over their data, will gain and regain consumer trust, which is the next challenge that many legacy companies face, especially with digital native consumers.[19]

And what if you break that trust? What are your options? Your job is to recover the customer relationship as soon as possible. So many companies think that they can just buy back trust by giving customers a few credit vouchers to shut them up. Imagine doing this for hundreds of customers every day. It would soon send you out of business. Earning back your customer trust, and therefore recovering your relationship with them, cannot be repaired with money. It's exactly the same as listening to the satnav rather than your partner, and giving them 50 euros or a gift, to ask their forgiveness when you've let them down, with no emotional understanding of why they are so hurt and upset. Instead, you need to do things like apologise authentically and listen with empathy. You also need to commit to look into, and address, the root cause of the reason why they are not happy with their experience.

The same applies with customers as it does with any other relationship in your life. When customers put their trust in your brand, it is a human thing, and you must repair it with a human touch. The materialistic way of recovering a relationship will only get you so far. Customers won't hate you for breaking their trust, but unless it's quickly restored, they will grow indifferent to you, going forward. The tangible cost of losing loyal customers as a result of breaking their trust, in whatever way it happens, is very high. Just think about the credit vouchers that you'd be giving away; the number of employees required in the customer service department; the cost of losing future sales from the angry customers who won't be easily bribed with your voucher; the cost of multiple press releases if the issue has escalated; the potential cost of securing new customers, which is much higher than retaining your loyal ones. Depending on the industry that you are in, dealing with a breach of trust can be anywhere from 5 to 25 times more expensive than never letting it happen to begin with.[20]

On the flip side, keeping a customer's trust reaps dividends. It's been proved over and over that loyal customers spend more. A 5 per cent increase in customer retention increases profits by 25 per cent to 95 per cent.[21]

With this digital tsunami bombarding us, more data can lead to more "mess" to wade through – which adds to your employees' ongoing to-do list. Think about what insights really help you to know your customers better. Which insights do you really need? And what tech tool can help you offer these insights more meaningfully for better personalisation?

A study carried out by the *Harvard Business Review* shows that the top three barriers to providing more tailored customer interactions are as follows:

1. Barriers of organisational silos, which make it difficult to understand and to improve the customer journey
2. Lack of compatibility across existing technology systems
3. Lack of clear vision from management[22]

These three points are enormous barriers to improving customer relationships, but I'd also add another:

4. Treating the customer like a wallet through the selling process.

The third and fourth barriers exist because we still tend to manage companies on the basis of numbers, which is a retro mindset.

So many companies keep on getting the shiniest piece of tech, without thinking whether it is compatible with their other technologies.

Software systems that don't communicate well with one another make it very difficult to get a holistic view of customers. I have been in companies where there is no sign of a customer relationship management (CRM) system in place. Yes, some companies think that, in the 21st century, they can still get away without one; some use Excel spreadsheets; and others still have 30-year-old software. How do you think such an old CRM system can operate effectively and interface with newer digital technologies? You probably know the answer.

During the pandemic, nearly 16,000 coronavirus cases went unreported in England, because they were recorded in an old version of an Excel spreadsheet that reached its maximum file size.[23] When this data was transferred into a central computer system, a chunk of the names got lopped off. *The New York Times* called it an amateur bookkeeper error – this from the National Health Service of the world's sixth-largest economy.[24]

Many companies add more and more tech at the expense of the customer without thinking how and why this can make for a very inconsistent experience. One of the reasons for this is operating with outdated legacy technology that doesn't integrate well. All the software that we use in the marketing and sales departments – such as content management systems (CMS), CRM systems, marketing automation tools – need to integrate well with customer experience management (CEM) tools. Unfortunately, legacy software makes it impossible to meet customer expectations.[25]

Outdated systems may prevent your company from adapting to the digital age and limit the effectiveness of your employees to help your customers in a more efficient way.

It's not just about the adoption of the right technology and avoiding legacy software, but about building a more agile technology infrastructure with cloud-based storage. This is not only cheaper, but it also links your data and your people in a faster and more agile way. The more fragmented your systems are, the more difficult it is to keep cyber threats from your door.

Today's cyber threats are incredibly sophisticated. Do you have all the different security measures in place for each and every one of your tech tools? And what about digital ethics? This may be needed for initiatives that involve collecting, storing and using customers' data.

Nowadays, as we've discussed, every piece of software and hardware is contributing to a global data tsunami. Yet, the "maximising engagement" culture has sparked a movement to overcome users' digital addiction. In fact, legislators in the United States started protecting consumers with the Detour Act against "dark patterns".[26] Dark patterns are practices that companies employ to subtly influence users to do things that they didn't mean to do. These include disguised ads, forced continuity, hidden costs and misdirection. Most consumers don't understand what is happening behind these tactics. These practices often push users towards accidentally giving up their data.[27]

There are already algorithms out there that decide prison terms, treatments for cancer patients, the 'social credit' on a population,[28] and even hire your employees. Should your customers know that they are interacting with robots? If you want to earn their trust, you must be transparent about how their data will be used and who is interacting with them. Finding the right tech for your customer-centricity strategy also means keeping the data you collect smart and clean.

The European Union will soon further regulate the use of AI by requiring more transparency on things such as chatbots and deepfake (media in which a person in an existing image or video is replaced with someone else's likeness).[29] Informing users that they are interacting with something artificial will be the law in Europe going forward.[30]

In Chapter 7, we'll look into how to be more transparent, simple, ethical and safe when dealing with your customer data – while adopting AI and ML for offering personalisation to your customers. Remember, the key ingredient in your machine-human customer relationship is *trust.*

TECH AND EMPATHY

With COVID-19, behaviours and expectations are changing even more radically and much faster than ever. Understanding your customers' lives and perspectives is critical; but customers' behaviour are unpredictable. They want all sorts of options at their fingertips. Whether it is their preferred method of communication or transaction, they are constantly changing the way they interact with companies. Sometimes they want to shop from your retail store, other times they prefer to buy from your e-commerce store, and other times still, they will use your retail store as a showroom but then buy products from your competitors. In short, they want you to know them while being transparent, clear, easy, trustworthy, empathic, quick, convenient and offering a product that is good quality, organic, safe and personal. And, of course, they want online and offline experiences.

Social distancing may have spurred you to move to fully digital or to a hybrid of digital and physical. Striking a must-have balance between the convenience of digital channels and the empathic in-person connection will become the new competitive advantage. Something of particular importance is that you'll have to deliver omnichannel experiences, blending both digital and physical environments into hybrid experiences.

As a result of the coronavirus pandemic, the number of people using digital channels has increased – children, the elderly, individuals with physical disabilities and sceptics – which all adds new layers of digital expectations.[31] There is thus an urgent need to redesign and rethink your customer journeys to accommodate your new customer behaviour.

In the 2021 customer experience predictions by Forrester, Joana mentioned that, going forward, customers will value experiences that provide an alternative to the digital saturation we have experienced prior, during and after COVID-19. This means delivering immersive experiences that bridge the online and offline worlds. For example, this may equate to smaller stores, where customers can place orders for home delivery.[32] There will be a lot of innovation in the retail sector to complement both environments. We will explore more of how the retail sector will evolve, in Chapter 9, while going into how innovation will be part of your customer-centricity strategy.

Of course, most of us purchased online at least once before the pandemic hit. But some lagged behind. For example, my mum, a Baby Boomer, did her grocery shopping online for the first time during this crisis. Now, she does it every two weeks, exclusively online. She enjoys the convenience and ease of it, and she tells me that, whenever she feels like it, she can always go back to the supermarket. These behaviours will not change, because people like my mum have finally enjoyed the convenience of digital.

The digital transformation we have been on has been a significant, skyrocketing journey. Yet, as we have seen in the Pillar of Humanity, people still want connection. Even though COVID-19 was the biggest and fastest digital transformation training, people also want the physical and in-person interaction. As companies, we need to think about how we can keep the human connection, because that is the heartbeat of business, and it always will be. That's why it is crucial that your brand starts to embrace what many call the "phygital" world.

Phygital blends both the online and offline worlds by taking the best aspects from each environment to create a complete and more satisfying cross-channel customer experience. But what happens if you are a digital company only?

Forrester's 2020 European Banking Customer Experience Index (CX Index™) measures how successfully 28 banking brands in the UK, France, Italy and Spain deliver customer experiences that create and sustain customer loyalty. Forrester's CX Index surveys customers to assess how three important aspects of CX quality (effectiveness, ease and emotion) impact three measures of customer loyalty (retention, enrichment and advocacy).[33] Joana tells me that Monzo, a UK digital-only bank, delivered 38.5 positive experiences for every negative experience – the highest ratio of positive to negative experiences in European banking in 2020.

As a virtual neo bank, how was Monzo able to build a strong emotional connection with its customers? Joana says, "Monzo is very much focussed on empathy and the customer's financial wellbeing, so it's much more than just helping customers manage their finances. Monzo embedded financial management tools into its mobile app. But that's not all. Everything is about empathy, so how they communicate with customers, how they write their scripts for their customer service agents and so on. These things are what have helped them to create a customer experience that is different from other banks."

During the COVID-19 pandemic, customer service departments were the channel of choice for many consumers. This function shrinks brand reputation because agents usually have very strict timing and processes to adhere to. Customer service agents are one important piece of the puzzle for successful human–tech balance because they bring the empathic human touch that we explored in Chapter 4. As you rethink the offline experience for the phygital era, you not only have to employ design tactics, such as clear navigation elements, descriptive buttons and simple language, but it's also imperative that you do it with empathy throughout the customer journey – because, again, empathy takes centre stage in customer experience.[34] Joana tells me that, "First Direct, a telephone and internet-based bank in the UK, performed the best on the customer service drivers in the European Banking CX Index. They made the decision to not outsource their customer service department, because they believe that having a human conversation with their customers is incredibly important, which has resulted in a differentiator for the brand."

So, what are the aspects that need to be in place within the phygital environment in order to remain customer-centric? We will look into the ways of creating a phygital customer experience in Chapter 8. We will look at how to minimise the bad interactions, inconsistencies and frictions that may upset your customers. We will cover how to minimise the steps and procedures that make your customers ghost you – and, most importantly, how to introduce convenience, automation and invisibility at the same time. Your tech strategy should have a direct correlation to your customer-centricity strategy, joined by the same objective of serving your customers better. For example, this may involve helping your customers more quickly or allowing employees to fulfil orders more efficiently. Finding the right tech for your customer-centricity strategy means being strategically selective.[35]

I am a little worried that businesses are favouring technology as opposed to people. The more digital things become, the more useful humanity can be due to the efficiencies and connections involved. But many companies think of their employees as their algorithms: the processes are in place, and employees are following the rules and doing what they are told. It's a bureaucratic, top-down approach that leaves little to no room for human connection.

In a chat with Don Peppers, customer-centricity authority and author of *Customer Experience: What, How and Why Now,* we talked about what we thought the future of customer centricity would be. Don says, "The future of customer centricity is people-oriented. As the world gets more and more automated, humanity will be even more important. In the 19th and 20th century, organisations were highly bureaucratic. In the 21st century, they will be more team-oriented, much more agile, more flexible and more human." Don shared an interesting example about the importance of interactions between employees and customers. He tells me that the CMO of an Australian company instituted a new policy in the contact centre. "If the person in the contact centre dealing with a customer problem thinks they know a good solution for the customer that's not scripted in the computer, the only permission they need is to get one other frontline employee to agree to that solution. They both sign it off, and then the employee dealing with the customer offers the solution to them. The CMO told me that they only had 40 or 50 of them in the 3 or 4 months that they had the programme going, and they hadn't had to reverse any. The contact centre people were all jazzed and enthusiastic about solving their customers' problems as they were in charge."

Don continued by saying that a bot couldn't have had a conversation of that kind with a customer, and certainly couldn't have had consciousness, as humans do. "Computers are involved, and they do the job when they can, but in the end, we trust people – and *our* people. The more you can be an objective counsellor when trying to fix a customer problem or meeting their needs, the more likely that customer will trust you and return to you in the future. And the more they do business with you, the better off they will be. A customer will create the most value for your business over the long term. And they will feel they're getting the most value from you when they can trust you always to act in their interest."

Being a machine-centric business is not the answer in a world where mass automation is being adopted by the minute, societal and stakeholder expectations are rising and disruptors are continuing to threaten entire sectors. In this pillar we will look at how the customer-centric company of the future puts its people at the centre and uses technology as an enabler.

Spoiler alert: *data, ease of use and innovation* are the three elements of the Pillar of Technology that make a customer-centric brand of the future.

PONDER AND ACT

When looking for a new tech app, answer these questions:

1. Is this a necessary technology to help the lives of your customers?
2. Is it useful for your employees? And for your bottom line?
3. Does this technology support your customer-centricity strategy?
4. Do you have more data than you actually need? What do you do with it?
5. Is data security a major part of your tech and customer-centricity strategies?

CHAPTER 7: DATA

BE DATA-DRIVEN

"Computers are useless. They can only give you answers."
– Pablo Picasso[1]

A few months ago, I was suffering from really bad back pain. This was due to the number of hours sitting in front of a computer at home without the proper desk equipment. As you can imagine, writing a book while taking care of my client projects, delivering virtual presentations and running a business, all from my one-bedroom apartment during a lockdown, became challenging and incredibly stressful for both the mind and the body.

After visiting my physiotherapist, her solution was to "rest, go for walks, take breaks, and buy yourself a new, shiny memory foam mattress". I took the physiotherapist's advice to the letter, and I started my research on Google for the "best mattress for back pain". After about an hour of scouring websites, checking reviews online, and signing up for appointments with several companies, I not only started seeing flashy adverts all over the web, but I started getting "buy now" emails about ... mattresses of course. A week after I made my purchase, I began getting salesy newsletters from my mattress company trying to sell me ... another mattress. Another one?! Hang on a second. Why on Earth was this company trying to sell me another mattress after I had:

1. spent about 15 minutes of my life compiling a customer form asking me multiple questions about my house, injuries, myself, etc.; and
2. bought a mattress from them the previous month.

As a single Millennial who lives in a one-bedroom apartment, where did they think I was going to fit another mattress? In the kitchen? The answer is: they were not listening to me, they were not personalising their emails, they were not merely upselling – for example, with pillows – and, most importantly, they were not asking me how I was getting on with my new mattress. Clearly their communication was completely off. It simply celebrated their products and didn't really spark any sort of conversation about my first night on my new mattress or whether it had improved my back pain.

This is a classic example of what many call the common marketing mindset: the communication is the same for hundreds of thousands of customers, both existing and potential. Many companies keep segmenting their customer base with buyer personas, thinking all customers within a particular segment are the same. Or they target different generational cohorts in the same way. As a Millennial, there are huge differences between me and my Gen Z sister. She lives with my dad and her mother, and she is still a high-school student, who makes dance videos on TikTok. I live on my own and run my own business.

As today's businesses are rapidly adopting mass automation, consumers – and especially younger generations of consumers – are increasingly turned off by any communication that seems impersonal, and they can sniff out those companies that are treating them like a number in the system. In fact, 66 per cent of consumers state that they feel like they are treated like numbers.[2]

How long do you think the brand-customer relationship lasted between the mattress company and me? Not long at all. I unsubscribed from the annoying and irrelevant communication, and said thanks so much for the comfy mattress.

Around 70 per cent of Millennials like me feel frustrated when they receive emails they deem irrelevant.[3] But not only Millennials. Digital and social media have reshaped the world – and our world as consumers. Each and every day, we are bombarded with information via texts, push notifications, emails, advertisements, social media posts and so on. Our brains have to automatically filter and digest large amounts of content that we are fed every day. This has completely changed the way we communicate with one another – and how we consume the media both online and offline. And, of course, it has shifted consumers' attention.

A recent indication of how our attention has dramatically changed is how social media networks now count video views in the first three seconds, meaning that most people, on average, stop watching after this point.[4] By examining my sister's and my behaviour, and also by speaking to marketing professionals, I have come to realise how companies must work harder to stand out and capture people's attention in the "three-second world". Customers generally care more about themselves and not about your product or your brand, and they pay little attention to irrelevant marketing.

With consumers being savvy enough to tune out when they know they are being overtly sold to, I don't understand why so many companies still put their shiny products in the spotlight of their communication – instead of connecting emotionally while discussing how they can bring value to the customers. Let's put it this way: you wouldn't go to the cinema because the advertisement tells you to "buy now" the tickets, but rather because the story, the concept or the experience intrigues you enough to see a film based on your interests, values and emotions. Right? I know this sounds obvious, but you'd be surprised how many companies *love* talking about *themselves.*

Your customers don't have time for irrelevant communication. Live by the principle that "they love to buy, but hate to be sold to". Treat them like individual human beings – and give them the messages they need, not the blanket messages you want to blast to the world.

Personalisation can save your customers time and grab their attention in the three-second world so that they don't have to filter through the myriad of information out there. Spotify, Amazon and Netflix have raised the bar when it comes to the personalisation that customers now expect. So, regardless of whether you are a small company or a big one, your customers expect you to offer them the highest levels of personalisation.

Personalisation can be in different forms, whether it is an AI-powered tech that recommends your products and services or a bespoke product created and personalised for each customer. To give you a practical example, personalisation is not just about getting the customer's name right in a newsletter (although that is important); it's more about getting into the interests, emotions, values, dreams, concerns, pains, etc. of that particular customer.

In Chapter 2, we talked to Alan Zorfas, Co-founder and Chief Intelligence Officer at Motista, who explained the benefits of creating emotionally connected customers as opposed to merely satisfied ones. Emotional connection with a brand or company occurs when people connect their own desires, values and aspirations to the brand. Emotional motivators of individual customers, such as wanting to "stand out from the crowd", "feel a sense of belonging", "protect the environment" and "feel secure", can drive their behaviour.[5]

When Alan and I talked about using emotional motivators for personalisation initiatives, he made an interesting analogy. "If you're going to meet with people that you already know, you wouldn't ask them questions such as where they're coming from, what's important for them, what their values are. You're naturally going to adjust the conversation based on what you already know about them as you want to increase your chances of connecting more deeply with them. Right? The same goes when using customer insights to dig into customers' emotional motivators. Sending customers personalised messages designed to resonate with what connects them emotionally will drive behaviour at each stage of the customer journey. You can use artificial intelligence to do wonderful things, but having the input of customers' emotional motivators is a much more significant investment of your personalisation strategy. In other words, it's important to make the customer feel like 'this brand really gets me, it really understands me!' So, by adding a layer of emotional connection to your offering, it feels much more personalised."

Knowing your customers inside out is becoming extremely important. This includes understanding their needs, their opinions, their behaviours, their emotions, their ever-evolving expectations and more. Personalising your interactions with customers happens through collecting customer data, analysing it and using it in a way that serves customers the right message at the right time on the right channel. Unfortunately, this doesn't always happen.

I interviewed Thimon De Jong, lecturer on social influence at Utrecht University and Founder of Whetston, a think tank on the future of human behaviour. Thimon and I spoke about all things AI. He shared an interesting view on the use of data in companies: "Companies have the tendency to outsource long reports from research firms every 6 to 12 months – which is okay – but the customer is not heard in a constructive manner. If you have a few psychologists and sociologists who represent the people's side on a full-time basis instead, they can own the role of voicing the emotions and needs of the customer all the time." Thimon continues by saying that companies "collect any kind of customer data which sits in big databases, hire a bunch of data scientists to measure that data, who then start asking, 'All right, what shall we do with all this data?', but where are those people who really understand human behaviour? The people researchers should be there before harvesting the data. They and data scientists should work in parallel to better understand the customer."

This is absolutely spot on and something that I have experienced and seen with my own eyes. Great human experiences require deeper human understanding. I have seen companies buying reams of sector data, which end up providing the same experience to every customer.

'GIMME' YOUR PERSONAL DATA

Every interaction with our phone or computer involves data. Every interaction on social media creates data. Walking down the street with our phone, even if we are not using it, generates data through its GPS. Every transaction we make and every digital media we stream includes data. *Everything* is data.[6]

International Data Corporation, a market research firm, estimates that there will be nearly 56 billion internet-connected devices by 2025.[7] Intelligent objects are becoming connected objects that use sensors to generate data about everything from our heart rates to volcano temperatures. Today, we have tons of customer data – both structured and unstructured. We can seamlessly collect smartphone and interaction data that yields deep insights into customers.

As a former marketer of both B2C and B2B sectors, in multinationals and start-ups, I know there is a lot of pressure from the leaders above to conduct broad outreach and prove the impact of the marketing initiatives to the whole organisation. This makes it extremely difficult to understand the needs of the customers and offer them experiences that they expect.

In the B2B sector, it's the same *music,* but the pressure is to generate as many leads as possible, rather than relationships. It's sickening to see this as a top priority! Customers today want to be seen as more than a lead. They want you to understand their needs for every stage of the buying process, anticipate these needs, give them real-time solutions and personalise human-like interactions.

Of course, we cannot expect teams of employees in different departments to be active all the time, innately know the customer's individual history, and deliver experiences in real time. The art of data science therefore has a great role in closing this gap. The science can find patterns across an overwhelming wealth of data and numerous touchpoints – in a consistent manner and across all channels.

OBSESSING OVER CUSTOMER INSIGHTS

Customer expectations have always evolved, and they will continue to change – whether due to the COVID-19 pandemic or another as-yet-unknown influence. As a customer-centric company of the future, your role is to find new ways to fulfil these needs and expectations – whatever they are and whatever their size. Your deeply embedded company purpose should give direction in a way that keeps every employee aligned.

Digital technologies can help you anticipate the needs of your customers so you can solve and fulfil them before they even arise. For many years, customer insights were limited to the marketing department, but having a 360-degree view of customer needs and expectations means understanding customer signals through gathered data from other departments, such as sales, customer care, operations and finance, too.

The banking sector has been among the most vulnerable industries to digital disruption.[8] Why, and what is holding the banking system back? The industry is plagued by a lack of a clear digital strategy, bad customer service, a lack of customer-centric culture and an inability to adapt to rapid technological changes. In fact, most incumbents still rely on IT systems that were installed in the 1970s, 1980s and 1990s.[9] The newcomers are not only challenging banks on their lower fees and high-tech abilities, but especially on their business model, which puts customers' needs first.[10]

I interviewed Zachery Anderson, Chief Data and Analytics Officer at NatWest. I wanted to find out how a major retail and commercial bank in the United Kingdom is challenging the status quo. Zack proudly shared that NatWest is transforming into a relationship bank for a digital world. That means investing very aggressively in evolving its digital capabilities, both in the commercial and personal spaces, to capitalise on the customer behaviour shift. To tackle the very new generation of consumers, NatWest has been communicating with them about loan offers through the Facebook chat feature – meeting customers where they are, which is one of the biggest challenges for traditional banks. Zack shared, "NatWest has been exploring a number of ways of communicating and engaging with customers based on their insights. For example, during the COVID-19 crisis, we set up a 24/7 emergency customer care line to help our customers who work for the National Health Service (NHS) or in social care. We used our analytics to identify them and made it available for them. We then used our analytics to support customers over 60 and in extended isolation to bank from home. Since our data could tell who had been coming into the branch on a regular basis, it then showed that they were no longer able to easily come into the branch, for whatever reason. So, we decided to check in on them and make sure that they had what they needed. We offered some specific services that allowed them to shop, have cash and make sure that they had somebody to talk to during the isolation."

For many, managing finances is not always easy and pleasant. Zack mentioned that NatWest's mission is to help customers build good financial habits, while taking financial stress off their plates.

Another unique aspect of an organisation with high potential of becoming a customer-centric company of the future is the capability to use customer data to anticipate customer needs. Zach continued, "NatWest is using payment data insights to remind customers of events in their lives – such as car insurance or a new electricity provider. We know that if you stick with an electricity provider for a long time, usually your rates go up as opposed to down, so we let you know that maybe it's time to look for a new one." I shared with Zack that I am a total disaster when it comes to remembering things like this, and useful prompts sent via the app could really make my life easier.

Something that really taps into the Millennial and Gen Z mindset is Mettle. As a result of the increasing demand of the gig economy, NatWest created a completely separate entity. Mettle is an entirely app-only proposition designed to help freelancers, digital nomads and the self-employed to digitally manage a business bank account without the need to visit bank branches and fill out hefty paperwork. In an interview, Alison Rose, CEO at NatWest, said, "Customers have been able to renew their mortgage online in a simple, straight-through process that takes as little as 10 minutes, compared with anywhere up to 23 days when the process was manual. Our mortgage retention levels improved to about 80 per cent in 2020 compared to about 70 per cent in 2019. We're now planning to extend digital decision-making across all our channels, creating greater speed and certainty for our customers."[11] This traditional bank is really surfing the digital transformation wave like a pro.

Being data-driven is about breaking the data silos and connecting all departments together, because customer obsession is not only the responsibility of the marketing or sales department, but of the whole company. A survey by Salesforce research revealed that 54 per cent of customers can sense when departments are completely disconnected – for example, when sales, service and marketing teams don't share information with one another.[12] Once all this data is analysed, it can provide a solid and holistic view of your customers.

It's thus critical to unify and democratise your data. By making it instantly accessible and understandable to everyone in the company, you can engage in faster decision-making and therefore build more agile teams.[13] Providing accessibility to customer insights across the company also means that you are not only serving customers better, but, at the same time, creating the path to customer-centric growth. This doesn't mean simply investing in more tech, but investing meaningfully. It requires flipping the operating model to align digital applications, data and your employees in one system. This provides your operations with the required agility to fulfil customer needs quickly and efficiently.

Leading companies with an eye towards the future are increasingly using predictive analytics techniques to connect more closely with their customers, anticipate behaviour and needs, and identify customer experience issues and opportunities in real time. These analytics can then predict future actions and suggest potential positive effects from those actions. For example, predictive analytics are used to train a mathematical model and find key patterns on customers' past data. The model, once trained on a large and consistent amount of historical data, can predict what will happen next.

In simple terms, analytics can answer the question: "What is most likely to happen based on my past and current data, and what can I do to change that outcome?"[14]

So, how can you use predictive analytics to improve your customer satisfaction? There are hundreds of examples – from the supply chain to the marketing department. The next sections will explore some of them.[15]

Using predictive analytics to reduce customer churn

Given the fact that it's more expensive to acquire new customers than to retain new ones, predictive analytics can be used to identify customer patterns that present high churn risk. This can help you proactively suggest incentives to customers, such as payment plans or lower price alternatives, to prevent customer churn before it takes place.

Using predictive analytics to anticipate your customers' needs

You can also use predictive analytics to precisely forecast customers' needs, even before they do. If you are a car manufacturer or dealer, for example, by looking at historical data, you can predict when a car is most likely to need servicing before a breakdown occurs. In this way your customers can receive real-time alerts about their car service.

Using predictive analytics to know your customer lifetime value

Are you interested in identifying your most loyal customers, or those with a high potential of becoming loyal? You can – and you can also expend more resources on these consumers or even offer them special incentives.

Using predictive analytics to improve human resource management
Predictive analytics can also be used to allocate your human resources more efficiently. In the retail sector, for example, by using past data about store footprints and customer behaviour, you can accurately anticipate how many staff members are needed. The same goes for the contact centre. This prediction will help you plan so that your customers can have a smoother, better and faster experience.

Should we automate everything we possibly could? To be effective, automation must be subtle and not perceived by the customer. The key to personalisation is not relying solely on either technology or people. No matter what AI software you get, there is a special type of intelligence that is unique to humans. Short-term metrics and outreach maximisation help you scale, but what makes the personalisation real is, once again, empathy.

Empathy is what will give your company a competitive edge in a crowded field. Some companies deploy robots that can offer artificial empathic responses or can fake emotions. But real human empathy can only be found in real humans.

WHEN IT GETS A BIT TOO CREEPY

Consumers love personalised experiences. In fact, 83 per cent report being willing to share their personal data to enable a personalised experience.[16] However, the way in which their data is used is crucial.

For the last 20 years, marketers have used personalisation tactics with the wrong objectives. We've given customers the convenience of personalisation, but we've also given them the worry that this convenience is getting too creepy.

Years ago, just before quitting my job, I was on the train on my way to London. I started chatting to a 20-something woman (Gen Z) who was sitting in front of me. When I said that I was a marketing manager for a multinational, her face changed, and she became very defensive. She told me, "at first it was very convenient when companies knew our buying preferences, but now it's really creepy and scary. I am extremely careful, because my personal data can be accessible to any company that's willing to pay for it. I get random telemarketing agents calling me, texts trying to sell me something, or emails from companies that I've never heard of before. I cannot go online without being tracked."

In 2018, Google unveiled its work on Google Duplex, a virtual assistant that uses hesitation markers and even adds human sounding fillers such as, "um", "ah" and "you know".[17] The device calls businesses to make reservations and schedule appointments with doctors, hairdressers, dentists, etc.[18] While many people applauded it, it did generate a backlash, because it sounded too human and people felt tricked.[19]

Now the question is: would your customers find it acceptable to engage with artificial machines sounding like humans, without their knowledge? If we want to leave digital ethics as a final item on the bottom of the agenda, like it was with sustainability for years, then the answer is "care about it as a nice thing to have". The problem is not AI or data itself, but how you deal with it. Governments and consumers around the world are calling for more restrictions and regulation on the collection of personal data. The California Consumer Privacy Act (CCPA), the Brazilian General Data Protection Law (LGPD) and the General Data Protection Regulation (GDPR) in Europe require businesses to provide more transparency with people's personal data.[20]

Rachel Botsman, an expert on trust, who we've seen in the previous two chapters, believes that the speed of technology makes it very hard to pause and think more about the micro-decisions that we make. But these decisions impact our reputation – including what we are and what we believe – and especially the people connected to us.[21] If you want to gain consumer trust while collecting, analysing and using their data for a long-lasting effect on your customer-centric strategy, the right answer is "you must be transparent, simple, safe and good". Although some companies are open about their data practices, most prefer to choose control and risk being sorry rather than to seek approval.[22]

It really shouldn't be this way. Following the four rules below will help you to create data practices that meet customers' expectations and earn their trust, while also leveraging their personal data.

Be transparent when using customers' personal data

Transparency is the way forward for building consumer trust. In fact, a study shows that 94 per cent of consumers have greater trust in companies that offer more transparency.[23] Being open about how and why your customers' data is being used can lead to opportunities for more engagement and higher trust. Additionally, you should give customers control in choosing what information they want to share with you.[24]

Be simple when using customers' personal data

Avoid using jargon and difficult terms in your data policies. Use simple and clear language that is user-friendly and easy to read and digest. Use bullet points and numbering to give space to your text. Keep the length of your data policies short, with clear headings. Don't forget to use practical examples of how you'd use the customer data.[25] I know that for you something may sound like common sense, but put yourself in the shoes of an elderly customer who has no clue about what "retargeting" means.

Be safe when using customers' personal data

Research shows that 79 per cent of consumers are concerned about the security of their personal data.[26] As data breaches and cyberattacks become more and more sophisticated, your job is to keep your customer data safe with a strong security plan. Stay ahead of cyberattacks by continuously monitoring customer data for potential threats. You should carry out cyber testing to highlight issues and weaknesses, and adjust accordingly. Frequently update your software and devices to the most current version to keep out the unwanted.[27]

Be good when using customers' personal data

Last but not least you should be good with the data you collect. This recommendation is my favourite. How can you use your customers' data to create value for them, and beyond? As a firm with a team of skilled data scientists, you have the capabilities, the analytical resources and the expertise to use data for social good. Remember, first and foremost, data owners must be aware.

As an example of using data to do good, let's return to Zachery Anderson at NatWest. Along with his team of data scientists, he has inspiring plans to address the climate challenge. With their consent, NatWest helps its customers track their carbon impact through an innovative, cross-industry partnership with a start-up called CoGo. The app analyses customers' banking data and matches every transaction to a specific industry, such as fashion, grocery, insurance. It then multiplies each transaction by an "emissions factor" for that industry, to work out the carbon footprint of that transaction.[28,29] Zack tells me, "Our ability to support our stakeholders to transition to a lower carbon economy is quite powerful, and it's in complete alignment with their expectations. In the motivation of our staff, for example, I run teams of data scientists and a number of little hackathons to establish how we could use our data to improve either the carbon operations of the bank or of our customers. The hackathons are completely oversubscribed, and all of our employees are extremely excited to understand how much their commute to work actually impacts the environment. This is the power of having a shared purpose. It is the motivation, the excitement and the impact of doing something good out of analytics." Zack's excitement was extremely contagious, to the point that I wished I was one of their employees fighting for the same cause.

Zack revealed to me that NatWest is committing to an ambitious and inspiring brand purpose; one that champions climate solutions and contributes to unlocking gains for the environment. So, the use of data for this purpose was not random, but intentional and planned. Zack ends the conversation by saying that "aligning our stakeholders and shareholder goals, and then having an impact on the environment and the world around us, is a pretty powerful set". NatWest is combining data analytics and their mission in a way that is strategic and customer-centric.

It's extremely interesting to see that traditional incumbents are slowly leaving behind the complexity of a legacy business. Could this be a step towards prioritising stakeholder value over profit?

PONDER AND ACT

1. How can you apply personalisation techniques to save customers time and increase customer loyalty?
2. How can you move towards connecting all customer insights from different departments and sharing them across the company to get a clearer 360-degree view of your customers?
3. How will you personalise customer interaction?
4. In what ways will you ensure that you are transparent, simple, safe and good with your customer data?
5. How will you use your customer data to create value and to support causes that deeply align with your purpose?

CHAPTER 8: EASE OF USE

THE EASIER THE BETTER

"Simplicity is the ultimate sophistication." – Leonardo da Vinci[1]

During my year travelling solo, I went to Vietnam. One day, I woke up to discover that all my direct debit payments had been declined, and my card wasn't working. After many calls to customer service, it turned out that the system of a traditional UK-based bank had picked up a supposed fraudulent attempt on a recurrent direct debit payment and had blocked my bank account and card. Basically, a system fault! Everything was frozen, and my card was refused for the rest of my stay – for my accommodation, food, travel – causing a huge nightmare.

After about three hours on the phone, being passed from one department to the next and being verified multiple times, finally, a not-very-gentle man, who apparently couldn't understand my Italian accent, told me that my card would be replaced, and I would receive a temporary one within five to seven working days at my resort in Phú Quốc island. *Phew, finally sorted.* You'd think!

On the eighth day, there was no sign of my card. Imagine being in a developing country, thousands of miles away from home, surviving on limited resources that you had saved in your emergency N26 account (just in case), with no online access to your main account. When travelling, it is good practice to split your funds across several bank accounts not related to your main account so that if a card gets stolen, blocked or lost, you have access to other means while the issue gets sorted.

I phoned customer service back, who, again, bounced me back and forth between departments and verified me multiple times, before saying they had no idea what had happened, but my card had been sent to my home in Cambridge, UK. This time, the kind lady – who apologised profusely for what had happened – transferred me to the Visa department to apply for an emergency card to be sent in 48 hours. Of course, Visa verified me again, and asked me to complete a "blocked card form" of 20 questions before sending the replacement.

Okay, fine. I can wait another two days in this pricey resort. Thankfully, it's already paid for! I thought.

After *four* days – that's 96 hours, not 48 – of waiting, anxiety and frustration, my emergency card finally arrived. I went to do some food shopping, only to discover that it didn't work in any ATM, retail or online transaction. I called customer service, and I was again directed back and forth for verification purposes and spent another couple of hours over the phone trying to understand what was going on and why the damn card wasn't working. Someone on the other side of customer service, who was supposed to block the card that was sent to my UK address, had accidentally blocked the emergency one being sent to Vietnam instead. My patience hit rock bottom at this point! I was reassured I would receive a new functioning replacement card as soon as possible, but, unfortunately, luck wasn't on my side. Once again, I was sent a useless replacement to my UK address. Some three weeks had gone by, and I still had no solution. Apparently, the system was automatically sending it to my billing address! My trust in a bank that attempted to serve me well for years was completely gone!

Of course, a bank also asks for feedback about the service you received. My feedback wasn't pretty, so the bank thought they'd offer me a paltry £50 (€58) compensation for the inconvenience! How do you think I felt? Angry, sad, frustrated, disappointed, bullied – you name it. What shocking service, right?

The first thing I did when I flew back to Cambridge was close my accounts with the traditional bank and transfer all of my direct debit payments and savings into my N26 account. The UK-based traditional bank had failed big time in serving my basic expectations, and it no longer deserved my customer loyalty.

In the highly competitive and disruptive financial sector, doing just enough is not good enough; we customers now expect interactions and problem solving to be simple, quick, effortless and seamlessly connected across physical and digital touchpoints.

As a consumer, there is also a moral to this story. Over the last decade, more than 300 digital banks have launched globally. If you are planning to travel on a long-term solo journey, choose a bank that cares about you and has a quick and smooth process to replace cards or issue funds as soon as possible, wherever you are. Losing your credit/debit card or getting robbed on the other side of the world with no support from your bank would be one of your worst nightmares.

Tom Goodwin, author of *Digital Darwinism,* mentions that, for a long time, legacy companies used to disrupt other businesses with a new, shiny version of their product and leverage the advantages of their market size and position. But today, size seems to be a liability. And considering the amount of choice on offer, a shiny product or service alone doesn't mean much to customers. Customer expectations are changing, and leaning on legacy alone is no longer cool! Customers don't tolerate poor behaviour, online checkouts not functioning, being passed from pillar to post when calling contact centres, long booking forms and so on. Tom says, "You can have both excuses and explanations for your inability to function like nimble businesses built today, but the stock market and customers won't care for long."[2]

In the past, legacy companies got away with giving customers okay-ish products and poor customer service. But with the level of customer expectations today, even the best version of your product is no longer enough.

In the Pillar of Humanity, we discussed how you can be a more human brand – where you go beyond the product and service that you sell – and how you can add value to people's lives as well as to society at large. In Chapters 2 and 3, we explored customer-centricity fellow expert Steven Van Belleghem's model based on four elements:

1. Good quality products and services
2. Transactional convenience
3. Partner in life
4. Save the world[3]

In our chat, Steven tells me that a first-class product is the new minimum today. And transactional convenience is becoming a commodity – a "must-have". Giving your customers transactional convenience moves the needle in the direction of empathy – which is something beyond merely offering a good product. It means that you have walked in their shoes to understand the frictions that impede them from having a smooth interaction with your brand.

Today, as I've reinforced in multiple chapters, customers expect these journeys with your brand to be easy, quick, effortless and seamless. Most brands map more than one customer journey. The more friction present in your journeys, the less your customers will be able to reach their desired destination and fulfil their needs.

Part of the solution for keeping customer journeys smooth can be summed up in one word: efficiency. The *Cambridge English Dictionary* defines efficiency as "the good use of time and energy in a way that does not waste any".[4] If I want to translate this as part of your customer-centricity strategy, it would be "the good use of your customers' time and efforts in a way that does not waste their energy". Time is one of our most precious resources, and if you are a customer-centric business, then you are also in the business of saving your customers' time and making their lives easier.

Millennial and Gen Z consumer behaviour is forcing companies to craft "phygital" customer journeys that straddle both physical retail and e-commerce stores. Creating a phygital strategy means taking the best components of the digital world, such as convenience and immediacy, and the best of the physical world, such as the human touch and interaction with the physical product. In order to achieve this, you should equip yourself with a digital interface that provides a seamless experience in the physical space too.

According to Steven, if you want to provide efficiency in the digital world, you should offer interactions through an interface that is "proactive, zero effort, invisible and personalized."[5] Let's look at each of these in turn.

Proactive. This means using a digital interface that can anticipate a customer's needs before the customer asks for something, and/or solves problems before they even arise. Being proactive may include sending nudges – for example, your central heating sends an alert when it needs servicing. You can then opt to be contacted by a customer representative to book your service as soon as this alert comes on.

Zero effort. This is self-explanatory. Your customer should be able to interact with you without effort or friction. Steven recommends appointing friction hunters within your company. These are people dedicated to examining any possible friction that your customer journey presents and removing it as soon as possible. Domino's Pizza is a great example of this. They looked at all customer insights and discovered that most customers order the exact same pizza each time, so they created a zero-click mobile app linked to their Domino's profile. Customers simply open the app, which will display a 10-second countdown until the order goes through, without being asked to tap, swipe or click anything.[6]

Invisible. We have seen how, these days, machines can automate things with little to no human intervention. If you want to use automation for communicating with your customers via a chatbot, this can provide stellar 24/7 service, *if* (big if) this is the highest performing automation. Many companies have jumped onto the chatbot bandwagon as another "nice feature to have", without considering the implications of not offering it properly. Chatbots are another branch of machine learning, and they can be quite useful in potentially helping the influx of basic customer enquiries. The problem with these automation features is that they mostly perform poorly, leaving the customer even more frustrated. Remember when I told the bot that my grandmother had died, and I was met with a cheery response? Point made.

Personalised. In Chapter 7, we saw how personalisation can be a winning strategy, which continues not only via the communication with your customers but also through the products that you offer. Personalisation has been the central focus of L'Oréal. The company engineered a small portable machine that allows customers to create personalised products such as foundation, lipstick or serum in under two minutes, wherever they are and as frequently as they want.[7]

'HEY GOOGLE, WHAT'S THE BEST WAY TO COMPETE WITH TESLA?'

Customer-centric companies orchestrate Steven's four aspects of an interface seamlessly in the phygital world. They ease the customer journey, generate trust and improve the customer experience.

To give you a complete picture of a company that joined all these elements in the phygital space, I interviewed Tim Heldmann, former Chief Marketing Officer at Polestar, a new, Swedish electric car brand owned by Volvo Cars and Geely. As a female Millennial, I don't remember ever looking forward to going into a car dealership – if anyone ever does! Buying a new car not only feels like a once-in-a-lifetime kind of purchase but also pressuring and intimidating in a male-dominated environment. The historical trip to the dealership was long, and the whole process of buying a car felt like pulling teeth: making an appointment; picturing cars that were mostly out of stock; dealing with pushy and shady commissioned salesmen that put you under unnecessary pressure, require you to fill out long paperwork and negotiate the terms of the deal when you feel unprepared.

Thankfully, many of these old practices seem to be changing.

Although the automotive industry has been very resistant to adapt to the digital world and new generation of consumers,[8] global disruption, technological advances and changing consumer behaviour are pushing the automotive sector to shift gears.

Polestar is one company that is changing the face of the traditional automotive dealership model by enhancing every aspect of the sale with a hassle-free experience. Polestar customers can define the entire customer journey, from the initial interactions with the brand to the delivery of their car.

Polestar is also the first car to come with an infotainment system powered by Android Automotive OS, with Google apps and services built in – which means that they are using technology to enhance their customer-centric approach, even after the sale.[9]

Tim told me that the Polestar team replicated a state-of-the-art in-vehicle infotainment (IVI) system that provides an "in the car" experience identical to how people interact with their smartphones. IVI is a combination of vehicle systems which offers passengers entertainment and information via audio and video.[10]

Polestar customers can download a wide range of media apps for listening to podcasts, the radio, audiobooks and music direct to the vehicle. Google Assistant is integrated into the car so that users can voice control with commands like, "Hey Google, play some music." Apple users are not forgotten. They can connect their phones via Bluetooth. These features provide an easy-to-use and fun driving experience.[11]

Polestar is an online tech company, because all purchases are made online. They created dedicated, intimate 250 sq m (much smaller than traditional dealerships) "Polestar Spaces" positioned in the heart of city centres around the world so that customers could touch, feel and interact with the products on their terms. The brand is also adding "Polestar Destinations" as its available retail spaces. Destinations are located at larger, easy-to-access, out-of-town locations (more like traditional dealerships) and will also perform handovers to customers who decide to purchase and pick up their cars rather than get them delivered at home.[12]

Tim told me, "Our people working in our retail spaces are a lot younger than those we used to hire years ago, so it's more like you're getting into a flagship store of a California-based tech company, where you really have a friendly chat about the car with them."

The amazing thing about Polestar's customer-centric strategy is that the product experts aren't paid on commission, are not buttoned up in a suit, which can feel intimidating, and they have genuine interest in serving customers. They are passionate and want to talk to them, rather than pressuring them into a hard sell by pushing an agreement under their nose. Polestar staff are very focussed on what the customer needs when they walk through the door, from helping them place an order online to answering any queries about the cars. Whether this is a five-minute chat or an hour-long discussion, eventually it is the customer who decides if they are going to place that order and when – with no sales pressure on the scene.

I visited the Polestar retail space in London Westfield, the biggest shopping centre in Europe. It was amazing how these product experts made the atmosphere so welcoming. It didn't feel like a car dealership at all. One reason is because Polestar has placed its retail space in a shopping centre among the high street retail brands of the world, so I didn't have to get a taxi out of London and book an appointment to purposely see the car. It was already there for me! When I sat in the car to get a feel for it and play with the iPad-looking central touchscreen, it was fun to ask Google Assistant: "Hey Google, what's the best way to compete with Tesla?"

You might be thinking: why is a car retail space located in a high-street-brand shopping centre in the heart of London? Because they wanted to make it very easy for the customer to come in and discover the car. I was already shopping in a nice and relaxed environment, where parking is easy, food is readily available, etc. Polestar has created such beautiful environments aligned to high street tech retailers and seamlessly connected through digital interactivity which feels invisible.

Tim said, "Our retail spaces are really adaptive to what the consumer wants. We have a lot of large screens on the walls that have a technology called 'proximity sensors', where the digital signage changes based on the proximity of the visitor. For example, when people look at the screen and come closer to it, it means they are interested, therefore they get additional information displayed. We wanted to minimise the intimidating feeling so that the customer can navigate through the space on their own. We created a complete, end-to-end, digital, seamless customer experience."

Polestar's customer journey starts either through the Polestar app or website in the comfort of the customer's own home and in their own time, or with the guidance of a Polestar product expert in a chosen retail space. Tim continued, "Once the customer has chosen the car specifications, these are saved in the customer's mobile app, ready to be ordered when it suits them. If the customer comes to one of our stores, they can place their phone on our near field communication (NFC) compatible devices, which are placed in every Polestar space. These help customers retrieve the saved car configurations."

It's great to see the digital sales model of a car manufacturer such as Polestar enabling its customers to explore, configure and purchase a car from a mobile app whenever and wherever they choose to – on their terms.

Tim also told me that this ease-of-use philosophy applies inside the car too. The car comes with a digital key, which is connected to the customer's smartphone, and as the customer approaches the car, the door unlocks. This means that the customer doesn't have to take bulky keys out with them. In addition, Polestar thought of an easy way of sharing a car with friends and family by enabling the digital key to be shared.

As Tim explained to me how they created a zero-effort customer experience, I told him that young generations like mine are a bit strange in the way we want things. The speed of technological advancement means that we don't get a chance to grow fond of the tools that we use in our daily lives. We want a hassle-free way of owning things, and we don't put car ownership particularly high on our list of priorities.[13]

He told me that Polestar thought of that too and created three options of owning a car. "One is the old-school buying model, where you have the cash and buy the car. The second is the classic leasing option. And the third is the subscription model, which is a monthly flat rate. If you choose this option, you decide how long you want to drive the car for – one, two or three years – and you get everything included in your monthly subscription. We deal with all the paperwork related to the insurance, we service the car for you, we bring it back to you, etc." Terms for the subscription model are shorter and more flexible. Unlike in the lease option, insurance and maintenance costs are included in the monthly rate. "It's plannable, hassle-free and digital. In addition, we offer a return policy of up to 30 days as we want to take the hassle out of our customers' lives," Tim ended.

As easy as that!

SEAMLESS-ING EVERYTHING

The pandemic has led to a surge in online shopping across the world, forcing brands to amalgamate physical and digital spaces. The line between what customers do online and offline is getting very blurred. Online transactions also include mobile e-commerce (also known as *m-commerce*).

Many companies assume that every household has a desktop computer or laptop, and that's where customers carry out their purchases from. Well, that's a wrong assumption! Research done in the US shows that mobile, as a share of total e-commerce spent in 2020, was 70.4 per cent, worth $2.91 (€2.49) trillion, and it's projected to be worth $3.56 (€3.04) trillion by 2021.[14]

Across all consumers, it's the young generations who use m-commerce more than others: globally, 43 per cent are Millennials, and 30 per cent are Gen Z.[15] During the pandemic, m-commerce had a huge spike. In the UK alone in 2020, one online purchase was made every second through a mobile device.[16]

However, Raffaella Stratta, Research Manager at Google, reported that 7 out of 10 people who started their mobile journey online ended up leaving that journey without making a transaction. This comes down to poor user experience – one that makes the process difficult and frustrating.

Every day that you're not optimising your mobile experience, you are potentially losing baskets of transactions and customers. Raffaella conducted a number of studies and came up with 10 barriers to buying on the mobile web:

1. Scrolling fatigue due to poor site navigation
2. Lack of autofill functionality
3. Slow site speed
4. Lack of product comparison feature
5. Poor presentation of products and services
6. Lack of transparency in key information[17]
7. Search struggle
8. Unwanted pop-ups
9. Perception that site is not up to date
10. Insecure payment options[18]

Lowering these barries represents a €15 billion-worth of incremental opportunities for those e-commerce retailers that get it right.[19]

Mobile is a very important channel, but it's not the only channel or device used in a customer's journey. In fact, 85 per cent of shoppers use more than one device to interact with a brand.[20] They start their journey on mobile and finish on another device, for example.

One of your challenges today is not only removing all the possible frictions but also understanding your customers' journeys and how they navigate from the first touchpoint to the last.

In my conversation with Joana de Quintanilha, Vice President and Principal Analyst at Forrester, we talked deeply about customer journeys. Joana told me that developing a data-driven approach is crucial to understanding customer journeys in real time and on an individual level.

Investing in the right technologies, working with the data team to unify and understand that data, and co-creating the journey with the customer creates major shifts for brands right now. This allows you to tap into the individual's journey, rather than just creating a general idea of who your buyer is.

Individualisation goes even deeper than *personalisation*. The audience is not "them"; it's "me". To truly individualise, you must be speaking to your customer as an individual and not as a buyer persona.

Personalisation can become individualisation, "but many companies aren't even at the point where they can really understand what's going on in the journey," said Joana. She suggests that you "accelerate the focus on key journeys and start unifying the data between, for example, the website and the call centre, and start making improvements. Then scale up from there but avoid boiling the ocean and doing everything at the same time." Unifying customer data is a crucial step for providing a more holistic and accurate view of the customer. This can be done by ingesting customer data from various operational systems and combining them into a single source.

My first time working in the field of customer experience was in my very first job, in the biometric division of NEC Corporation. Under the biometric technologies umbrella, we deployed NEC NeoFace facial recognition solutions for different uses: from surveillance to hospitality, and from verification in airports to customer experience improvements in the retail sector. For example, in a shopping centre, if a shopper stopped in front of a screen with embedded NeoFace technology, the software would map the shopper's facial features and identify their gender, age, ethnicity and even detect their emotion so that it could show them relevant products. If the person showed lack of interest in that product, the software would change to another product that might be more suited to the user's features, and show them where the item could be found within the shopping centre. In other cases, NeoFace would match a VIP customer face against a database of recorded images and welcome them with special treatment or simply grant automatic access to an office, or via a private or public entrance.

At its best, this was an enormous improvement in customer, employee, passenger and citizen experience. It helped people navigate obstacles in their everyday lives and made processes smoother.

At its worst, facial recognition data can be erroneous, and, most importantly, it threatens our human rights and privacy, often without our knowledge or consent. Facial recognition didn't last long, at least in Europe. With the imposition of the GDPR regulations in 2018, Europe limited the use of facial recognition in public areas, and today the Council of Europe has called for strict rules to avoid the risks to privacy and data protection – and it plans on banning it altogether.[21]

In other continents and countries, facial recognition software is making hyper-personalisation of the customer experience a dream come true and a blessing for both companies and customers. In restaurant chains in California, customers can order meals at kiosks, where the software recognises their faces and immediately fills the screen with previously ordered food items. In a number of hotels in Asia, guests can easily bypass the traditional check-in process. For example, they can open their room doors, access business centres, turn on the TV via the setting they created during their previous stay and pay their bill without the touch of a button.[22]

British Airways uses facial recognition software for passengers boarding flights from the US rather than asking them to show their passports and boarding passes. How cool, right? Other forms of biometric solutions include voice, fingerprint and iris recognition.[23]

Today we can buy our favourite toothpaste via Internet of Things (IoT) devices like Alexa, authenticate payments with our fingerprints, unlock shared cars from a mobile app, switch off our house lights from our phone and more. These technologies are improving our lives in many different ways, by giving us convenience, saving time and removing stress. The biggest headache is the way our data is used and all the privacy repercussions.

Also, since COVID-19 has made us pay more attention to what we touch, companies should take these concerns seriously. According to a Capgemini study carried out in 2020 on 5,000 customers in more than 12 countries, most people (77 per cent) prefer touchless interactions instead of a high-end touch screen.[24] This means that customers favour interactions with technologies that have zero user interface (Zero UI). In simple terms, this means interacting with a device or application without using touchscreens, keyboards or devices.[25]

If your payment process still requires your customers to touch PIN pads to pay for their transactions, this is an indication that they will soon start to favour brands that understand the importance of safety and hygiene. Removing this type of friction is now critical, so companies are moving towards touchless options like biometric, voice and proximity payments.

If you are jumping on such technology, consider how you can provide accessibility to all. Not everyone can speak or see. BNP Paribas and Visa are partnering up to give the option of biometric payments, for example. The biometric card is equipped with a sensor that allows customers to make transactions of any amount with their fingerprint rather than having to touch a pad.[26] This allows for more efficient, more convenient, more personalised, more secure and quicker processes.

DESIGN FOR ALL

Boston Consulting Group says that Human Centered Design (HCD) is more important than ever. This is an essential perspective in successfully designing products, policies, customer journeys and customer experiences. By using an HCD perspective, we are able to better understand people's needs, motivations and pain points. The COVID-19 pandemic has brought into the digital space millions of new users finding their way through online channels, products and services, so it's important to design for all, with an inclusive mindset. With so many changes in such a short time, we need to use our empathic touch to understand the human side of our customers.[27]

A company that is great at using a human-centred design approach is Apple. Apple has been designing inclusively with accessibility in mind since long before the pandemic started. They strive to understand users' needs, motivations and roadblocks.

Apple's accessibility features are made specifically for four main categories of impairments: *vision, hearing, physical and motor,* and *literacy and learning.*[28]

To give you a better sense of inclusive design, I chatted with my friend Mario, who is a visually impaired Apple customer. Mario told me, "Most blind people like me use Apple products because Apple really understands our struggles that affect how we interact with the world. When Apple introduced their accessibility features, especially the VoiceOver [a screen reader built into the iPhone], it allowed me to have a great experience regardless of my capabilities. I can pretty much do everything on my own now. I can do my own shopping, surf the web, chat with people, go on social media and a lot more. It has been life-changing, and I can't thank Apple enough for including people with disability in their design process."

Accessibility means giving access to products and services to people who are normally presented with barriers due to the way that our society designs spaces. For example, Starbucks is planning to distribute large-print and Braille menus for blind and low-vision customers.[29]

When you design for all, it leads to innovation. In the next chapter, we'll see how other companies are using accessibility as part of their customer-centric strategy – and how ease of use can be applied outside of digital settings.

PONDER AND ACT

1. How can you differentiate your offering by eliminating as many frictions as possible from your customer journeys?
2. In what ways can you balance the convenience of digital with the human touch of in-person experiences?
3. Consider how you might offer interactions through an interface that is proactive, zero effort, invisible and personalised. In which of these areas could you make the most impact on your customers?
4. Think of a mobile-first strategy to integrate into your customer-centric strategy. What ideas come to mind?
5. Think of human-centred design as a mindset and philosophy. What needs to shift for this to become a priority in your company

CHAPTER 9: INNOVATION

ROME WASN'T BUILT IN A DAY

"All truths are easy to understand once they are discovered; the point is to discover them." – Galileo Galilei[1]

The lift, or elevator, has been part of our history since the Egyptians, Romans and Babylonians. One of the earliest examples was built in Rome approximately 1,500 years ago, in the Colosseum. It was used to transport killer animals, such as lions and tigers, into the arena to fight gladiators. This served as entertainment for the Romans.[2]

The invention of the lift went from using sophisticated ropes and pulley systems to having a "driver", who regulated its speed, to automatic lifts in the early 19th century. Automatic lifts were, of course, easier to use, but the problem was that nobody trusted them. People didn't like the idea of hanging by a cable in the air without a driver and lift drivers didn't like the idea of losing their job with the advent of automation. In 1945, people occupied the streets of New York in a protest against technological advancement.[3] There was nothing to do to stop the development; although slow, it took about 50 years for people to get comfortable enough to trust the automated lift.

The passenger experience had to match their expectations, which would vary based on social, circumstantial and ethnographic differences. However, the common expectation was to have a "good ride".[4]

I first heard about this story in a great talk delivered by Thimon De Jong, lecturer on social influence at Utrecht University and expert on the future of human behaviour, who features in Chapter 7. Thimon says that the protests actually helped to accelerate the adoption of automatic lifts. How? It prompted efforts to help people to accept the automatic lift. A number of psychological elements were introduced, such as music to calm anxiety. To make them seem more accessible, marketing campaigns depicted grandmothers with their grandchildren. The emotional elements portrayed were that the lifts were safe and easy to use.

"I can see the COVID-19 crisis as a big opportunity to push the launch of new technologies or fast forward the reintroduction of some that have been set aside," said Thimon. He has a good point here and shared that, sometimes, innovations get introduced too fast, which is the main reason for failure. It's important that people get used to new technologies in phases – as with the lift.

This reminds me of the eminent communication theorist and sociologist Everett Rogers' theory, the *diffusion of innovations,* in which he describes that certain types of individuals are inevitably more open to adaptation than others.[5] Whether it is a driverless lift or a driverless car, the issue here isn't about the technology but about trusting that the technology will do its job well.

The COVID-19 pandemic has disrupted many industries as well as consumer behaviour. When it hit, many businesses were forced to finally confront their vulnerabilities. But it also helped them spot opportunities for learning, changing and innovating. Organisations that were trapped in the status quo have been forced to quickly create experiments, think differently, fail, learn, re-learn and move forward. In other words, they are being pressed to innovate.[6]

I interviewed Steve Spiro, Chief Executive Officer at Halotherapy Solutions and Chairman of the Global Wellness Institute, a non-profit organisation with a mission to empower wellness worldwide. Steve shared, "Halotherapy Solutions has always been a B2B company selling salt rooms, booths and cabins to high-end spas, wellness facilities and fitness centres around the world. But due to COVID-19, a lot of these facilities, unfortunately, either closed temporarily or permanently. Even if we don't want to launch a new product, we need to be prepared in case our competitors come out with something new. Fortunately, before the pandemic, we had been testing new technologies, and we had been working on new innovations. The pandemic has pushed us to expand the consumer business with a portable device that people could carry with them or simply use at home. We were unfortunate on the B2B side; however, the B2C side presented an opportunity to accelerate a product that we had parked for some time. We had to quickly pivot our business model on the consumer side, also because we wanted to help billions of people breathe better."

Halotherapy is an ancient holistic approach that mimics the microclimate of a salt cave, where dry salt air is dispersed into an enclosed environment (room, booth, cabin) and turned into microscopic particles which are breathed in and absorbed by the skin to reduce inflammation.[7] Steve told me that they are "growing very, very quickly because, with COVID-19, people have become a lot more aware of the importance of respiratory health, hygiene and building their immunity". And, as he shared, that's what salt therapy does. Steve continued, "So, we've been focussing primarily on people with respiratory conditions, and we have been repositioning in two ways. First, we are converting a lot of our salt room, booth and cabin clients (B2B) to become resellers. In this way, the end consumer can contact a local spa, wellness facility or fitness centre in their community and see if they're selling the unit to install at home. We're also talking to retailers to sell the units directly to the end consumers. And second, we've created HaloPocket, a pocket-size halogenerator, where you put about a quarter of a teaspoon of salt into the cylinder, you press a button to grind it up, you hold it in your hand, and breathe the salty air."

As a customer-centric business of the future, you must use crises and technologies to drive innovation and quickly adapt to a constant wave of change. But must we wait for a crisis to successfully pursue customer-centric innovations? No! And, in fact, I advise that you don't. You must keep finding innovative ways to meet customers' continuously evolving needs. Customer-centric innovation can take place in different forms: from finding new ways to serve customers to enhancing multi-channel customer journeys.

In the previous chapter, we explored the benefits of removing frictions from customers' journeys. Joana de Quintanilha says, "Journeys are customers' lived realities. Journeys are not a business process or marketing funnel. Each one belongs to the customer. It must be viewed from their perspective. A customer may be on multiple journeys, at different levels, and for different purposes and tasks."

When done well, *journey mapping*, also called customer journey mapping, not only reveals customers' lived realities but also sparks empathy and helps drive tangible actions. Customer journey mapping is the process of representing a visual illustration of the steps that your customers go through when they interact with your brand.[8]

Joana told me that future-state journey mapping helps companies create new offerings, unlock new areas of value, and envision possible future outcomes from the near to the long term. Unlike current-state journey mapping, the purpose of future-state journey mapping is to innovate by conceiving entirely new customer experiences. This ranges from designing a new product for launch this year to achieving groundbreaking differentiation that will be a decade in the making.

Future-state journey mapping requires that you choose the time horizon up front, bring in blue-sky thinkers as well as technology and subject-matter experts, and coordinate with a broader range of stakeholders on an iterative roadmap. The journey map documents the vision and aligns it with workstreams. So, as projects and pilots generate feedback, or as feasibility changes, both documents – the journey map and roadmap – will need periodic updating. Treat both as living documents that are part of a test-and-learn, iterative cycle.

THE RENAISSANCE

To stay ahead of your competition and your customers' needs, you must be constantly innovating. Most companies believe that they are customer-centric just because they map out their customer journeys and eliminate any frictions. As we have seen in the previous chapter, this is a very important piece of the puzzle. However, nearly all companies start mapping out their journeys from the product or service perspective. This is still a product-centric focus – which is not enough.

As has already been mentioned many times in this book, customer centricity also looks at finding ways to enhance customer experiences – meeting consumers in their everyday lives to provide enrichment and ease. Often, companies map a customer journey from the moment the customer lands on their website or store. But this is not really the beginning of the journey from the customer's view. It starts much sooner.

An Asian bank thought of their customer journey beyond their services. The excitement in buying a house is not in getting the mortgage. The real excitement is in looking for the house, the area, the furniture, etc., and buying a new house, which, in terms of customer journey, begins long before applying for a mortgage. The bank walked in the customer's shoes and thought of ways of helping people find their dream house in the first place. They created a mobile app that helps buyers with their property hunting and buying decisions. A potential buyer visits a house for sale, uses their smartphone to scan the area, and the mobile app suggests the most suitable offerings nearby. Once the dream house is found, the mortgage calculator suggests if the buyer can afford it.[9]

American startup Booster has reinvented the way people fill up their cars. Going to the petrol station is an inconvenience for most of us. The traffic to get there is stressful, the journey is a waste of time and the queuing is a pain. Booster's hassle-free solution to remove this completely from people's minds is to fill up their cars while they're at work.[10]

The process is simple: the customer orders fuel via the Booster mobile app; they pop the fuel door, either manually or via their car's app; a professional Booster serviceman refuels their tank; the serviceman shuts the fuel door and notifies them via the Booster app when it's all done.[11] It won't be long before cars automatically order their own petrol when they sense the tank is getting low – until fossil fuel cars become a thing of the past.

As is the case for many sectors and markets, the rush to offer products and services digitally has been very aggressive, especially now that half of the world's population has been pushed to make online purchases. This increases the pressure on retailers to keep innovating both their product and services while addressing their customer experiences.

Retailers around the world are realising the need to constantly refresh their propositions, as the need to engage with consumers in more creative, sophisticated and personalised ways grows. In this way, the retail sector has never been as competitive and challenging as it is now, since the coronavirus pandemic. Consumers are not only buying what reflects their beliefs, but they are also becoming more tech-savvy.

According to *The Economist,* being increasingly digital doesn't mean that the physical store will vanish, but it does means that shopping data and shopping patterns are breaking down the relationship between mass consumption and production. The 21st century consumer landscape is a world in which the consumer decides whether to buy online or in store and whether to shop via platforms or from individual brands. It's a very tough time for retailers!

Consumers want a more personal and direct relationship with brands and less interaction with the middleman. And companies understand that the middleman creates uncontrollable frictions. That middleman who, for centuries, created piles of hidden costs is being squeezed out. Nike is cutting ties with many department stores, such as Urban Outfitters, and wholesalers, such as Zappos and Amazon.[12]

Nike is a manufacturer, a retailer, a media powerhouse and, most importantly, a brand that is unafraid of taking bold decisions. They understand how their customers think in the world of omnichannel retailing.[13] An omnichannel strategy doesn't prioritise digital over physical, or vice versa, but it provides customers with a fully integrated shopping experience.

The shoe brand has been expanding its retailer footprint with smaller-format stores that are digitally enabled in order to connect and enhance the retail experience.[14] In a statement, the company declared, "As part of our recently announced Consumer Direct Acceleration strategy, we are doubling down on our approach with Nike Digital and our owned stores, as well as a smaller number of strategic partners who share our vision to create a consistent, connected and modern shopping experience."[15] This is one way Nike is moving towards an omnichannel strategy that capitalises on seamless transactions that allow frictionless, direct-to-consumer shopping experiences, easy payment solutions, and quicker pick-up and delivery options. By selling through a wholesaler, it's more and more difficult to control the customer relationship and engagement in times when customers want a brand to be a partner in life.

This is how much friction can be removed by customer-centric brands. The strategy allowed Nike to take back control of its distribution, deepen its connection with consumers, expand its focus on the community and invest in data analytics.[16] But also, 40 per cent of Nike's revenue now comes from direct-to-consumer shopping.

Over the past year, Nike has welcomed 70 million loyal customers as "members" who connect via the digital app, which offers everything from running advice to guidance on purchasing trainers through vending machines. If Nike's members were favouring yoga on the app, data traffic analysis would show this and the company would therefore produce more yoga apparel.[17]

The pandemic has boosted online shopping, but remember: customers aren't favouring one over the other when it comes to physical or remote purchasing. They want the convenience of shopping both ways, depending on their mood, time and circumstances. This has given room for innovation, reinvention and renaissance – so that customer-centric innovators have an easier path forward.

Despite the opportunity to capitalise on this online shift, the world of retail is in turmoil right now. Some say that we will see empty shopping centres and high streets, along with unemployment, as a result of big e-commerce oligopolies that are widening the gap.

Still, I take the more optimistic view and think that the retail renaissance will be an opportunity for brands to reach customers directly, create a more frictionless shopping experience and apply more innovation. It will also be an opportunity to gather consumer data to produce products that match what customers want, avoiding surplus inventory.

The Economist recently reported that the future of retail will be a place of interaction between retail "stylists" and consumers. Retailers have the opportunity to create smaller and more intimate places in which the community of customers can gather.[18]

How will retail change specifically? The convenience of e-commerce is spoiling consumers with shopping from the comfort of their home. This means that, even when the effects of the pandemic are over, retail brands will need to work harder to attract consumers back into physical spaces. Innovations in the retail sector are thus a priority for companies. Burberry is using QR codes on in-store product tags to help consumers find styling tips, exclusive fashion content and more.[19]

Innovation also extends to at-home purchasing of, traditionally, retail products. Estée Lauder has been leveraging Augmented Reality (AR) tech to create a hyper-realistic virtual experience of trying on beauty products at home so that consumers can continue to engage with the brand in a personalised way. The technology enables customers to "try on" products using the camera of their smartphone or desktop device.[20] The company is now extending this interactive technology to its skincare line, with a self-guided digital skincare diagnostic tool.[21]

Over the last five years, there's been a growing trend for new retail concepts like experiential shopping – but it will be even more important going forward. Freitag, a Swiss bag and apparel brand, offers a "build-your-own-bag" experience in its interactive space in Zurich. The space is a "micro-factory" that allows customers to choose fabric and straps, and watch them being cut and stitched together.[22] In this way, customers get involved in assembling their bag.

Farfetch has unveiled the "store of the future" by blending the physical and digital experience, and strengthening the emotional connection. Customers can scan their smartphones when they enter the store, which allows the shop assistants to view their profiles, purchase history and online wish lists. Clothing racks are "connected": they record the items the customers pick up, store them in the customers' smartphone app, and create an in-store wish list. Items can then be removed from the app or purchased another time. Smart mirrors – those that interact with the customer – allow shoppers to request items in another size or colour, find alternatives, or even pay before leaving the fitting room.[23]

Dan Frommer, Founder of *The New Consumer*, a publication on the intersection of technology and consumer brands, states, "The mindless shopping is going to stay online, whether the intentional shopping – the browsing, discovery, socializing, learning – will continue to happen in stores."[24] In fact, innovative retailers have been redesigning stores to be places where customers can engage in entertainment options such as reading corners, happy hours and yoga rooms.

I agree with Dan, in that I don't think that, after a year of isolation, customers will stubbornly only want to purchase online. As we said in the Pillar of Humanity, we belong to tribes, and we prefer to gravitate towards places that create human connection and interaction.

INNOVATION + SUSTAINABILITY = INNOVABILITY®

Regardless of which channel your customers prefer to buy from, you should put sustainability high on your agenda – because that's what your consumers do. Whether they are getting a package through the door or driving to get to your retail store, new consumers are not just value-conscious: they are also increasingly projecting their ethical and political ideology onto what and how they buy. Today, as we've touched on in previous chapters, younger generations of consumers in particular want to know a company's environmental credentials and supply-chain standards. They want to know whether the company's values and beliefs match theirs. These are all indications that the consumer revolution will change capitalism for the better.[25]

From the Enron scandal in the 2000s,[26] to the BP oil spill in 2010,[27] the energy industry has suffered a really bad reputation, which is also due to the negative impact on the global environment and its communities. Global warming, biodiversity loss and resource depletion are just a few of the consequences that we are facing as a result of fossil fuel consumption. Fossil fuels in 2019 accounted for 84 per cent of energy supply around the world, while renewables accounted for a mere 11 per cent.[28] And the energy sector is responsible for 73 per cent of greenhouse gas (GHG) emissions worldwide.[29] Doing "business as usual" with a little greenwashing won't change anything. Reducing the output of carbon dioxide (CO2) is the world's biggest priority right now.

Enel is an Italian energy company that provides a wide range of energy-related services in more than 30 countries across five continents. The company is committed to leading the global transition to clean energy. It coupled innovation with sustainability and moved from a siloed, internal R&D approach to an open innovation model called Open Innovability®, in which everyone within the company, in every department and in every country, can be an innovator.[30]

Enel aims to create a world where energy is fully sustainable. They recognised the way to get there is to keep developing innovative technologies and business models. In fact, sustainable development cannot occur without innovation, and innovation is not actually innovation unless it's sustainable. Given that, Enel combined innovation and sustainability in every aspect of the company's business and coined the neologism Innovability®. The Open Innovability® approach is grounded in the belief that collaboration is the best way to solve the most complex issues that society faces – and ultimately to create value for all stakeholders.

Enel X is the Enel Group's business line dedicated to making the energy transition possible by creating sustainable and innovative solutions that support decarbonising energy. Enel X has been working on innovative solutions linked to the energy transition, which are also well grounded in customer needs.

I interviewed Marco Gazzino, Head of Innovability® at Enel X. Marco told me that Enel X wants to help everybody make more intelligent decisions about the way energy is created, stored, managed and consumed. Enel X is doing this by delivering smart, simple and fast solutions and services able to get the most from the energy transition. This includes innovative solutions of different kinds – from city analytics through the use of big data to a platform for remote patient care; from intelligent street lighting to e-mobility solutions. Marco shared that simplicity and ease of use are at the heart of Enel X innovation.

I remember years ago obtaining quotes for a few solar panels to go on my roof. They were big, difficult to install, expensive and not feasible for a small city apartment. Enel designed a simple, convenient and afford-able smart solar panel that can be installed on any apartment balcony in the heart of every Italian city. The panel easily and quickly connects to a regular electric socket, so it's a completely hassle-free and low-cost solution which is accessible to every household.

Circular economy is a strategic driver of Enel Group as it perfectly puts into practice Enel's Innovability® strategy. The Ellen MacArthur Foundation defines it as "a systemic approach to economic development designed to benefit businesses, society and the environment".[31] It involves gradually decoupling economic activity from the consumption of non-renewable resources, and designing waste out of the system.[32]

Enel X has adopted this vision since it was established and has a specific programme designed to boost the circular economy. This programme embeds sustainability in its products and boosts circularity by design. For instance, JuiceBox, an at-home charging point for electric vehicles, is made of recycled plastics and can itself be recycled. Public chargers are also designed for easy and modular maintenance. This helps reduce the waste when sub-components need to be replaced, and it helps recover parts when the units are dismantled.

Enel X and Enel Group's Innovability® strategy also has a global network of innovation hubs located in the world's leading innovation ecosystems: Tel Aviv, Madrid, Boston, Rio de Janeiro, Moscow and many others. Innovation hubs are powered by a global online platform designed by the company, which crowdsources the best international talents, ideas and technologies with high potential to be transformed into real energy-transition solutions.

In four years, innovators from more than 100 countries submitted more than 8,000 proposed solutions; 200 of which were successfully selected and awarded. Those selected have the opportunity to work with Enel in the development of their solutions. They get access to Enel's network of laboratories, internal and external experts, investors and industrial plants from around the world, where they can test, receive valuable feedback and develop their solutions in a timely and more effective manner.[33] Enel's innovative ecosystem of startups, venture capitalists, industry leaders and universities works as a guide to a virtuous path to collectively respond to customer needs and emerging challenges that affect humanity and our environment. In fact, innovation hubs also work as the "antennae" for scouting customers' needs in the ecosystem where they are based.

Marco further explained that Enel X considers the end customers and users a fundamental and integral part of the innovation ecosystem. Onboarding customers is therefore a key factor throughout the innovation process – from idea generation to solution deployment. For this purpose, Enel X adopted a protocol called the "customer observatory". This protocol is rooted in the very basic foundation of customer centricity – listening to customers' needs. Enel's customer observatory embodies a radical new approach to the stale and old-fashioned R&D department. This new approach nurtures the culture of innovation driven by customer need and also powers initiatives such as neuroscience and behavioural economics.

To illustrate the methodology of the customer observatory, Marco told me about a project that particularly caught my attention – Juice-Ability. JuiceAbility is a smart, dedicated cable that allows people with disabilities to charge their electric wheelchair batteries in a few quick and simple steps from any of Enel's 14,000 e-vehicle charging stations across Italy. He said, "One of the biggest fears of people with disabilities is not being able to get home because of the lack of wheelchair battery life. From the innovation hubs, we scouted the Italian startup Avanchair, a mobility equipment supplier, which brought up this issue.[34] Following the methodology and operations of our customer observatory protocol, we partnered up with Avanchair and A.N.G.L.A.T., the Italian association for representing and protecting the rights of people with disabilities primarily in the field of mobility and accessibility.[35] Both partners helped us uncover users' needs right down to the smallest of detail. During all the innovation stages of JuiceAbility, Enel and our partners gathered a number of wheelchair users in the co-creation processes."

How did the company come up with the right product features for these special consumers? By aligning the customer observatory with a customer co-creation strategy. The strategy allowed customers to add value and feel valued by becoming involved with the core of the business. Co-creating brought the solution to life using empathy and simplicity as the foundation of the project. This involved four steps:

1. Supporting particular customers in sharing their opinions and ideas, and fulfilling their needs.

2. By envisioning the initial customers' needs, Enel came up with a minimum valuable product (MVP) or functional prototype that satisfied the very basic need of people with disabilities – carrying a portable wheelchair battery charger.

3. With the help of Avanchair, A.N.G.L.A.T. and wheelchair users, Enel was able to test the MVP in various rounds of co-creation and refine its user experience. For example, they flattened the handle that allows users a better grip and ability to reach the electric charging point.

4. The co-creation process helped in shaping the final product, which was then approved by the Italian association.

Enel's customer observatory approach is considered an integral part of the company's innovation ecosystem. Listening to customers, in addition to providing indispensable feedback for go-to-market, has significantly contributed to generating new concepts and solutions.

Enel X not only debuted the innovative solution at the Consumer Electronic Show (CES) 2020, but it is also aligned with the United Nations' 10th sustainable development goal (SDG), which aims to reduce inequality. The wheelchair is, of course, connected to an Enel X mobile app called JuicePass, which allows users to find a charging point on a map and manage the various charging services available at these locations.[36] We are living in the era of co-creation!

In the Pillar of Humanity, we have seen how trust in brands is at an all-time low. Co-creation helps to address this trust deficit. When we treat customers as more than mere consumers, inviting them to become active contributors and part of the business, we make them insiders. In fact, 86 per cent of them say that brands that co-create are more trustworthy.[37]

Enel's Open Innovability® approach not only collaborates and listens in order to create sustainable products that fulfil society's needs, but it embodies the community spirit that we talked about widely in Chapter 2.

As well as catalysing innovation, Enel has shown how a multinational can change its culture with the excellent best-practice example of implementing the Open Innovability® model, as well as creating shared value (CSV) for all stakeholders and the communities in which it operates.

The next chapter will open up a new pillar, that of culture, and touch upon how Enel managed to become Europe's "climate centurion", as *The Economist* called it.[38]

Furthermore, in the chapters ahead, we will talk more directly about leadership and the crucial relationship between employees and customers.

PONDER AND ACT

1. Which are the most important customer journeys for you to map?
2. How can you make sure the customer is actively involved in the journey mapping process?
3. How can you use innovation to create more creative, sophisticated and personalised customer experiences?
4. How can you develop innovative solutions that contribute to saving the world?
5. In what ways could you spark innovation by involving your customers in co-creating activities?

PILLAR OF CULTURE

CHAPTER 10

YOUR SOUL SEARCHING

"Noli foras ire, in te ipsum redi, in interiore homine habitat veritas. Do not wander far and wide but return into yourself. Deep within man, there dwells the truth." – Augustine of Hippo[1]

It's 5 am! I am donning my white clothing and practising my private meditation in the dorm. Some 20-plus other women are sleeping on the floor; others are getting ready for the day like me. There are only two toilets available, and the showers have no hot water. I hardly slept; it was another night of cockroaches running around the dorm, and I can't stand them. I quickly head to the main hall for a small ceremonial rice offering to the monks, followed by the morning spiritual practice of group meditation and chanting.

I am at the Wat Pa Tham Wua Buddhist monastery in Mae Hong Son, a small village in the northwest of Thailand, 17 miles (27 km) away from the Myanmar border. This beautiful forest monastery is nestled in a mountain valley and surrounded by lush jungle, caves and palm trees.

After the rice offering and lesson about Dharma (the nature of reality regarded as a universal truth taught by the Buddha),[2] we go for a 40-minute meditation walk. Through and around the monastery, little ponds dot the grounds, and beautiful trees with big yellow flowers are in full bloom. It's my ninth day here – the last day of this Vipassana meditation silent retreat.

Every day is full of hours of meditation, Dharma talks, food offering to the monks and doing chores in the monastery. It sounds very busy, but it's not the case, because silence is the number one rule at the monastery – strictly no talking to anyone but yourself. Silence also means no phones, no writing, no reading, no eye contact and no smiling at anyone.

The silence is there for a reason: to find a higher state of consciousness and fall into an inner dimension of *beingness*. There is a lot of time with the *self* to think, contemplate and ask a lot of deep questions, such as *"Who am I?"* and *"What am I here for?"* Something similar in Western society might be a soul-searching retreat, where one examines their conscience, especially with regard to motives and values.[3]

While Buddhism believes living beings have no soul, in Hindu, a soul is the *atman,* and in Judaism, it's the *neshama.* Having been born and raised in a Catholic country, and having listened to the teachings of Western philosophers, I've been told that a soul is "the real self" or the "essence of a human being, that which confers individuality and humanity".[4] In other words, it is the totality of our values, beliefs and behaviours, and therefore central to who we are.

Augustine of Hippo, a theologian, philosopher and one of the most important fathers of the Latin Church, believed that every soul is "the principle of life" and the governor of a particular body. Augustine had a Neo-Platonism and Aristotelianism view of the relationship between soul and body. He believed that the soul gives the body the ability to move and the means to act in accordance with its volitions.[5]

Body and soul are thus not antagonists but are interdependent. In other words, the body needs the soul in order to live, and the soul needs the body in order to be a soul at all.[6] This is thought to be the same for every organism's life.

I'd like to extend Augustine's doctrine to businesses of any kind and size. The soul is the *culture* of a business, and the body is the *brand, assets, meetings, processes, technologies, products, forecasting* and so on. For better or worse, both the soul (the culture) and body (everything else) of a business are inextricably linked.

An interesting article published by the *Harvard Business Review* states, "Culture expresses goals through values and beliefs and guides activity through shared assumptions and group norms." The culture of an organisation outlines the attitudes and behaviours of the people that form that organisation. Companies have the full ability and energy to thrive when their culture is properly aligned with the people's personal values, drives and needs towards a shared purpose.[7]

I first heard about "the soul of a business" a few years ago from a Fortune 500 CEO, as she was trying to revive her company. Many companies start their "soul searching" initiatives as a last resort when they are in a haemorrhagic state – when a lot of damage has already been done – when the body of the business is giving up, and the only thing left is the soul.

THE WAY WE DO THINGS AROUND HERE

Soon after I returned from my gap year, I started my own consultancy business. A client invited me to a leadership meeting. The CEO was presenting the company's strategy and objectives to carry them through the next five years. Around 1,000 employees formed the audience. The presentation was mainly focussed on techniques and strategies to increase profits. There was no word spent on the company's role in society, on the employees or on the customers. I quietly wondered how many of those employees jumped out of bed every day, excited by the thought of *maximising shareholder value*.

I soon figured out that maximising profits was company policy. I could easily picture sales representatives, shop assistants, e-commerce managers, marketing people and so on being trained to make money off customers from every possible angle. The company didn't have a problem with customer engagement, as they thought they did, but more with their culture. This was a big weakness – and ultimately an area of vulnerability.

Of course, making money is vital. Otherwise companies would not survive. But making it an obsession and the sole objective can be quite dangerous. It creates competition among employees, and it implies that that business is soulless.

Broadly speaking, a company's culture can be encapsulated in the age-old saying, "the way we do things around here" – which is basically the sum of values and beliefs that shape employees' behaviour at all levels.[8] When the culture is intentionally managed and people-centric, it can empower your employees' behaviour – as it creates a common understanding of values. This feeds a purpose and emotional connection that employees feel by being part of your brand.

In Chapter 4, we explored how and why empathy is so contagious. Have you ever wondered why couples that have been together for a long time behave and talk in a similar way? Or, if you are eating out with friends, you tend to be influenced by what they are ordering? It's called the *chameleon effect*, in which human beings mimic one another's behaviour in a group, whether consciously or not.[9] This shows how a culture can become toxic – or a positive differentiator in your organization – as it spreads from person to person.

If "the way we do things around here" at your company is not conducive to a thriving, customer-centric company of the future, you really need to take action. Many companies never think of changing their approach to inject values, beliefs and culture norms. They never undertake a soul-searching exercise, and their leaders find it difficult to understand their company's culture. In fact, a survey carried out on more than 7,000 business leaders across 130 countries revealed that only 28 per cent know their company's culture.[10]

Typically, in the past, a company's culture was a task for the human resources (HR) department. The HR team would craft a sort of mission statement that the senior management had thought of, then it would put together some sort of birthday celebration calendar for every employee and organise the Christmas party.

If changing a company's culture was this easy, it'd be too good to be true. Unfortunately, this approach no longer works – if it ever did. Why is that? Millennial customers (83 per cent) want to buy from brands that align with their values[11] and Millennial employees would take an average pay cut of $7,600 (€6,500) for a "better quality of work life" that includes career development, purposeful work, work-life balance and company culture.[12] These needs and expectations drastically impact the shape of your company's culture.

The good news is that a company's culture can be assessed, formed and changed over time. But where do you start?

Culture isn't only about thinking of a few intangible beliefs; it's about being responsible for developing and maintaining the way that everyone's beliefs shape their behaviour. There isn't a fixed framework through which cultural transformation should happen. Every company is different, and some things may work for you but not for others. Regardless of what framework or model you use, or which path you take on this journey, the most important thing is that you are *committed* to pushing the transformation forward for years to come – and instilling this commitment and effort into the rest of the organisation.

Commitment to the customer-centric culture is baked into the very fabric of your organisation, and it plays a critical role in aligning functions, values and enabling a strong purpose.

THE HEART OF BUSINESS

Hubert Joly joined Best Buy as the new CEO at a time when the company was more dead than alive; when everyone thought that Amazon would suck the retail chain's blood. In his recently released book, *The Heart of Business,* Hubert explains the transformation that he undertook to revive the company. He created an environment that was forced to radically rethink the company culture, its purpose and its soul.

Hubert says that companies are not soulless entities, but human organisations made of individuals working together in the pursuit of a common purpose. His approach totally transformed Best Buy, prompting a seismic shift from profit to purpose – treating profit as an outcome, not the goal. This approach started with having a noble purpose at the top which, according to Hubert, became like a North Star against which every decision was made and measured.

Hubert's transformation continued with employees who were at the heart of the business. Employees could rally around the noble purpose. They could also nurture and care for authentic relationships both with their colleagues and their company's stakeholders. Lastly, the finances were addressed.

When considering new business ideas, four questions were asked:

1. Does it fit with our purpose as a company?
2. Is it good for the customer?
3. Can we deliver?
4. Can we make money?[13]

In Hubert's transformation, employees were at the centre. This happened since company culture is the cumulative effect of people's common values, beliefs and behaviour, and these collective sets of norms could blend the strategic thinking of top leaders with the knowledge and experiences of frontline employees.

Your company's culture, in this way, is how you can achieve your objective or purpose. Cultures are successfully transformed by those leaders who care about the wellbeing of their people. Customer-focussed cultures, like Hubert's, are created by a collective work, when the people in charge of taking care of customers are taken care of themselves. We will see more about employee wellbeing in Chapter 11.

During an executive team dinner, Hubert asked everyone to bring pictures of themselves as young children to tell personal stories about those times, to share how their personal purpose connected to their jobs, and how they wanted to be remembered. This exercise would help Hubert to understand what energised the team at Best Buy.[14]

Members of the C-suite are not just leaders; they are human beings with their own dreams and life purposes. From this exercise, Hubert found out that for the majority of his executive team, their purpose was about "doing good for others", and Best Buy could be used as a platform to enrich people's lives.[15]

This exercise cascaded. A Boston store manager asked every single person on his team to write their dream on a whiteboard. He was keen to find out because, by discovering their motivation, he could truly connect with each and every one of them. In fact, he used this exercise to find a way to link their dreams to the company's purpose. The store manager's commitment gave his team energy that, when combined with their capabilities, led to that store's superior performance.[16]

Who's responsible for a cultural transformation? To find out, I interviewed Denise Lee Yohn, brand leadership expert and author of *Fusion: How Integrating Brand and Culture Powers the World's Greatest Companies*.[17] Denise told me that many companies have a gap between the existing culture and the desired culture, and while company leaders should take responsibility for cultivating the desired culture, ultimately everyone in the company is responsible. As she stated, "It starts with assessing where the gaps are between your *current culture* and your *desired culture*."

But where do you begin? Denise explains, "When defining your desired culture, you need to define what is the unique culture that you want to have and really define its unique characteristics. What are the unique values? What are your unique purpose and motivations?" I asked Denise about how to operationalise this shift, and she laid out five strategies:

1. Look at your organisational design and operational processes, and ask yourself: are these really cultivating the kind of culture that we want? Since culture is developed by internal behaviours,

look at how different groups interact with one another and do their work. For example, forecasting, budgeting, developing new products, going to market and so on are all processes which are fundamental operations that impact your culture.

2. Create culture-changing employee experiences. Just as you would design and manage customer experience, intentionally design and manage your employee experiences to cultivate the kind of culture you want. For example, if you want your customer experience to be seamless, tech-enabled and intuitive, but your employee experience is bureaucratic, slow and manual, you won't get there. Create a culture to cultivate that alignment.

3. Look at policies, procedures and all kinds of small, mundane aspects of your operations that can have a huge impact. For example, to promote a culture that values safety, employees at Chevron, a utility American multinational, are asked to open every meeting with a "safety moment" – such as an update on new safety procedures at a plant, or advice on how to ensure their own personal safety. Another example: Insight Global, an IT consultancy, names its conference rooms after key moments in the firm's history to remind people of its cultural foundations.

4. Foster employee-brand engagement. You need to make sure that every employee, regardless of their role – in other words, not just the marketing team – understands what your brand stands for, who your customers are, how you're different, and how you're positioned to create more value for customers. For example, training and tools to help employees develop customer empathy can be a great thing.

5. If you have a vital, valuable culture but not a very strong brand, you can actually apply a lot of what you're doing internally to customers. This will achieve integration and alignment between culture and brand. When Recreational Equipment, Inc. (REI), an outdoor gear and apparel retailer, needed to strengthen its brand differ-

entiation, it looked to its culture. Because it always encourages its employees to enjoy the outdoors, it decided to close its retail stores on Black Friday, the biggest shopping day of the holiday season in the US, and give them the day off to have fun outside instead of working inside. It then created an #OptOutside brand campaign, in which it also encouraged customers to get outdoors instead of shopping indoors. The campaign effectively differentiated REI's brand and drew in new customers, as well as employees.

For a customer-centric culture to be sustainable, the system of values, norms and beliefs of all employees should deeply align with corporate practices. This cross-collaboration is needed to manage and keep strong relationships with customers and among employees.

When instilling values across the company, you need to ensure that every employee (not just the customer-facing ones) live and breathe the company's values and can prioritise them by importance. Disney Resorts is a prime example of this. In every resort, every employee knows Disney's four key values for delivering exceptional customer experience: safety, courtesy, show and efficiency. At Disney, safety comes first, and every employee knows what actions and behaviours are aligned with each value.[18]

A cultural transformation doesn't happen overnight; it takes a lot of pushing through, commitment from everyone involved and, especially, accepting that there is no end point. Culture is dynamic and must be constantly nurtured.

"IF WE DON'T CHANGE, WE DIE"

In Chapter 3, we saw how important it is to have a strong purpose, and how companies shifting towards a purpose create shared value (CSV) for all stakeholders. Mark Kramer, co-creator of the concept of shared value and Senior Lecturer of Business Administration at the Harvard Business School, put it very nicely: "While some believe that capitalism is a zero-sum game in which a win for companies means a loss for society or vice versa, the model of shared value is the exact opposite. Shared value means that everybody wins: companies need a healthy society, and society needs healthy companies. In this sense, CSV can be interpreted as a substantial extension of Adam Smith's concept of the *invisible hand*, according to which the pursuit of personal gain within the free market naturally creates benefits for society."[19] Companies create shared value when the communities in which they operate are also prospering. And these communities can be highly influenced by a culture – and what is done within it.

Cultural transformation starts with having a strong purpose, which is a big piece of the puzzle and an actual "walk the talk" initiative. Boston Consulting Group says some companies "do almost nothing to integrate purpose into the day-to-day experiences of their employees and customers. This 'surface purpose' amounts to a thin veneer that doesn't ingrain new beliefs and behaviors. Despite the hype, the organization remains unchanged".[20] Other companies, such as illycaffè – the Italian coffee company that we read about in Chapter 3 – are born around a shared value purpose. And others, such as Enel – the Italian energy multinational that we learned about in the previous chapter – underwent a cultural transformation that deeply embedded sustainability values and a focus on innovation at the core, while supporting the creation of shared value for all stakeholders.

Authentic purposes like those of illycaffè and Enel motivate employees, strengthen relationships with stakeholders, foster stronger organisational alignment and positively impact society. Enel's stated purpose is: "Open power for a brighter future. We empower sustainable progress." Its purpose is tightly aligned to creating shared value by tackling four of the world's biggest challenges listed in the United Nations' SDGs. The company has been pursuing such a purpose through helping mitigate climate change (SDG 13). Its activities are directed towards decarbonising energy production and consumption with innovative solutions (SDG 9), giving access to affordable and clean energy to everyone (SDG 7), while creating sustainable cities and communities (SDG 11).[21]

A number of projects involved Enel's continuous presence and engagement with local communities, proving how they were "walking the talk". For example, in the Chilean Atacama Desert, the company developed a geothermal plant, which taps into the earth's internal thermal energy. When creating the plant, Enel also created job opportunities for indigenous communities.[22] Other examples include closely working with rural communities in Brazil to understand their contexts and needs, which was the best way to connect those remote communities to the electricity grid. Through creating shared value, Enel introduces access to electricity via new technologies, while creating employment, job training and business opportunities at the local level.

The shared value creation model of Enel has the following aims:

1. Maximising the potential positive impacts of the company's operations.
2. Minimising the negative impacts in any specific community.
3. Reducing environmental impact.
4. Creating a circular economy to foster socio-economic development.[23]

To date, the company is creating lasting shared value through its entire value chain by analysing economic, environmental and social contexts to identify local business issues.[24] Enel is now planning to invest €190 billion to prepare for an all-electric future by 2030, by virtually tripling its renewable-energy capacity and transforming its grids in Europe and Latin America.[25] Last but not least Enel is committed to carbon neutrality by 2050.[26]

As Ernesto Ciorra, Chief Innovability Officer* at Enel, says, "If we don't change, we die."[27]

Cultural transformation happens only when we do things differently. It can represent a revival – not just for the business itself but also for the values and souls of human beings.

Everyone at Enel works around the company's shared value purpose, which inspires and guides employees to do their jobs. A strong and effective company purpose, based on creating shared value, reflects employees' motivations for doing the company's work every day. As we've seen in Chapter 3, people get together to collectively strive for a cause that they wouldn't strive for separately.[28]

The biggest barrier to success for many companies that have tried to be customer-centric for years is that their culture has failed to represent this philosophy. Customer centricity is led by a strong customer-centric culture, and culture is made of the people working inside the organisation.

In Chapter 9, we discussed how Enel made innovation part of their customer-centric culture. In my conversation with Marco Gazzino, Head of Innovability® at Enel X, he told me that Enel X's key milestone towards a customer-centric culture via the design of innovative solutions was the initiation of the seven design principles. These guide everyone at Enel X when designing and developing a solution.

- The first guiding principle is the *human touch*, meaning putting people at the centre of experiences by involving them in every step of the design and development process.
- *Simplicity and flexibility* principles ensure that the solution developed is easy to use and that the experience is seamless at every touchpoint.
- The *reliability* principle ensures that customers can count on Enel X; the company delivers on its promises.
- *Cool factor*, *emPOWERment* and *360-degree* impact are the principles related to the uniqueness of the brand – by which it creates "wow experiences", frees people's potential, and fosters inclusion and sustainability.

These design principles are not only key to ensuring customer centricity but that all solutions developed are coherent with Enel X's purpose of *empowering sustainable progress.*

A customer-centric culture will determine the way that you as a company decide to live and breathe. Business leaders should lead the way to customer centricity by ingraining a customer-centric mindset in every employee and making sure that customers' and employees' needs are put first.

Cultural transformation requires a 360-degree change, where the customers are at the centre of every decision-making process, and people are the cornerstone of a successful transformation. The Pillar of Culture will explore this.

Spoiler alert: *people, leadership* and *the bottom line* are the key elements of this pillar for becoming a customer-centric business of the future.

In the next chapter, we will look at the connection between employees and customers – and why it's vital to have high levels of motivation and engagement among employees. This engagement can revive the company's soul, creating superior customer experiences and relationships. We will also see how KLM Royal Dutch Airlines undertook its cultural transformation by focussing on its employees before anything else.

PONDER AND ACT

1. Does your cultural transformation include a shared value creation purpose?
2. Do your current values and beliefs promote a customer-centric culture?
3. How can you invest time in reinforcing the company's purpose with the input of employees?
4. If your culture needs to change, how is your leadership team approaching this?
5. How will you begin spreading the customer-centric culture across departments?

CHAPTER 11: PEOPLE

THE COMPASS

"Give the ones you love wings to fly, roots to come back and reasons to stay." – The Dalai Lama[1]

One evening in 2017, as I was driving back home from the office, it was absolutely pouring down – one of those times where no matter how fast the wipers are moving, you just can't see a thing.

But my vision was not only limited by the heavy rain but by the tears flooding my eyes. I looked at myself in the rearview mirror and saw a miserable and unhappy me. What was going on? My job was affecting my whole life. At one time, I had loved my career as a corporate marketer, but there was something about it that wasn't working any more.

It had taken me years to climb the corporate ladder across different companies, and this was my sixth month in my promotion. Despite the position of seniority, and how much more money I was making, the excitement of the new promotion was short-lived. It brought me little joy, as I dragged myself out of bed in the morning and from meeting to meeting during the day.

I spent countless hours of career coaching to find the root cause of my unhappiness, which needed fixing. We are taught that our careers should be financially secure, but we rarely focus on ensuring that our job is personally fulfilling. When trying to find a solution for the dissatisfaction, we often think that it's because we want a higher salary, so we either ask for a pay rise or change companies to find that satisfaction. We may feel that something changed for a short time, but then the dissatisfaction starts to creep back in.

I grew up influenced by my aunty, who often told me, "It doesn't matter what job you do in the future, and however much money it brings you, what matters is if that job can fulfil your life and the lives of others." Was money enough to make me feel happier in my daily job? Was this job fulfilling my own purpose? Was it making a positive difference in the world? Was this job meaningful and impactful? No, it wasn't.

In the previous chapter, I mentioned that Hubert Joly, former CEO at Best Buy, believes that companies are human organisations made of individuals working together in pursuit of a common purpose.[2] In shiny statements, every company claims to have a great purpose and values; but so often they remain just statements. The main reason why I left my corporate career was because my own purpose and values didn't align with those of my employer. It was less about their stated values and more about their extreme focus on profit – and the leaders' evident disconnection with customers and employees.

During my drive home, I began to realise that my aunty was right all those years ago: work is tough if it is not fulfilling. I reflected on her words as they rattled around inside my head, and there was my answer.

In 2019, Larry Fink, CEO of BlackRock, wrote a letter to CEOs stating, "Purpose is not the sole pursuit of profits but the animating force for achieving them. Profits are in no way inconsistent with purpose – in fact, profits and purpose are inextricably linked."[3] Larry's view is supported by a study carried out by the *Harvard Business Review* on more than 1.5 million employees across thousands of companies. The study confirmed that a strong corporate purpose gives employees a sense of meaning and impacts the way they do their jobs. In fact, companies with a higher purpose have a faster growth rate, higher profitability and are able to outperform the market by 5 to 7 per cent per year,[4] providing that senior management spreads the sense of purpose across the organisation and provides clarity on how to achieve it.[5]

When employees' purpose and values align with those of the company they work for, this automatically creates an emotional connection.

Why do I keep talking about a company's purpose so much? Because when employees are deeply engaged in the work they do, they will look after their customers well and be excited to contribute to the company's purpose. This correlation demonstrates why we shouldn't just think about building a sense of belonging for customers, but also for employees. A recent survey carried out by the *Harvard Business Review* on 984 business executives showed that 92 per cent of respondents agree that companies with highly engaged employees have happy customers, and 81 per cent strongly agree that highly engaged employees perform better.[6] In other words, engaged employees create engaged customers.

What is the level of employee engagement around the world? Well, according to a Gallup study, only 22 per cent of employees are engaged.[7] Employee engagement is "the strength of the mental and emotional connection employees feel toward the work they do, their teams and their organization."[8]

Most companies see employee engagement as initiatives limited to salary increases, ping-pong tables in the recreation room, free cakes and doughnuts, holidays, etc., but very few think of connecting with their employees emotionally. Employee engagement should not be seen as a "thing" of the HR department but as important, holistically, across the whole organisation. Gallup says that the main driver for increasing employee engagement is purpose because, as it was in my case, people want purpose and meaning from their job.

So, why are 78 per cent of employees worldwide actively disengaged at work, despite so many companies claiming to have a higher purpose? Employees want a genuine relationship with their employer, who can coach them to the next level and who genuinely cares about the development of their career and lives.[9] We will see more of the role of leadership in Chapter 12.

A *Harvard Business Review* study on 20,000 workers at 50 major companies around the world states: "Why we work determines how well we work." The study concluded that a company culture that emphasised play, purpose and potential for its employees, and minimised economic (financial reward) and emotional pressure, created more motivation for employees and therefore better customer outcomes.

In addition, performance review systems where employees are stack-ranked or rated against one another increase emotional and economic pressure, and end up reducing total motivation and performance.[10]

Boosting employee engagement is a tricky thing for many companies. Pay hikes acted as an acceptable motivator for people working in the shareholder primacy era and the business-as-a-machine era, and are still used today. What's wrong with rewarding employees with financial incentives? Well, it can encourage unethical behaviour, fuel employee turnover and foster envy and discontent, according to Wharton University of Pennsylvania management professors Adam Grant and Jitendra Singh.

Companies should instead focus more on intrinsic motivational approaches. Grant and Singh say, "That means designing jobs that provide opportunities to make choices, develop skills, do work that matters, and build meaningful interpersonal connections."[11]

Intrinsic motivation involves the employee's willingness to perform better, while gaining satisfaction and enjoyment from their work. Extrinsic motivation is instead powered by external factors such as financial rewards, fame and praise.[12]

How does intrinsic motivation affect performance? In 1977, psychologists Edward Deci and Richard Ryan shared their theory of motivation, which says that there are three basic needs that human beings have which, if met, motivate our behaviour:[13]

Relatedness. Our sense of belonging and connectedness to others.

Autonomy. Our desire to feel free, as opposed to controlled, when making decisions.

Competence. Our sense of being capable and our desire to learn new things.[14]

Workplaces that help employees meet these three psychological needs magnify their intrinsic motivation and therefore their performance, bringing meaning to the job and recognition.

In previous chapters, we have seen how you should be a partner in the life of your customers. But if you want to close the gap between your customer experience and your employee experience, you should really be a partner in the life of your employees as well. Company purpose aligned with relatedness, autonomy and competence directly influence how much personal energy we are willing to spend in our job. Since purpose is a very important element of your journey to centricity, I have decided to stack it at the top of the intrinsic motivational approach.

Purpose: "Why we work determines how well we work"

In 2015, KLM Royal Dutch Airlines undertook their cultural transformation by focussing inwards – on the people inside the organisation. They believed that what provided genuine value to their passengers and business clients was closely intertwined with empowering employees to be "the best of themselves". This was done by creating an optimal, engaged, diverse and inclusive workforce that executed the company's strategy and aligned with their cultural map. KLM's cultural map, the "Compass", was created to consolidate employees' values and behaviour into the KLM purpose. Prior to the cultural transformation, KLM didn't have a common purpose. In fact, if you'd asked random employees what it was, they'd have all given you a different answer.

The creation of the Compass started from understanding the company's *why*. People from different parts of the organisation – from senior management to front-end staff – were gathered together for a number of workshops in which each and every employee was given a chance to have their say.

One part of the KLM Compass comprises five elements that belong to the organisation as a collective entity:

1. Why: Our purpose
2. Who: Our identity
3. Ambition: Our goal
4. What: Our offering
5. How: The KLM spirit[15]

After being encouraged by inspirational companies that had authentic purposes and values, everyone was asked to write down their views on the values they wished they had with regard to each element. Everyone enjoyed it because their opinion on such an important matter was highly valued. The other part of the Compass was instilled by everyone involved, and was formed of four elements:

1. Desired customer experience
2. Optimal staff behaviour
3. Optimal working climate
4. Optimal leadership[16]

The Compass created a very powerful foundation in the employees' everyday lives, because everyone contributed in defining it and felt engaged in working behind it.

Relatedness: Our sense of belonging and connectedness to others
Being a partner in the lives of employees also means valuing them by respecting gender equality, combatting discrimination and promoting diversity and inclusivity.

Throughout my whole career, up until I eventually decided to leave my corporate job, I always worked in male-dominated industries, and for years I sat in meetings and boardrooms as "the only woman", "the youngest" and "the foreigner" – often between white, middle-aged men. This had some benefits, such as being remembered and cared for due to my unique status. However, it also meant that I had to fight harder in order to climb the corporate ladder, it was hard to see myself in long-term senior positions, and I often felt like the outlier.

Being the only one in the room – or the minority in a group, regardless of race, sexual orientation or background – can be lonely. A lack of diversity can negatively affect a company in other tangible ways. Different studies show that organisations with greater diversity are more productive and have better performance. A study by McKinsey examined proprietary data sets for 366 public companies across a range of industries from the United States, the United Kingdom, Canada and Latin America. The study found that companies in the top quartile for racial and ethnic diversity are 35 per cent more likely to have better financial returns, while the figure is 15 per cent for those in the top quartile for gender diversity. More diverse companies are also better able to win top talents and improve their customer orientation and employee satisfaction, which consequently leads to increasing returns.[17]

I wrote the manuscript for this book between 2020 and 2021, and believe me it was very hard to find female senior executives to interview.

But why? Women are born with essential leadership capabilities that many companies see as "just soft skills". KLM launched a female leadership programme and the Talent to the Top manifesto, which actively seeks to appoint more women of all backgrounds and cultures to top positions within the company.[18] KLM has coaching and mentoring initiatives to promote women's career progression in leadership positions. These can help achieve the target set by the board of directors in 2020: they aim to have 33 per cent of women within the group executive committee, and 40 per cent of the top 10 per cent of management-level positions held by women by 2030.[19]

KLM also celebrates diversity by supporting members of the LGBTI community. In 2019, it hosted the annual Workplace Pride Conference, run by a non-profit organisation dedicated to improving the working conditions of LGBTI employees worldwide. In 2010, the company set up Over the Rainbow, the KLM LGBTI community that brings together gay, bisexual and transgender employees.[20] Through this community, KLM provides advice to ensure fair treatment, regardless of sexual orientation.

KLM has been striving for a culture in which every employee feels valued and safe. The company is not only the second-largest private employer in the Netherlands, but it was chosen as the most attractive employer in 2019.[21]

This open mindset of diversity fluency (how proficient people are in understanding differences for diverse groups[22]) makes employees feel more valued and safer, while providing a higher sense of belonging. But it is also a competitive advantage to attract and retain diverse talent.

A decade ago, I had just joined a tech multinational in the UK. My colleague, Pablo (not his real name), had just started at the company too. He was of a similar age and background, likewise a foreigner, and held the same job as me.

He shared his salary with me in confidence. In Latin countries, sharing salary information is considered normal, but this little cultural difference might not have been taken into consideration by the UK-based company. When Pablo told me how much he was earning per year, I was shocked to find out that his salary was 50 per cent higher than mine. Why on Earth was there that much difference, considering that we had similar qualifications, backgrounds and work experience?

Was I happy about it? Of course not. I was frustrated, envious, disappointed and resentful. This is what pay inequality brings to an organisation. Professors Adam Grant and Jitendra Singh state that employees judge the adequacy of their salary not in absolute terms, but in terms of how it compares with their colleagues'.

Our salaries don't just give us the means to support our families; they signal our value to a company.[23] Furthermore, 25 per cent of Millennials say that they'd stop purchasing from companies because of the pay difference between senior executives and average employees.[24]

Frontline employees are superheroes. They are the ones dealing with our customers on a daily basis. They are the most important people when it comes to customer relationships and delivering positive customer experiences, yet they are often forgotten. Seth Godin, entrepreneur and bestselling author, says, "The experience people have with your brand is in the hands of the person you pay the least."[25]

Relatedness creates a sense of community and belonging – a feeling of being valued by others. During my university studies, I was employed as a part-time team member at Nando's in Cambridge, UK. The popular South African restaurants represent more than just your average fast-food chain. Essentially, I was a little bit of everything: a waitress, host and cashier. We would take turns with the duties. For example, I would greet customers at the door and show them the best seats in the house, then I would take their orders, serve their meals and make sure that they had everything they wanted.

As a 20-something working there, I found Nando's not only fun but like a family and home. When I joined the company, I needed to pay for my university studies and support myself while far away from my homeland. But, like any human being away from their family, I wanted a sense of connectedness to a group that I could call my second family. Nando's gave me both the money and the family feeling I needed. In fact, we used to get together every Sunday and in the holidays. Children and partners joined too.

It's not easy to explain why Nando's was a special place to work, aside from spending Sundays together. I believe it came down to "the way we work around here" – and the connection that team members felt with one another and with the managers and supervisors. It was much more than just a temporary job needed to fulfil my basic needs; we all genuinely cared for one another.

Interestingly, according to a Gallup study, leadership alone accounts for 70 per cent of employee engagement.[26] Nando's people – including the leaders – never took things too seriously. People with higher responsibilities called us team members or buddies, and they really treated us like friends. It was an optimal working environment, where I could be true to myself and feel at home. It was a "sticky" environment which I found hard to leave when I had to.

Autonomy: Our desire to feel free, not controlled, when making decisions
Daniel Pink, bestselling author of a number of business and human behaviour books including *Drive: The Surprising Truth About What Motivates Us*, says, "Human beings have an innate inner drive to be autonomous, self-determined and connected to one another. And when that drive is liberated, people achieve more and live richer lives."[27]

Autonomy is about empowering your employees with freedom and control over their work, and their lives at work. In customer-centric companies of the future, giving autonomy to employees means letting them use their natural ability to do the right thing for customers in a particular moment. If employees are not given that freedom and autonomy, because they need to cross layers of approval, you are decreasing the chance of creating superior customer experiences and that much-needed bond between employees and customers.

At the Ritz-Carlton, for example, employees at all levels are empowered to "delight guests" who have raised an issue, by spending up to $2,000 (€1,725) per guest, per incident. The Ritz-Carlton says that employee empowerment is less expensive than it seems, because the full $2,000 is rarely used. The money is really a symbol to show trust towards employees in doing the right thing in resolving a guest issue well. And it's meant to delight customers. This not only gives them autonomy but freedom in using their creativity in memorable ways to elevate the guest experience.[28]

Autonomy breeds creativity and innovation, which don't happen in command-and-control settings. According to research, stress levels at work are also directly related to how much control people have in their roles.[29] By giving autonomy to your employees, you'll boost employee engagement, establish mutual trust, and raise customer satisfaction and loyalty. Autonomy also means giving employees more flexibility in how they manage their time, how they work and where they work from.

At Best Buy corporate, employees were allowed to work from wherever they wanted, whenever they wanted, as long as they delivered the expected results. In management, this is called ROWE (results only work environment). ROWE eliminates the conventional practices of set hours, office presence and required attendance at meetings, and creates a relaxed and comfortable environment, where employees have total autonomy and flexibility. The only measure of value is the results they deliver. Of course, there are disadvantages to this, but many organisations say these are outweighed by the advantages. Those that have adopted and kept ROWE are seeing cost savings, financial gain, increased productivity, employee retention and improved workplace morale.[30] This is another boost to the trust between company and employee.

Best Buy removed ROWE in 2013 because, in the middle of a turnaround, Hubert Joly said he needed everyone's strength in the same place at the same time.[31] Now that COVID-19 has forced many companies to adopt remote working, many have adopted the ROWE mindset. That said, remote working and ROWE conditions might not be for everyone or for every organisation.

Professors Grant and Singh say that employee motivation can be increased by granting more autonomy in tasks, work schedules and work methods.

Competence: Our sense of being capable and our desire to learn new things
Professors Grant and Singh continue that competence involves developing specialised knowledge, skills and expertise.[32] Companies with a strong learning culture are 92 per cent more likely to be more innovative, 56 per cent more likely to be the first to bring innovation to market,

52 per cent more productive, and 17 per cent more profitable than their competitors.[33] Have you ever left a company thinking, *I didn't see the opportunity for growth there*? This is exactly what happens in the minds of individuals who are not given the tools for growth.

Millennial and Gen Z employees in particular see learning opportunities as one of the most important drivers for choosing their company of employment. Nando's wanted the whole family to be happy and succeed in their working journey, whatever their job was. Regardless of how high up they were, if my workmates wanted to pursue a career in hospitality, the company provided all sorts of training, from leadership to cooking. Each employee was given training not only on how to grill the chicken, but also on how to interact with customers. Nando's culture was about "being a family", and it made sure that we all kept an eye out for one another, inspired one another, and celebrated every small or big win with one another.

In 2021, Nando's was ranked the 12th best place to work in the UK by Glassdoor. Past and current employees voted by completing a company review about their job, work environment and employer. One feedback form read, "It is a kind, caring, friendly and down-to-earth company, who will do all they can to help you further your career."[34] As you can see, employee reviews matter just as much as customer reviews.

I have been part of companies where I was given the opportunity to get some sort of training, but they weren't really designed with the employee-customer relationship in mind. Having a load of training available for the sake of it will not make any difference.

The COVID-19 pandemic has fast-forwarded digital adoptions in the workplace to the extent that many employees were dumped with new digital tools to work with – creating a new need for training. Despite the advantage of these digital technologies, the sudden change led to huge gaps of acceptance between employees, because we all have different needs, challenges and technical proficiency.[35] A study showed that 62 per cent of employees feel they lack the necessary skills to do their jobs, and their employers don't support them with the right training.[36] This includes providing the right support for the tech tools that are needed to interact with customers, and the right support when tech brings frictions – which happens very often.

Removing frictions from your employees' work will lower their stress levels and ensure that their experience remains positive. Your people should be at the core of your customer-centricity strategy because they will be the ones who will make a successful customer-centric transformation happen.[37]

Delivering consistent, superior customer experience means doing the same for your employees. As we have seen so far in this book, customer-centric companies of the future have a strong mentality that serving customers is the priority. When this mindset naturally aligns with employees, they find their work personally fulfilling.

As you become a customer-centric business of the future, you should start hiring with the customer in mind, and this means that during the acquisition process, prospects should be asked questions to understand their customer orientation. This is how you'd align every new employee with customer-centric thinking.[38]

We talk a lot about improving the customer experience, but most employees fall into one of the following categories:

- They don't know what it means to put customers at the centre of the organisation.
- They don't know how to improve or offer a superior customer experience.
- They don't know how their daily job contributes in any way to making customers' lives better.

This happens when companies' departments are siloed, every department only cares about their own performance, and employees of each department only care about their own tasks.

As a customer-centric company of the future, you should devote a significant amount of time and resources to educating and communicating the customer value proposition to your employees. What are the company's plans to make customers' lives easier and better, and how will the company be a companion in customers' lives? It's not only about communicating this approach, but actually making sure that employees at all levels understand how their job delivers value to customers – and listening to all employees as they provide input on how their jobs can improve the customer experience. This not only educates and coaches all employees but it also instils the company's purpose and value proposition holistically when serving customers.

Breaking silos starts by making customer feedback and data easily accessible across all departments. This creates a sense of collective achievement when customers are happy about the experience they had. It also creates a sense of accountability whenever customers are not happy.[39]

THE EMPLOYEE REVOLUTION

You must be getting the impression by now that we are in the middle of a work revolution. With the rise of tools that remove barriers within and between companies – coupled with the work-from-home phenomenon – the gig economy and the new generations of employees are forcing companies to rethink their approaches to talent acquisition and management.

If today's customers have the choice of where to buy from, employees have the choice of who to work for. For companies, it has been a challenge to find highly talented people. In fact, 82 per cent don't believe they recruit highly talented people, and for those who do, only 7 per cent say they can retain them.[40]

During my gap year, I travelled to many destinations across Asia and Europe where I came across the digital nomad phenomenon. These are location-independent individuals (mostly Millennials and Gen Z), often from developed countries, who leverage tech tools to perform their jobs while living a nomadic lifestyle.[41] Most of these individuals were independent contractors, tech entrepreneurs, remote workers and freelancers who had got sick of corporate life, so they were working and travelling at the same time. Digital nomads can achieve a better work-life balance, while enjoying their jobs and lives.

One thing that many Millennial digital nomads and I had in common was that we had all left our corporate careers. And many Gen Z digital nomads had never worked in a company. In 2019, 57 million American workers (35 per cent of the US workforce) were estimated to be freelancers and more than half of Gen Z had started their careers freelancing.[42]

Now that it's easier for employees to ditch companies in favour of more flexible work, it's more imperative that those companies do what they can to retain their workers. According to the Work Institute, the total cost of voluntary turnover in the US was $617 (€527) billion in 2018, which is a staggering 27 per cent of the total workforce that, at this rate, will hit 35 per cent by 2023.[43] Crises such as COVID-19 have led us to think more deeply about our lives, purpose, relationship with our work, and especially how to care for others more than we did previously.

This heightened compassion for others means that another factor increasingly influencing consumer behaviour is how companies treat their employees. In fact, the 2020 Edelman Trust barometer shows that 3 in 10 respondents around the world say that this is one of the most important factors in deciding whether to become a loyal customer. In addition, 90 per cent of the people surveyed said that companies should protect employees' wellbeing and financial security during the COVID-19 pandemic, if they want to earn customers' trust – even if this means sacrificing financial gain.[44] This attitude is here to stay.

Sustainability therefore doesn't only mean taking a stance on global issues but also proving the humanity of your company by treating your people well. This is another test for brands as Millennials like me have high standards for determining which organisations make the cut. In fact, in a report conducted by Deloitte, 62 per cent of us around the world believe that companies have no ambition beyond wanting to maximise profits, and 70 per cent agree that businesses focus on their own agendas rather than considering the wider society.[45]

Yet, companies' contributions to environmental and social good are a major attraction for career choices. When a company strives to do good to other people, the environment, and society as a whole, the connection between the company and its people is much easier to make and to retain.

Changing decades-old systems is not an easy task. It takes time and commitment from the leaders across the company. A customer-centric culture is not only aligned to a strong brand purpose, but has an optimal working environment that makes sure that all people are valued and understood, and that they belong and matter. Society's needs are many, large and growing, and the new generation of young people – whether they are customers or employees – is asking businesses to step up.

In this chapter, we have seen what truly creates shared value through workforce practices but, although they are crucial, employees alone cannot create the conditions for the customer-centric company of the future.

Over the next chapter, we will explore your role as a leader. Just as a compass shows true north, a customer-centric leader shows the right path, engages others to follow, and empowers each employee and customer to become proud ambassadors of the brand.

PONDER AND ACT

1. Based on the concepts in this chapter, how can you ensure that you look for values and a customer orientation when recruiting and selecting new employees?
2. How can you close the gap between the employee experience and the customer experience by sharing customer insights with your people?
3. How can (or do) you involve all employees in identifying ways to improve the customer experience?
4. What opportunities exist to create relatedness, autonomy and competence to engage and retain employees?
5. What can you do to ensure that you are a fair employer, or what are you already doing?

CHAPTER 12: LEADERSHIP

THE RESET BUTTON

"It should be borne in mind that there is nothing more difficult to arrange, more doubtful of success, and more dangerous to carry through than initiating change…" – Niccolò Machiavelli[1]

"We have been able to almost destroy our environment. From this point of view, how can we say that we are better organisms?" These are the words of leading plant neurobiologist Stefano Mancuso, also head of the International Laboratory of Plant Neurobiology at the University of Florence. Stefano believes that human beings have the wrong assumption that they are the most perfect and intelligent beings on our planet. In fact, since homo sapiens have been around for only 300,000 years, they are not best compared with other species that have lived on Earth for an average of 5 million years.

According to Stefano, humans' chance of survival is very low, because of the way we are organised. The animal kingdom and human society are structured in a centralised and hierarchical way. This is basically the same way our body is made with a brain and various organs, each of which is very fundamental for our survival. "We use this in our universities, our companies, even our class divisions," says Mancuso.[2]

We find pyramid-like organisations, with a top-level control centre, pretty much everywhere. Stefano believes that hierarchical organisations are weak. Why? Because if one critical component is missing, the whole thing collapses. Plants, for example, don't have centralised organs like humans and animals do. Instead, they are horizontal, diffusive and decentralised.[3]

Stefano says that we homo sapiens have a lot to learn from plants. For example, a forest is made up of a huge network of interconnected roots, through which plants communicate in a genuine "mutual support network". This network is not based on competition, like in the case of the animal and the human worlds, but on reciprocal help. Plants are highly sensitive to their surroundings and able to respond quickly to dangerous situations to make sure that they can collectively improve the situation. In the case of a fire, for example, they are able to communicate to one another and produce more water in order to survive.[4] This is the collective behaviour that has allowed them to survive for hundreds of millions of years.[5] As we tend to compete, plants can teach us a better way to survive – to cooperate instead.

The words of Stefano Mancuso are also very relevant in the business world, where leaders of hierarchical organisations, managed through command-and-control cultures designed more than a century ago, are reluctant to give up some of their power. Command-and-control models were designed for a stable, slow-moving, predictable world, a world that no longer exists. Hierarchical pyramids are slow, static, outdated, siloed, bureaucratic and so on.

According to Gary Hamel and Michele Zanini, authors of *Humanocracy*, formal hierarchies consist of a bureaucratic blueprint. They say, "Power is vested in positions, authority trickles down, big leaders appoint little leaders, strategies and budgets are set at the top, central staff groups make policy and ensure compliance, job roles are tightly defined, control is achieved through oversight, rules and sanctions, managers assign tasks and assess performance, everyone competes for promotion, and compensation correlates with rank."[6]

There is no way we could create a customer-centric business of the future without pushing the reset button on the way we, as organisations, are wired, and flattening the hierarchy. In traditional, hierarchical, pyramid-like businesses, the C-suite does the thinking, dictates the goals and creates politics, while the rest of the employees execute tasks like robots, without understanding the *why* behind those tasks. This type of business is broken down in siloed departments that are powered by competition and hostility, because employees don't know one another and don't understand what anyone else does.

In a highly disruptive and changing world where customers' expectations change incredibly quickly, as we've discussed throughout this book, we need agile, customer-centric companies. Flattening the hierarchy means decentralising the authority by empowering employees to execute freely, which speeds up decision-making processes. It also means forming dynamic networks of teams that can rapidly communicate information and collaborate in a cross-functional way.

Such a network of teams involves an evolution from the traditional structure, in which team members can self-organise and collaborate more quickly and flexibly. These self-managed teams should consist of a maximum of 15 people with different skill sets, which makes them highly multidisciplinary. The tasks and responsibilities for each member are not based on job descriptions or positions, but on interests and talent. Teams are granted a lot of autonomy and self-control, but whatever they do must be in line with the purpose and values of the network or company for which they work. Although each team has a clear focus on a particular objective, the network of teams is designed around a strong purpose that glues all teams together and provides guidance and direction.[7]

Smaller teams such as these can empower and engage with one another better, deliver results faster and stay focussed on their mission more than traditional teams could. The leaders ensure their team is aware of other teams' activities and has immediate access to customer insights.

By giving employees more freedom, teams can be more agile, communicate more freely, and make better and faster decisions. This also builds genuine relationships and trust among teams.

Societal institutions, such as governments, the military and the church, have long had pyramid-like structures. In 2004, General Stanley McChrystal took command of the Joint Special Operations Task Force and understood that the conventional, hierarchical, command-and-control structure of the US military served well only during the early stages of the Iraq War. No matter how well equipped, highly trained and technically sophisticated the US military was, Al-Qaeda in Iraq was able to move more quickly, strike ruthlessly and win battles. How? By having fluid tactics and organic, decentralised networks in place.

General McChrystal realised that "winning" would become more about internal culture and a new approach to management.[8] He restructured to a new military system that decentralised the decision-making authority ("empowered execution"), where every member became empowered to execute. He also developed a real-time information-sharing system by breaking down silos between the CIA, FBI and NSA, which, up until that point, would not share information widely and fast enough to the soldiers on the ground who could use it ("shared consciousness").[9] The information centre also worked for dedicated teams that could monitor and see patterns in Al-Qaeda's random attacks. Each team had a "liaison officer", who was responsible for information flowing quickly to other teams.

There is not a structure that will work for every company out there, but these principles can be applied to your business too. Teams should have a cross-functional relationship, rather than one that is dysfunctional and competitive. How can you create connections across teams? You unfortunately can't write a process to work in every case, but, once again, you can set the culture.

Spotify, the music and podcast streaming company, is a great example of a unique organisational structure. It is not the classical, hierarchical, top-down management approach with layers of bureaucracy, but a people-driven, autonomous approach that emphasises the importance of an agile culture and network. Spotify is home to more than 6,000 employees who are organised into agile teams called squads, which form a self-organised and cross-functional network. They are granted autonomy for what to build, how to build it and with whom in order to successfully complete their mission. Yet, they are all aligned with the company's purpose, which, of course, is more important than any individual squad's task.

Several squads are then organised into a lightweight matrix called a tribe, which links them together via individuals who serve as "chapters". Tribes are designed to be less than 150 people, which, according to sociologist Robert Dunbar, is the optimum (and maximum) number that any individual can know well and communicate with.[10]

While the squad is the primary group, which in the Spotify case focusses on the product delivery and quality, the chapter is basically what we call a line manager in a traditional setting. The chapter should be a servant leader who focusses on mentoring and coaching, since their primary role is to facilitate learning and competency development through the squads.

Since Spotify believes in the player-coach model, chapters are not only leaders but also squad members. Squad members can move between squads and retain or change their chapters as they move.

Spotify's structure is based on a community that communicates in informal and unpredictable ways, so the company has introduced a third element, known as a guild. Guilds are informal communities of interest where people across the whole company gather and share knowledge within a specific area. Guilds don't have much structure; in fact, anyone can join or leave at any time. I recommend watching a video about them for inspiration.[11]

FAIL FAST ➡ LEARN FAST ➡ IMPROVE FAST

Unless you are a small business starting from scratch, you'll have strong advocates of the status quo who don't see the need for breaking walls. A lot of senior management tend to be older, because they are considered more "experienced". But this doesn't account for how the world of business keeps changing rapidly. Younger generations of employees and customers live, work – and buy – differently to most senior leaders. In other words, they offer less experience within a corporate setting, but more experience with crucial platforms and practices.

Most of the clients who I ask "What do you think you need to change in this business?" answer with "I don't know" or "Not much, really". They might not be against change, but they just don't know any other way, because they are comfortable driving the business forward via the status quo.

Another issue in pyramid-like organisations is that most of the solutions to customers' concerns are with the people at the lower levels who understand what is working and not. But these people often get ignored, because information flows top-down and not bottom-up.

In my conversation with Victoria Roos Olsson, Senior Leadership Consultant at FranklinCovey, we spoke in depth about successful leadership. Victoria said, "It's incredibly important to create a culture of feedback that goes two ways, where frontliners meeting customers every day come back and say, 'Hey, this didn't work' or 'I had this reaction three times on the floor today.' Leaders should proactively ask for feedback to create that safe space for team members to see what's working and what's not. Unless you have a culture of feedback based on trust, this will not come automatically. Leaders also have the critical job of sharing the vision – 'the why behind the what'. And not just in a yearly employee meeting or passing on an email from the CEO, but in an ongoing dialogue, as a constant in everything."

Those who interact with our customers might not have the right answer for every problem, but they bring additional perspective and creativity as the ones interacting with the outside world. Walls that need breaking down include those that divide the top from the bottom. Those on the top (C-suite leaders) and bottom (anyone else) must be connected to find the best solutions for the business, and therefore the customer. The bottom must understand the decisions of the top before serving the customers, and the top must understand what happens at the bottom for the strategy to work.

More often than not, strategic decisions from the top get passed down, but that information doesn't trickle *all the way* down. It gets stuck somewhere in the middle, because some middle manager forgot to communicate it to their team. This creates disconnection from the leaders at the top, who rarely communicate directly with the bottom.

Listening and communicating both ways has never been more important because, in the 21st century, C-suite leaders and line managers don't and can't have all the answers up their sleeve.

Spotify's structure goes beyond the obsolete matrix organisations of the 1950s that still exist today. Their cross-functional mechanism not only enables self-management but it also balances autonomy and accountability, which therefore enhances innovation and minimises bureaucratic rules ("empowered execution").

In Chapter 11, we saw that the level of employee engagement around the world, according to Gallup, is a mere 22 per cent.[12] Engaged employees are more productive, provide better customer experience and show higher levels of commitment to their team and the business.

Usually, it's not the employees who are the issue, but the leaders. Unfortunately, many leaders struggle to release autonomy in people's jobs, because they believe that their power is a zero-sum game, and they are terrified that it will create chaos if they loosen the reins.[13]

Spotify's concept of "aligned autonomy" seeks to address that concern of leadership by striking the right balance between autonomy and accountability. Squads have full visibility of the project's successes and failures through internal and customer feedback. Squads conduct retrospective meetings to reflect on what works, what doesn't and how to improve.

To make this work for both the individual and the whole squad, Spotify re-engineered its performance management system to separate performance reviews from coaching and feedback so that people don't feel pressure about their performance. Anyone, regardless of their position, can provide feedback on how an individual may improve, which enhances continuous learning and personal growth.[14]

Spotify's concept of aligned autonomy is what they call "loosely coupled, tightly aligned squads", in which "the stronger alignment we have, the more autonomy we can afford to grant". The leader's job is to communicate what problem must be solved and why and let the people collaborate to find the best solution for the problem.[15]

Spotify's model is, of course, the result of how their leaders think, learn and behave (their mindsets). Spotify adopts what Stanford psychology professor Carol Dweck calls a "growth mindset", as opposed to a fixed mindset.[16] A growth mindset can help employees be customer-obsessed and fail and learn fast. A fixed mindset can cause employees to think that they have reached the limit of their abilities, which puts boundaries on what they can do for customers. Spotify's founder, Daniel Ek, puts it nicely: "We aim to make mistakes faster than anyone else."[17] This means recovering and learning from failure, rather than avoiding failure.

If people at Spotify don't know the best way to do something – which as human beings is likely to happen – they are encouraged to try different approaches and run several small A/B tests. This doesn't always mean that things go in the right direction. Some squads have "fail walls", in which failures get analysed and shared to allow everyone to learn and improve from them.

A fail-friendly environment is never about who's at fault, but about what happened and what was learned ("shared consciousness"). A test-and-learn approach provides more data-driven decisions and eliminates decisions driven by opinion, ego or authority. This creates a platform for building collective intelligence.

On a scale from authoritative to liberal, Spotify ranks itself more on the liberal side. It has a people-first culture of empowering others and giving credit. No matter how talented someone is, there is very little ego about their individual accomplishments.[18]

ZERO-EGO GAME

I asked Victoria Roos Olsson what makes a good leader. She debunked an existing leadership myth. "Many have the idea that we're either born leaders, or we're not. I'd like to scrap that, because being a good leader is not necessarily innate. It's about communication skills; it's about being able to create that one-to-one relationship; it's about your empathic touch with others. These are all things that can be learned and relearned. From the leader's perspective, the most important thing to understand is that my success is not because of my individual results, but because of the commitment and effort that I invest in helping my team succeed in their roles. This is the starting point of good leadership." Victoria continues by saying, "Good leaders should set the picture of 'where we are going' and be the translator and storyteller of that picture."

We shouldn't scrap the older and more experienced leaders, managers and supervisors like an old car, but I am a believer that the wisdom any of them acquired through decades of experience should be passed down via coaching or mentoring. The core skills of coaching involve an ability to listen and ask really good questions. It's all about unleashing the talent and potential.

Employees' level of engagement – their happiness and, therefore, their retention – is strongly based upon their relationship with their line manager. Coaching is not about getting employees to agree on what has already been decided. The manager-as-coach asks questions to spark insights instead of providing answers, supports employees instead of judging their performance, and facilitates their development instead of dictating what must be done.

This illustrates the one-to-one relationship that Victoria talked about. It sounds too good to be true, because most managers and leaders don't feel they have the time for "soft" approaches, and it can feel like they are being deprived of asserting authority. But coaching is effective. Employees are more empowered to unleash innovation and commitment.

As a member of the C-suite, you should provide middle managers the reset tools and support to become better coaches and mentors. On top of targets, budgets and numbers, middle managers' mission is to grow and motivate employees' capabilities that build customer success. This also means making coaching a part of the company's culture. To do this, you must be the first to embrace it.[19]

Victoria has been training, developing and coaching leaders around the world for the past 20 years, and she has noticed a common pattern. She said, "Often, leaders are so absorbed in numbers and figures that they don't truly live and role model the behaviour they're looking for. The messengers of this behaviour are also the middle managers, but it's not enough that they pass the message on. They also truly need to live it."

Another leader of note applied Carol Dweck's growth mindset principles to encourage employees to shift from a historical "know-it-all" mindset to a "learn-it-all" curiosity. Satya Nandella took the reins of Microsoft in 2014 when, after four decades, it had become stodgy and stagnant. He started by modelling the behaviours that he expected middle managers to adopt, including eliciting thoughts from anyone he talked to, and listening empathically – whether they were a top executive or a frontliner. He encouraged everybody to fail and learn from mistakes, showing that his role represented support rather than judgement.[20]

Modelling is a powerful approach, because it shows that you, the leader of the organisation, are actually "walking the talk". And it works, because when people don't know how to behave, they copy the behaviour of those in power.[21]

As part of the shift in the coaching-oriented approach, the Microsoft leadership team removed the "precision questioning", or performance questioning, in their mid-year reviews, which had provided the typical barometer of people's progress and performance. Microsoft turned precision questioning into coaching-oriented questioning, such as:

- "What are you trying to do?"

- "What's working?"
- "What's not working?"
- "How can we help?"[22]

Mid-year reviews and performance questioning are largely unproductive, fear-inducing rituals in command-and-control business cultures. They are a deterrent to the supportive conversations and dialogues that employees need in order to grow and develop – and support the business mission.

According to neuroscientific studies reported in the *Harvard Business Review*: "When the amygdala registers a threat to our safety, arteries harden and thicken to handle an increased blood flow to our limbs in preparation for a *fight-or-flight response*. In this state, we lose access to the social engagement system of the limbic brain and the executive function of the prefrontal cortex, inhibiting creativity and the drive for excellence."[23]

Coaching conversations and real-time feedback are a much more constructive way of growing the next generations of leaders. Committing to the growth of your people is equal to receiving commitment through their loyalty, which will translate into customer success.

BE A HUMAN LEADER

Daniel Goleman is an internationally known psychologist who first introduced the term "emotional intelligence" (EI) to the business world 25 years ago with his bestselling book *Emotional Intelligence*. EI is important when it comes to relationships – both with ourselves and others.[24] We often associate leadership qualities with intelligent quotient (IQ), toughness, determination, etc. However, Goleman believes that effective leaders are distinguished also by a high degree of emotional intelligence.[25] "IQ and technical skills are important, but emotional intelligence is the *sine qua non* of leadership," he says, in a 1998 article written for the *Harvard Business Review*.[26]

This doesn't mean that EI matters more than IQ, and vice versa.[27] According to Goleman, EI includes four skills:

1. *Self-awareness* is literally that. It's your capability to understand and recognise your emotions, and how they affect your actions and the actions of your team.
2. *Self-management* is your capability to control your emotions and maintain positive self-control, particularly in stressful situations.
3. *Social awareness* is your people skills and, more precisely, your ability to understand your people's emotions and the dynamics in play within your organisation (empathy).
4. *Relationship management* is your adeptness to connect with others in ways that are influenced, coached and mentored by you. It's also your ability to avoid conflicts and/or resolve them effectively.[28]

Why is EI important? Because, as a leader, you set the tone in your organisation. Another important factor: as we get further into the age of artificial intelligence (AI), we need more people with higher levels of emotional intelligence. Sensing and managing emotions – especially in relationships – is far beyond the ability of AI, at this point.

In our business world, we create a lot of processes, structures and rules. We tell people what to do and not do. All of these "creations" are barriers that stop people from being themselves, which in turn stops them from making that emotional connection with you, their colleagues and your customers.

Your role as leader of the organisation is to create psychological safety so that your people feel trusted, supported and safe to use their emotional intelligence. Psychological safety creates an environment in which people feel they won't be punished or humiliated for sharing ideas, questions, concerns or mistakes.[29]

I have heard leaders say, "This is just the way I am." Or, "That's just his/her way." Well, that's a fixed mindset, my friend. The good news is that you can change that mindset and grow your EI.

There are people who have more emotional quotient (EQ), as well as more IQ, than others. The only way to increase them is by challenging ourselves.

Goleman's research proves that EI can be learned. According to his popular article written for the *Harvard Business Review,* Goleman mentions that EI is "born largely in the neurotransmitters of the brain's limbic system, which governs feelings, impulses and drives". Our limbic system learns via motivation, practice and feedback – as opposed to the learning in our neocortex, which governs our analytical and technical ability. "The neocortex grasps concepts and logic. It is the part of the brain that figures out how to use a computer or make a sales call by reading a book."[30]

Creating a network of teams means breaking down the barriers, connecting with people and making sure they connect with one another, with us and with customers.

But before connecting with others, in order to help them develop and grow, we truly need to step out of our comfort zone and do the same for ourselves first. It's like when we fly on an aeroplane. The flight attendant gives us the safety instruction to put our oxygen mask on first, before helping others.

To become a stronger leader, we also must break down the barrier between our most important parts of the body: our head and our heart.

How can we lead with both our head and our heart while enhancing EI across the organisation?

1. By hiring a coach that can train us to increase our EQ.
2. By identifying EI competencies of star performers and hire more people with these competencies.
3. By providing EI training that focusses on the limbic system to help existing people develop those identified EI competencies. Researchers call this "competence modelling".[31]

Building more EI doesn't happen without sincere desire and effort. When I spoke to Massimiliano Pogliani, CEO of illycaffè, something he said which stuck in my head was: "I have an open-door policy. Everyone can come and talk to me at any time, about any topic, and no matter their job title. There is no need to book a meeting with my assistant. We must lead by example, and it's only by doing this that we increase the level of trust between the people inside and outside of the organisation. Trust is an intangible asset that is built up over time and maintained in a coherent manner."

Human leaders are also those who talk to their customers all the time and are genuinely interested in meeting them, listening to them, empathising with them, learning from them and trying out new ideas. It has always astonished me how many leaders claim to be customer-centric, yet have rarely met a customer. Jens Hofma, CEO of the UK arm of Pizza Hut, a global pizza restaurant chain, dedicates four hours to waiting on tables every other week. He finds this the best way of interacting with both customers and staff.[32]

I have heard from old-style leaders that EI is a "woman thing". What does that even mean? Having emotions and being able to control them is a "human thing" and not just a "woman thing". Lack of EI can result in lack of employee engagement and high turnover, which is also a human thing. Without EI, leaders won't be at their strongest, regardless of analytical skills, training and IQ.

In a global survey of 64,000 people, two-thirds responded that "the world would be a better place if men thought more like women". Among those feminine traits, respondents chose "plans for the future", "expressive", "loyal", "flexible", "patient", "collaborative", "passionate", "empathic" and "selfless". Are feminine qualities *that bad*? People surveyed found masculine qualities not to be that bad either. They valued being "decisive", "resilient", "analytical", "independent" and "proud".[33]

I believe that, regardless of gender, both women and men can create profound change in the way they lead. We don't need competition amongst genders, individuals or teams; we need to press the reset button to create a more equal world in which long-term stakeholder value replaces old stigmas and short-term profit. It's only by cooperating that we can drive our evolution. Plants have been teaching us to cooperate and not to compete for centuries, but we have completely underestimated them.

PONDER AND ACT

1. How can you create a network of teams through which people can cooperate in a cross-functional way?
2. What changes can you implement to create a "fail fast → learn fast → improve fast" culture, where feedback flows easily? Is failure currently tolerated? If not, why?
3. How can you move towards letting go of authority and power, and giving employees the freedom to decide the best solution for your customers?
4. How could you increase your team's emotional intelligence?
5. How can you begin to break existing barriers between top and bottom, and especially between your head and your heart?

CHAPTER 13

THE BOTTOM LINE

*"Prove yourself brave, truthful and unselfish, and someday you will
be a real boy."* – The Blue Fairy, The Adventures of Pinocchio[1]

Since being back in my countryside home in my native Sardinia, a lot
of events and objects have triggered memories. One item of particular
interest is an old book of my favourite children's stories that my grandmother used to read to me: *The Adventures of Pinocchio.* Pinocchio was
written in 1883 by Italian author Carlo Collodi.[2]

Reading Pinocchio through the lens of a 30-something-year-old
woman not only brings back sweet childhood memories but also a strong
lesson for me as a customer-centricity advisor. I believe the story goes
much deeper than "don't lie, or your nose will grow".

Pinocchio is a wooden puppet, carved by his father, Geppetto, who
prays that Pinocchio will become a real boy. One night, the Blue Fairy
grants Geppetto's wish; but in order to be a real boy, Pinocchio needs a
conscience. He is given a talking cricket for a conscience. Despite this,
Pinocchio becomes entrapped by a fox and a cat, who lead him into
many mischievous adventures. There are many other characters in the
tale, but these are the most significant ones to focus on, as I apply them
to the business world.

If Pinocchio – the puppet – is the business, I see Geppetto as the stakeholders. These are the people who want to buy from and work for trustworthy and genuine companies. I see the fox and the cat as the puppeteers that control the strings of greed within the current capitalism system, representing the short-term mindset and profit maximisation that control businesses. Although a business has a soul and a conscience, there is always something – like the fox and the cat – that tempts it to unethical behaviour.

There is one discrepancy that stands out in the story as a metaphor for businesses. Although Geppetto never stopped loving Pinocchio despite his naughtiness, today's stakeholders are not typically like this and are capable of walking away from a company in the blink of an eye.

If you read headlines and statements of corporations worldwide, you might conclude that we are doing well with customer-centricity today. These businesses have, apparently, fundamentally changed their *raison d'être* (purpose). Their customers are at the heart of their decision-making, and they are benefitting society at large.

Yet, despite the headlines, most leaders are still remunerated based on metrics – such as revenue, share prices and profit. When a company struggles to reach its targets, its typical move is to announce cuts – of any sort – and then proceed with massive lay-offs and restructuring so that share prices rise. Often, this happens not just because the company is not making enough money to cover costs, but because they are not making as much money as they had estimated. As a result, people lose their jobs.

How can we possibly think that anyone who survives being laid off can still trust the company and go to work every day, facing customers, with a smile on their face? Despite corporate promises to the contrary, today's business leaders are more responsible for the growing value of the company's stock than for growing the value of their customer base.

WHAT'S THE VALUE OF YOUR CUSTOMERS?

As we have seen throughout this book, the necessary change to customer-centricity is not realised by sticking a new statement on the wall or sending out a few press releases and publicity campaigns. Changing the narrative from shareholder value to stakeholder value doesn't happen overnight. It can only happen when we also transform the performance measurement system.

While it's admirable that companies want to change, at the operational level, there is still so much to be done. Change is unlikely to happen until we transform the way businesses are held accountable, because mandatory accounting systems and financial disclosures were created with shareholder value maximisation in mind. While, on the face of it, it's apparent that customers generate all the value in most businesses, investors and business leaders do not always act as if this is the case.

In this chapter, we will explore two highly intertwined problems that are the result of this disconnect.

#1 The wrong side of accounting practices

Financial and management disclosure generally fails to provide insight into a customer's profitability and lifetime value – or their drivers. The root of this problem can be traced back to 1890, with the advent of modern financial accounting. Milton Friedman's shareholder primacy doctrine made it even worse, not entirely because of Friedman's beliefs, but because of how they were interpreted. Pursuing shareholder value became synonymous with satisfying investor growth and profitability expectations. This prevailing ideology needs a serious update.

In 2010, Roger Martin, former dean of the University of Toronto's Rotman School of Management introduced the concept of the "age of customer capitalism", which posited that organisations that put their customers first would create greater value for their shareholders. Business leaders, however, worried that focussing on customers would erode short-term gain. Moreover, while Martin made a logical case, he did not back up his assertion with analysis of investor returns. The concept therefore failed to gain much traction.[3,4]

Rob Markey, senior partner at Bain & Company, who we discussed in Chapter 1, told me that the "profits versus customer" framing is to misunderstand how businesses really work. "Accounting was developed with no concept of the customer and with information technology gaps that make it difficult to see customers across the different systems in a business. This is compounded by corporate valuation, which has ignored the exponential impact of growing customer value in favour of the linear impact resulting from cost reduction or price increases. Investor pressure lies at the bottom of this false dichotomy, and accounting practices have created the conditions for this investor pressure." Government-mandated audits and financial disclosures are currently based on financial data (for example income statements, balance sheets and line item cash flow statements) – which show a murky view of a company's health and performance.

#2 Investors have an incomplete picture of a company's health
Investors do not fully understand or make use of customer value as a way to establish a business's investment value. This results, largely, from the fact that accounting fails to make the relevant information available through mandatory, reliable disclosure. Without a complete picture of a company's health, too much emphasis is placed on meeting short-term earnings and revenue goals. Therefore, stock prices swing far too wildly based on small changes in current period earnings and revenue, but far too little based on underlying changes in customer behaviour and customer economics (new customer acquisition, acquisition costs, retention, cross-selling, price realisation, etc.). Because of the sensitivity of stock prices to earnings, business leaders pay far too much attention to 'managing earnings' in the short term, which undermines long-term customer relationships. Business leaders manage earnings, for example, by

imposing high nuisance fees, decreasing services to poor levels, cutting labour costs, reducing product quality, etc. These activities often result in eroding customer trust, weakening brand reputation, making the company vulnerable to customer-centric competitors and reducing the long-term economic value of the customer base.

Rob believes that companies' performance and health should also be evaluated on *customer value*. Customer value, in Rob's framework, is the lifetime value of a company's entire customer base. It can be increased by acquiring new customers, earning more revenue from its existing loyal ones, retaining them longer, and improving the cost of acquiring and serving them.

Over the course of this book, we have explored three pillars – *humanity, technology* and *culture* – and how they can help you become a truly customer-centric business; one that is able to acquire and retain customers and therefore increase the lifetime value of your customer base. As a result of the two problems mentioned in this chapter – being on the wrong side of accounting practices and investors having an incomplete picture of a company's health – boards, CEOs and management teams do not place enough emphasis on managing and growing customer value. However, established and growing public companies – such as American Express, E.ON and Allianz – are using customer value metrics for reporting activities. Investors are increasingly interested in the success of a company based on customer value.

As stated throughout the book, the shareholder primacy era has been under criticism for many different reasons. Our job as leaders is to educate shareholders about the long-term gain that comes with a focus on customer value.

David Thodey, former CEO of Telstra, an Australian telecommunications company, committed to becoming customer-centric at the expense of short-term business performance. The company educated its investors on the importance of strengthening customer relationships; it then received these investors' full support on customer-centric initiatives.

204 THE BOTTOM LINE

Over 6 years, the business gained 10 points of market share, and the stock price rose by more than 70 per cent. When Thodey retired in 2015, the business fell back into focussing on cost position rather than initiatives for earning customers' trust.[5]

Rob argues that in order to effect change, we must start by improving the rules for disclosure of customer-value-related data, and by encouraging investors to use this data for business valuation. This, he argues, will consistently pressure business leaders to remain focussed on growing long-term customer value rather than just short-term earnings.

Peter Fader, Professor of Marketing at The Wharton School of the University of Pennsylvania, in Chapter 1 explained the importance of customer heterogeneity – the concept that every individual customer is unique. This ties into the "human" element we've discussed throughout this book.

Peter partners with Daniel McCarthy, Professor of Marketing at Emory University's Goizueta Business School. They both have been innovating around the use of customer lifetime value (CLV) in a way that helps companies to predict the future behaviour of customers. They are both founders of Theta, a company with a different approach to corporate valuation. Like Rob, they believe that projecting a company's future cash flow solely on the basis of traditional financial statements doesn't give shareholders the insights needed to value companies in the right way. Peter and Daniel use a technique called customer based corporate valuation (CBCV), which makes more accurate cash flow predictions from the bottom-up, instead of the traditional top-down, approach. Since all revenue comes from customers, CBCV brings more focus on how individual customer behaviour drives the company's revenue. It uses best-in-class models to give more accurate projections of a company's revenue and a more holistic view of the company's economic health by using four critical quantities:

1. How many customers are acquired in the future and at what cost?
2. How long will current and future customers stay before churning?

3. How many orders they will place?

4. How much they will spend on those orders?[6]

This practice can be used for both subscription-based businesses, such as Netflix and gyms,[7] and non-subscription businesses, such as retail.[8]

Peter and Daniel performed CBCV analysis of this kind on privately held and publicly traded companies – Farfetch, Lyft and Slack, among others – on behalf of investors who often guess about crucial drivers of corporate value.[9]

Shareholders have the right to know these important insights that are missing because a company's disclosure is limited to financial statements or only the customer data that they want to disclose. Reporting on customer value could help override the pressure that comes from delivering quarterly earnings. Shifting this focus may also help to erode the short-term mindset.

Rob, Peter and Daniel are on a mission to change the traditional corporate financial disclosure requirements. They petitioned the Financial Accounting Standards Board (FASB), a body based in the United States that develops financial accounting standards through transparent processes. Their letters proposed that the FASB consider creating disclosure standards and guidelines for metrics that would help investors and executives more accurately gauge the health of a company's customer base.[10]

One such letter stated that "the customer (whether it is a consumer or a business) is the primary 'atomic unit' to understand the current and future health of an enterprise, and clarity about them is invaluable for key decision makers inside and outside the firm".[11]

The pressure that leaders face to deliver quarterly earnings is the main driver of the short-term bonus culture. This comes at the cost of long-term value creation for customers and the rest of your company's ecosystem.

If financial statements don't show a pretty picture, consider this your opportunity to focus on creating stronger bridges between your business and all stakeholders – especially by sharing customer-centric transformation and value.

CUT THE STRINGS

As businesses, we may start with pure intentions, but if we let traditional influences control the strings of our behaviour, we will forever remain "puppets", even when we become "real boys". Yet, we have an opportunity, and now's the time to shift.

Never has it been more apparent that humanity is essential than in 2020. Crisis after crisis has demonstrated that the shareholder primacy model of 19th century capitalism is ineffective for the 21st century.[12] It has contributed to weakening business resilience and widening inequality, and left a stain of environmental and social destruction for future generations.[13]

I trust that, if you have read to this point in the book, you want to consign to history this system and era – when a limited set of metrics and pressure by shareholders controlled our destiny. It's time to get serious about writing a better capitalism tale – one in which companies perform and behave as trustful, real and unselfish entities.

The rule if you want to become truly customer-centric is that there are no rules. It's about changing mindset, behaviour, structures, culture and old practices. These might have worked for centuries, but they no longer work in a landscape where multiple variables are evolving quickly, dramatically and simultaneously – and where younger generations are disrupting businesses' trajectories.

Let's cut the strings!

YOUR CALL TO ACTION

Dear Reader,

I am very happy to see that you have reached the end of my book. It has been a pleasure sharing my work and mission with you. I hope to have inspired you and encouraged you to undertake your journey to centricity – a transformation that involves putting customers first and thinking more about value creation for all stakeholders. We've covered a lot of ground in this book. We've looked at the way businesses have been operating over the last century, and why those models no longer work in the 21st century.

We have seen that profit is a vital asset, but shouldn't be seen as the only focus at the expense of stakeholders, society and the planet. Running a company by looking through the lenses of revenue, cost and sales performance leads to destroying employee engagement and customer relationships. We explored the gaps between boardrooms and employees, and employees and customers – and how you can build the bridges. We've said that the automation of as many customer interactions as possible is wrong. Tech should be used as an enabler and not as a replacement for real human connection. Last but not least we've detailed how to be a more human brand with a long-term perspective, to have a positive impact in the society we are part of and to be relevant in tomorrow's world.

In an ideal customer-centric world, everyone wins: customers have more meaningful relationships with companies, employees benefit from making customers' lives better, shareholders see a return on their investment, leaders manage healthier organisations, and society enjoys increasing growth and sustainable value. This is the kind of value maximisation that I want to see out there. Above all, we need to achieve this in a consistent and coherent way. We have been talking, reading and writing about value creation for some time now, but the gap between words and actions is still too wide.

The one thing, above all else, that I would wish you take away from this book can be summarised in one word: *change.*

Change is key, because change happens even faster as you begin moving – which means it will always exist. What is here today won't be here tomorrow. Technology is creating a future that we cannot yet control. Products and services are being replaced at lightning speed. Companies are being disrupted by other companies, day after day. New generations of consumers and employees – with clear expectations and priorities – are making their mark on the world by being clear about how they want to be treated. Technology, products and profit come and go, but it's the purpose, mindset and soul of the business that stays.

My dream and mission are to see the customer-centric concepts and best practices that I've illustrated in this book become a reality for all businesses. It's up to each of us to push this movement forward as we all have a role to play.

How will you contribute?

WHAT TO DO NEXT

One of the common questions I get from business leaders is, "How do we know how customer-centric we are?" To help you take a temperature check on the level of customer centricity in your organisation, I have put together a barometer. This is a quick survey that is, of course, based on my Journey to Centricity framework. At the end of it, you will get a customer-centric score that will give you an idea of the level of customer centricity in your company. Since you will each have a different perspective, I'd recommend you let everyone take it, put together the results and then start planning your journey to centricity. You can find the barometer at www.ileniavidili.com/barometer. As with anything, let me know if I can help.

If you enjoyed this book, you may like my shorter writings as well. You can read my most recent articles in my free newsletter. Subscribers are also the first to hear about my latest projects, workshops and speaking engagements around the world. If you'd like to carry on the conversation, sharing ideas and opinions on how to become a more customer-centric business, I'd love to hear from you. I am also quite active on LinkedIn: you can either write to me there, or you can get in touch via ilenia@ileniavidili.com.

Thank you for reading.

Ilenia Vidili

THANK YOU

Who would have thought that writing a book would be this challenging and exciting at the same time? Although my name is on the cover, many people have contributed to making this book become a reality – from when it was just an idea, to the writing, to the publishing. For the content of this book, I am first and foremost grateful to all the interviewees, who have been extremely generous in sharing their experience and thoughts with me. Thank you for your trust, kindness and time in answering many of my questions. Writing about you, and with you, has been a joy and a privilege, as well as an endless source of learning. Thank you.

Huge thanks go to the Women in Customer Experience (WiCX) community, a safe space for women all over the world to meet, share, learn and grow together. Thanks for the great support and encouragement. Some of these incredible women helped in reading drafts in their entirety, providing invaluable feedback and useful comments: Ana Luisa Romero, Lara Khouri, Lisa Dancer and Susanna Baqué. Thanks also to those who helped with particular sections. Your insights and perspectives have been a great help. Any remaining errors are entirely my responsibility, of course.

I can't be grateful enough to my dearest friends: Assemgul Bektemessova, who helped me understand, accept and manage my rollercoaster of emotions at each and every stage of writing this book; Ignazio Pisanu, who believed in me when I didn't, provided a much-needed honest critique and supported me all the way to the finish line; Rosa Mary Espinosa Ferrer, for listening to me in good and bad times; Battistina Marras, for encouraging me when I needed it the most; my family for their constant support, especially my mum, for her wisdom, kindness, generosity and positivity no matter what project I happen to be working on. Thanks again for your help, Mamma! Thank you to all my friends and loved ones for being there for me at every turn. I hope those who I have missed will forgive me, and still accept my warmest thanks.

All my gratitude goes to each and every one of you, my readers. Thank you for being interested in this topic, and thank you for spending time with me by reading this book. I hope it helps you find your path to centricity! It would be an immense pleasure to hear your thoughts and feedback. You can send these directly to me at ilenia@ileniavidili.com.

Thank you for following me on LinkedIn, Facebook and Instagram and perhaps listening to me digitally and in person. I'll keep sharing content, writing articles and sending newsletters. You can keep up to date or sign up at www.ileniavidili.com.

Again, many thanks
Ilenia

ABOUT THE AUTHOR

Ilenia Vidili is a passionate customer-centricity advisor, author and keynote speaker. She has focused on consumer behaviour since her university studies in International Business Strategies, in Cambridge, UK. She's conducted corporate marketing for NEC, Bayer, ARM and a broad range of start-ups.

With over a decade of experience in both business-to-consumer and business-to-business companies, Ilenia realised that the gaps between companies and their stakeholders were far too wide. Today, she is the Founder of The Smarter Crew, a customer-centricity consultancy and training company helping businesses to close those gaps by *thinking differently, combatting inefficient processes, turning product mentalities into people mentalities*, and *improving customer focus*.

Ilenia gives enthusiastic global keynotes in multiple languages on embracing customer centricity as the key to unlocking the future of businesses. She has inspired business leaders and C-level executives of the likes of Coca-Cola, L'Oréal, Savills, Harrods, and many more. She also contributes as a columnist for the *CEOWORLD* and *Entrepreneur Media* magazines.

Having lived and worked in many countries, Ilenia holds a global perspective on today's crucial business challenges. She believes that there has never been a more critical time for "change" and advises decision-makers to connect their minds and hearts when leading businesses. Driven by bringing humanity to business, her mission is to see a brighter future – where companies embrace a higher purpose, create value for all stake-holders and contribute positively to society.

ENDNOTES

This is a long list of references for each chapter of the book. I have taken great care to check and double-check these sources. However, as literature and digital references change over time, this list may need to be updated.

Also, however hard I strived, you might find a mistake somewhere in this book – whether I have attributed a concept, theory or idea to the wrong person, or I haven't given the right credit where it is due. If you spot anything, please help me improve this book. Email me at ilenia@ ileniavidili.com and I'll fix the issue as soon as possible.

INTRODUCTION

1   The Illusions Index. (n.d.). *Duck–Rabbit*. Retrieved September 21, 2021, from https://www.illusionsindex.org/i/duck-rabbit

CHAPTER 1

1   Goodreads. (n.d.). *A quote by John F. Kennedy*. https://www.goodreads.com/quotes/159557-change-is-the-law-of-life-and-those-who-look

2   5 August 2018 Lombok Earthquake. (2021, September 3). In *Wikipedia*. https://en.wikipedia.org/wiki/5_August_2018_Lombok_earthquake#:~:text=Officials%20stated%20that%20at%20least,than%20417%2C000%20people%20were%20displaced

3   National Geographic Society. (2019, April 5). *Ring of Fire*. https://www.nationalgeographic.org/encyclopedia/ring-fire/

4   Toynbee, A. J. (1987). *A Study of History. Vol. 1: Abridgement of Volumes I-VI by D. C. Somervell*. Oxford University Press.

5   Digital revolution. (2021, October 7). In *Wikipedia*. https://en.wikipedia.org/wiki/Digital_Revolution

6   Corporate Finance Institute. (2021, February 22). *Baby Boomers*. https://corporatefinanceinstitute.com/resources/knowledge/other/baby-boomers/

7   Schnitzer, K., & Fabiano, J. (2020, August 14). *These are the 5 main Generation X characteristics you see in the workplace*. Ladders. https://www.theladders.com/career-advice/these-are-generation-x-characteristics-in-the-office-and-their-new-label#:~:text=Generation%20Xers%20embrace%20work%2Dlife,hours%20and%20a%20hard%20grind

8   Goldman Sachs. (2021). *Millennials Coming of Age*. https://www.goldma-nsachs.com/insights/archive/millennials/

9   Dimock, M. (2019, January 17). Defining generations: Where Millennials end and Generation Z begins. Pew Research Center. https://www.pewresearch.org/fact-tank/2019/01/17/where-millennials-end-and-generation-z-begins/

10   Francis, T., & Hoefel, F. (2018, November 12). *'True Gen': Generation Z and its implications for companies*. McKinsey & Company. https://www.mckinsey.com/industries/consumer-packaged-goods/our-insights/true-gen-generation-z-and-its-implications-for-companies

11   Spitznagel, E. (2020, January 25). *Generation Z is bigger than millennials — and they're out to change the world*. New York Post. https://nypost.com/2020/01/25/generation-z-is-bigger-than-millennials-and-theyre-out-to-change-the-world/

12   *Millennials. Demographic change and the impact of a generation*. MSCI THEMATIC INSIGHTS. (2020). https://www.msci.com/documents/1296102/17292317/ThematicIndex-Millenials-cbr-en.pdf/44668168-67fd-88cd-c5f7-855993dce7c4#:~:text=In%20 2020%2C%20approximately%201.8%20billion,1980s%20to%20the%20 mid%2D1990s

13   Deloitte. (2021). *A call for accountability and action: THE DELOITTE GLOBAL 2021 MILLENNIAL AND GENZ SURVEY*. https://www2.deloitte.com/content/dam/Deloitte/global/Documents/2021-deloitte-global-millen-nial-survey-report.pdf

14   Friedman, M. (1970, September 13). *A Friedman doctrine-- The Social Responsibility Of Business Is to Increase Its Profits.* The New York Times. https://www.nytimes.com/1970/09/13/archives/a-friedman-doctrine-the-social-responsibility-of-business-is-to.html

15   Vidili, I. (2020, October 22). *The Future Of Business Is Customer-centric: 3 Pillars to Create A Customer-centric Strategy.* CEOWORLD magazine. https://ceoworld.biz/2020/10/22/the-future-of-business-is-customer-centric-3-pillars-to-create-a-customer-centric-strategy/

16   Christensen, C. M. (1997). *The Innovator's Dilemma: When New Technologies Cause Great Firms to Fail.* Harvard Business School Press.

17   Van Belleghem, S. (2017). *Customers the Day After Tomorrow: How to Attract Customers in a World of AIs, Bots, and Automation.* Lannoo Campus.

18   Nambiar, R., Aggarwal, S., & Kumar, G. (2015). *When Digital Disruption Strikes: How Can Incumbents Respond?* Capgemini Consulting. Retrieved October 18, 2021, from https://www.capgemini.com/consulting/wp-content/uploads/sites/30/2017/07/digital_disruption_1.pdf

19   Porter, M. E., & Kramer, M. R. (2011, January). *Creating Shared Value: How to reinvent capitalism—and unleash a wave of innovation and growth.* Harvard Business Review. https://hbr.org/2011/01/the-big-idea-creating-shared-value

20   Edelman. (2020). 20th ANNUAL EDELMAN TRUST BAROMETER. https://cdn2.hubspot.net/hubfs/440941/Trust%20Barometer%202020/2020%20Edelman%20Trust%20Barometer%20Global%20Report-1.pdf

21   Business Roundtable. (2019, August 19). *Business Roundtable Redefines the Purpose of a Corporation to Promote 'An Economy That Serves All Americans'*. https://www.businessroundtable.org/business-roundtable-redefines-the-purpose-of-a-corporation-to-promote-an-economy-that-serves-all-americans

22   Schwab, K. (2019, December 2). *Davos Manifesto 2020: The Universal Purpose of a Company in the Fourth Industrial Revolution*. World Economic Forum. https://www.weforum.org/agenda/2019/12/davos-manifesto-2020-the-universal-purpose-of-a-company-in-the-fourth-industrial-revolution/

23   Schwab, K. (2019, December 1). *Why we need the 'Davos Manifesto' for a better kind of capitalism*. World Economic Forum. https://www.weforum.org/agenda/2019/12/why-we-need-the-davos-manifesto-for-better-kind-of-capitalism/

24   Schwab, K., & Vanham, P. (2021). Stakeholder Capitalism: A Global Economy that Works for Progress, People and Planet. Wiley.

25   Markey, R. (January 2020). *Are You Undervaluing Your Customers?* Harvard Business Review. https://hbr.org/2020/01/are-you-undervaluing-your-customers

CHAPTER 2

1   Goodreads. (n.d.). *A quote by Aristotle*. https://www.goodreads.com/quotes/183896-man-is-by-nature-a-social-animal-an-individual-who

2   European Commission. (2021, November 8). *Sardinia*. Sardinia - Internal Market, Industry, Entrepreneurship and SMEs. https://ec.europa.eu/growth/tools-databases/regional-innovation-monitor/base-profile/sardinia

3   Toti, D. (n.d.). *Sa Paradura: Safety In Numbers*. Gabbiano Azzurro Hotel
     & Suites. https://www.hotelgabbianoazzurro.com/en/Blog/-Sa-Paradura-
     safety-in-numbers

4   Blue Zone. (2021, August 27). In *Wikipedia*. https://en.wikipedia.org/
     wiki/Blue_Zone

5   Buettner, D. (2020, July 7). *Power 9® Reverse Engineering Longevity*. Blue
     Zones. https://www.bluezones.com/2016/11/power-9/

6   Betti, F. (2020, March 24). *From perfume to hand sanitiser, TVs to face
     masks: how companies are changing track to join fight COVID-19*. World
     Economic Forum. https://www.weforum.org/agenda/2020/03/from-
     perfume-to-hand-sanitiser-tvs-to-face-masks-how-companies-are-
     changing-track-to-fight-covid-19/

7   United Nations. (n.d.). *Global Issues*. https://www.un.org/en/sections/
     issues-depth/global-issues-overview/

8   United Nations. Regional Information Centre for Western Europe.
     (2020, June 29). *Sustainable Development Goals (SDG 1)*. https://unric.
     org/en/sdg-1/

9   Alberti, F. B. (2019). *A Biography of Loneliness: The History of an
     Emotion*. Oxford University Press.

10   Barreto, M., Victor, C., Hammond, C., Eccles, A., Richins, M. T., &
     Qualter, P. (2021, February 1). Loneliness around the world: Age,
     gender, and cultural differences in loneliness. *Science Direct, 169*,
     Article 110066. https://www.sciencedirect.com/science/article/pii/
     S0191886920302555#bb0145

11   https://www.google.com/search?biw=1304&bih=836&tbm=nws&sxsrf=
     ACYBGNTL_xMYGpHrk9r5bQaLi63lBs44IQ%3A1571695696286&ei=
     UCyuXcyEEbGd5wKmx4WwCg&q=%22loneliness+epidemic%22&oq=
     %22loneliness+epidemic%22&gs_l=psy-ab.3...4828.6314.0.6495.3.3.0.0.0
     .0.139.398.0j3.3.0....0...1c.1.64.psy-ab..0.0.0....0.6EEGBItbpoA

12   Howe, N. (2019, May 3). *Millennials And The Loneliness Epidemic.*
     Forbes. https://www.forbes.com/sites/neilhowe/2019/05/03/millennials-
     and-the-loneliness-epidemic/?sh=6087e8327676

13   Ewens, H. (2016, September 21). *What Young People Fear the Most.*
     VICE. https://www.vice.com/en/article/nnyk37/what-vice-readers-fear-
     the-most-hannah-ewens-love-loneliness

14   BBC. (2018, October 1). *16-24 year olds are the loneliest age group
     according to new BBC Radio 4 survey.* https://www.bbc.co.uk/mediacen-
     tre/latestnews/2018/loneliest-age-group-radio-4

15   Cigna. (2018). *Cigna U.S. Loneliness Index.* Multivu. https://www.
     multivu.com/players/English/8294451-cigna-us-loneliness-survey/docs/
     IndexReport 1524069371598-173525450.pdf

16   European Commission. (2018). *Loneliness – an unequally shared burden
     in Europe.* https://ec.europa.eu/jrc/sites/jrcsh/files/fairness_pb2018_
     loneliness_jrc_i1.pdf

17   Hammond, C. (2018). *Who feels lonely? The results of the world's largest
     loneliness study.* BBC Radio 4. https://www.bbc.co.uk/programmes/artic
     les/2yzhfv4DvqVp5nZyxBD8G23/who-feels-lonely-the-results-of-the-
     world-s-largest-loneliness-study

18 John, T. (2018, April 25). How the World's First Loneliness Minister Will Tackle 'the Sad Reality of Modern Life'. Time. https://time.com/5248016/tracey-crouch-uk-loneliness-minister/

19 Warren, K. (2021, February 22). *Japan has appointed a 'Minister of Loneliness' after seeing suicide rates in the country increase for the first time in 11 years.* Insider. https://www.insider.com/japan-minister-of-loneliness-suicides-rise-pandemic-2021-2

20 Holt-Lunstad, J., Smith, T. B., & Layton, J. B. (2010, July 27). Social Relationships and Mortality Risk: A Meta-analytic Review. *PLOS Medicine.* https://journals.plos.org/plosmedicine/article?id=10.1371%2Fjournal.pmed.1000316.

21 Mushtaq, R., Shoib, S., Shah, T., & Mushtaq, S. (2014, September). Relationship Between Loneliness, Psychiatric Disorders and Physical Health? A Review on the Psychological Aspects of Loneliness. *Journal of Clinical and Diagnostic Research, 8*(9). https://www.ncbi.nlm.nih.gov/pmc/articles/PMC4225959/

22 John, T. (2018, April 25). How the World's First Loneliness Minister Will Tackle 'the Sad Reality of Modern Life'. Time. https://time.com/5248016/tracey-crouch-uk-loneliness-minister/

23 Ozcelik, H., & Barsade, S. (n.d.). Work Loneliness and Employee Performance. https://faculty.wharton.upenn.edu/wp-content/uploads/2012/05/Work_Loneliness_Performance_Study.pdf

24 Murthy, V. (2017, September 26). *Work and the Loneliness Epidemic.* Harvard Business Review. https://hbr.org/2017/09/work-and-the-loneliness-epidemic

25   Orlowski, J. (Director). (2020). *The Social Dilemma* [Film]. Netflix.
https://www.netflix.com/it-en/title/81254224

26   Katz, L. (2020, June 18). *How tech and social media are making us feel
lonelier than ever.* CNET. https://www.cnet.com/features/how-tech-and-
social-media-are-making-us-feel-lonelier-than-ever/

27   Cigna. (2018). Cigna U.S. Loneliness Index. Multivu. https://www.
multivu.com/players/English/8294451-cigna-us-loneliness-survey/docs/
IndexReport_1524069371598-173525450.pdf

28   Alberti, F. B. (2019). *A Biography of Loneliness: The History of an
Emotion.* Oxford University Press.

29   Gilbert, J. C., Houlahan, B., & Kassoy, A. (2019, August 22). *Don't believe
the Business Roundtable has changed until its CEOs' actions match their
words.* Fast Company. https://www.fastcompany.com/90393303/dont-
believe-the-business-roundtable-has-changed-until-its-ceos-actions-
match-their-words

30   Leonhard, G. (2016). *Technology vs. Humanity: The coming clash between
man and machine.* p.17. FutureScapes.

31   First Round. (2019). *State of Startups 2019.* https://stateofstartups2019.
firstround.com/

32   Van Belleghem, S. (2020). *The Offer You Can't Refuse: What If Customers
Want More Than Excellent Service?* Lannoo Campus.

33   https://www.rapha.cc/it/en/rcc

34   Zealley, J., Wollan, R., & Bellin, J. (2018, March 21). *Marketers Need to Stop Focusing on Loyalty and Start Thinking About Relevance*. Harvard Business Review. https://hbr.org/2018/03/marketers-need-to-stop-focusing-on-loyalty-and-start-thinking-about-relevance

35   https://stircambridge.co.uk/

36   Maslow, A. H. (1943). A Theory of Human Motivation. Psychological Review, 50(4), 370–396.

37   Bacon, J., & Bussgang, J. (2020, January 21). *When Community Becomes Your Competitive Advantage*. Harvard Business Review. https://hbr.org/2020/01/when-community-becomes-your-competitive-advantage?ab=at_art_art_1x1

38   *Left & Right Hemispheres*. (2019, September 26). Brain Made Simple. https://brainmadesimple.com/left-and-right-hemispheres/

39   Forrester Consulting. (2019, June). *How Customers Think, Feel, And Act: The Paradigm Of Business Outcomes*. https://cloud.kapostcontent.net/pub/d2a85d5e-c053-4bfc-ae8d-f1a9c0b2af31/whitepaper-how-customers-think-feel-and-act-the-paradigm-of-business-outcomes?kui=MtTZamfFfmzvSS4fnSaD4Q

40   Shaw, C. (2016, August). *Customer[s] Are Irrational: Don't Fight It; Embrace It*. Beyond Philosophy. https://beyondphilosophy.com/wp-content/uploads/2017/10/Colin-Customer-Are-Irrational-Don%E2%80%99t-fight-it-Embrace-it-rev3.pdf

41   Zorfas, A., & Leemon, D. (2016, August 29). *An Emotional Connection Matters More than Customer Satisfaction*. Harvard Business Review. https://hbr.org/2016/08/an-emotional-connection-matters-more-than-customer-satisfaction

42   Zorfas, A., Magids, S., & Leemon, D. (2015, November). *The New Science of Customer Emotions*. Harvard Business Review. https://hbr.org/2015/11/the-new-science-of-customer-emotions

43   Zorfas, A., Magids, S., & Leemon, D. (2015, November). *The New Science of Customer Emotions*. Harvard Business Review. https://hbr.org/2015/11/the-new-science-of-customer-emotions

44   Zorfas, A., Magids, S., & Leemon, D. (2015, November). *The New Science of Customer Emotions*. Harvard Business Review. https://hbr.org/2015/11/the-new-science-of-customer-emotions

CHAPTER 3

1   Goodreads. (n.d.). *A quote by Confucius*. https://www.goodreads.com/quotes/52891-give-a-bowl-of-rice-to-a-man-and-you

2   Fink, L. (n.d.). *Larry Fink's 2018 Letter to CEOs: A Sense of Purpose*. BlackRock. Retrieved 14 September, 2021, from https://www.blackrock.com/corporate/investor-relations/2018-larry-fink-ceo-letter

3   Porter, M. E., & Kramer, M. R. (January 2011). *Creating Shared Value. How to reinvent capitalism—and unleash a wave of innovation and growth*. Harvard Business Review. https://hbr.org/2011/01/the-big-idea-creating-shared-value

4   Kramer, M. (2011, February 18). *CSR vs. CSV - What's the difference?*
     FSG. https://www.fsg.org/blog/csr-vs-csv-what%E2%80%99s-difference

5   The Economist. (2021, April 24). *How to save coffee from global warming.*
     https://www.economist.com/science-and-technology/2021/04/22/
     how-to-save-coffee-from-global-warming

6   illycaffè. (n.d.). *One day at a time, one step at a time.* https://www.illy.
     co.th/sustainability/

7   Porter, M. E., & Kramer, M. R. (January 2011). *Creating Shared Value.
     How to reinvent capitalism—and unleash a wave of innovation and
     growth.* Harvard Business Review. https://hbr.org/2011/01/the-big-idea-
     creating-shared-value

8   Packaged Facts. (2020, January 7). *Gen Z and Millennial Consumers
     Naturally Favor Organic Foods and Beverages, reports Packaged Facts.*
     Cision PR Newswire. https://www.prnewswire.com/news-releases/gen-z-
     and-millennial-consumers-naturally-favor-organic-foods-and-bever-
     ages-reports-packaged-facts-300982951.html

9   illycaffè. (2020, September 3). *illycaffè is a partner of Esof 2020.* https://
     www.illy.com/en-us/company/store-events/press/press-releases/illycaffe-
     partner-esof-2020#

10   illycaffè. (2019). *Sustainable Value Report illy 2019.* Value Report illy.
     http://valuereport.illy.com/pdf/2019/Sustainable-value-report-illy-2019-
     ENG-Cap7.pdf

11   Ethisphere® Institute. (2021). *The 2021 World's Most Ethical Companies®
     Honoree List.* World's Most Ethical Companies. https://worldsmostethi-
     calcompanies.com/honorees/

12   illycaffè. (2020, March 4). *illycaffè becomes a "Società Benefit" (Benefit Corporation) and confirms its commitment to the wellness of people and the planet by modifying its charter.* https://www.illy.com/en-us/company/store-events/press/press-releases/illycaffe-benefit-corporation

13   Certified B Corporation. (2021). https://bcorporation.net/

14   Bateman, A., & Bonanni, L. (2019, August 20). *What Supply Chain Transparency Really Means.* Harvard Business Review. https://hbr.org/2019/08/what-supply-chain-transparency-really-means

15   illycaffè. (2019). *Sustainable Value Report illy 2019.* http://valuereport.illy.com/pdf/2019/Sustainable-value-report-illy-2019-ENG-Cap6.pdf

16   https://fondazionernestoilly.org/

17   https://www.illy.com/it-it/live-happilly

18   United Nations. (n.d.). *THE 17 GOALS.* https://sdgs.un.org/goals

19   illycaffè. (2019). *Sustainable Value Report illy 2019.* http://valuereport.illy.com/pdf/2019/Sustainable-value-report-illy-2019-ENG-Cap2.pdf

20   *2018 Edelman Trust Barometer.* (2018). https://www.edelman.com/sites/g/files/aatuss191/files/2018-10/2018_Edelman_Trust_Barometer_Global_Report_FEB.pdf

21   Nava, O. (2020, January 15). *What Greta Thunberg can teach brands about decoding Gen Z.* We Are Social. https://wearesocial.com/uk/blog/2020/01/what-greta-thunberg-can-teach-brands-about-decoding-gen-z/

22   *Greta Thunberg.* In *Wikipedia.* Retrieved 5 September, 2021, from
      https://en.wikipedia.org/wiki/Greta_Thunberg#:%7E:text=She%20
      received%20numerous%20honours%20and,(2019)%2C%20and%20
      three%20consecutive

23   Garrido, M. (2019, June 6). *Brand Activism Is Driving More Meaningful
      Connections.* Adweek. https://www.adweek.com/agencies/brand-activ-
      ism-is-driving-more-meaningful-connections/

24   Dunlop, A., Reichheld, A., Zucker, J., Gross, M., Kang, C., & Martin,
      L. (2019, August 7). *We're only human: Exploring and quantifying the
      human experience.* Deloitte Digital. https://www.deloittedigital.com/us/
      en/blog-list/2019/we-re-only-human--exploring-and-quantifying-the-
      human-experience.html

25   Solis, M. (2020, August 20). *Ben & Jerry's Showed America What Real
      Corporate Activism Looks Like.* HuffPost. https://www.huffpost.com/
      entry/ben-jerry-ice-cream-corporate-activism_n_5f1b11dec5b6296
      fbf423019

26   Fleming, M. (2020, August 19). *Ben & Jerry's move to take on Number
      10 over migrants pays off.* Marketing Week. https://www.marketingweek.
      com/ben-jerrys-government-migrants-brand-health/

27   Response Media. (n.d.). *Beliefs and Brands: The Pros and Cons of Taking
      a Stand.* https://www.responsemedia.com/beliefs-brands-pros-cons-of-
      taking-a-stand/

28   *Two-Thirds of Consumers Worldwide Now Buy on Beliefs.* (2018, October
      2). Edelman. https://www.edelman.com/news-awards/two-thirds-
      consumers-worldwide-now-buy-beliefs

29   Patagonia. (n.d.). *Patagonia Action Works*. Retrieved 6 September, 2021, from https://eu.patagonia.com/gb/en/actionworks/about/

30   Deloitte. (2020, October 15). *Deloitte Digital announces Global Marketing Trends for 2021*. https://www2.deloitte.com/uk/en/pages/press-releases/articles/deloitte-digital-announces-global-marketing-trends-for-2021.html

31   Malnight, T., Buche, I., & Dhanaraj, C. (2019, September). *Put Purpose at the Core of Your Strategy*. Harvard Business Review. https://hbr.org/2019/09/put-purpose-at-the-core-of-your-strategy

CHAPTER 4

1   Northwestern University. (2006, June 19). *Obama to Graduates: Cultivate Empathy*. https://www.northwestern.edu/newscenter/stories/2006/06/barack.html

2   Bates, L. A., Lee, P. C., Njiraini, N., Poole, J. H., Sayialel, K., Sayialel, S., Moss, C. J., & Byrne, R. W. (2008). Do Elephants Show Empathy? Journal of Consciousness Studies, 15(10–11), 204–225. https://dspace.stir.ac.uk/bitstream/1893/946/1/2008%20Bates_et_al_JCS.pdf

3   Morell, V. (2014, February 23). *It's Time to Accept That Elephants, Like Us, Are Empathetic Beings*. National Geographic. https://www.national-geographic.com/animals/article/140221-elephants-poaching-empathy-grief-extinction-science

4   Holland, J. S. (2014, February 18). *Surprise: Elephants Comfort Upset Friends*. National Geographic. https://www.nationalgeographic.com/animals/article/140218-asian-elephants-empathy-animals-science-behavior

5   Psychology Today. (n.d.). *Empathy*. Retrieved 6 September, 2021, from https://www.psychologytoday.com/intl/basics/empathy

6   Heilbroner, R. L. (2021, July 13). The Theory of Moral Sentiments of Adam Smith. Encyclopaedia Britannica. https://www.britannica.com/ biography/Adam-Smith/The-Theory-of-Moral-Sentiments

7   World Economic Forum. (2019). *The Global Risks Report 2019 14th Edition*. http://www3.weforum.org/docs/WEF_Global_Risks_ Report_2019.pdf

8   Konrath, S. H., O'Brien, E. H., & Hsing, C. (2011). Changes in Dispositional Empathy in American College Students Over Time: A Meta-Analysis. *Personality and Social Psychology Review*, *15*(2), 180–198. https://doi.org/10.1177/1088868310377395

9   Booth, R. (2018, October 4). *Majority of Britons think empathy is on the wane*. The Guardian. https://www.theguardian.com/society/2018/oct/04/ increasing-number-of-britons-think-empathy-is-on-the-wane

10   Northwestern University. (2006, June 19). *Obama to Graduates: Cultivate Empathy*. https://www.northwestern.edu/newscenter/stories/2006/06/ barack.html

11   Avenson, B. (n.d.). *Why Empathy is Declining and How to Inspire More*. Ornish Lifestyle Medicine. Retrieved September 6, 2021, from https:// www.ornish.com/zine/why-we-empathy/

12   Association for Psychological Science. (2017, July 17). *Individualistic Practices and Values Increasing Around the World*. https://www.psycho-logicalscience.org/news/releases/individualistic-practices-and-values-increasing-around-the-world.html

13   The Sunday Magazine. (2019, June 7). *Empathy makes us human, but research suggests it may be on the decline.* CBC Radio. https://www.cbc.ca/radio/sunday/the-sunday-edition-for-june-9-2019-1.5165327/empathy-makes-us-human-but-research-suggests-it-may-be-on-the-decline-1.5166354

14   The Council of the European Union. (2018). Council recommendation of 22 May 2018 on key competences for lifelong learning. *Official Journal of the European Union*, 189/1-189/13. https://eur-lex.europa.eu/legal-content/EN/TXT/PDF/?uri=CELEX:32018H0604(01)&rid=7

15   Nook, E. C., Ong, D. C., Morelli, S. A., Mitchell, J. P., & Zaki, J. (2016). Prosocial Conformity: Prosocial Norms Generalize Across Behavior and Empathy. *Personality and Social Psychology Bulletin*, 42(8), 1045–1062. https://doi.org/10.1177/0146167216649932

16   Zaki, J. (2019). The War for Kindness: Building Empathy in a Fractured World. Crown.

17   Making Caring Common Project. (2021, March). *5 Tips for Cultivating Empathy*. Harvard Graduate School of Education. https://mcc.gse.harvard.edu/resources-for-families/5-tips-cultivating-empathy

18   Winerman, L. (2005, October). The mind's mirror. *American Psychological Association*, 36(9), 48.

19   Rifkin, J. (2010). *The Empathic Civilization: The Race to Global Consciousness in a World in Crisis*. Tarcher/Penguin Putnam.

20   Royal Society for Arts [RSA]. (2010, March 18). *Jeremy Rifkin - The Empathic Civilisation* [Video]. YouTube. https://www.youtube.com/watch?v=1-7BjeHepbA

21   Parmar, B., & Frost, S. (2016, September 15). *People or process: which does your company put first?* World Economic Forum. https://www.weforum.org/agenda/2016/09/empathy-index-human-resources-business/

22   Zaki, J. (2019). *The War for Kindness: Building Empathy in a Fractured World.* Crown.

23   Krill, A. (2011). *Fixists vs. Mobilists in the geology contest of the century, 1844–1969.*

24   Lesley University. (n.d.). *The Psychology of Emotional and Cognitive Empathy,* https://lesley.edu/article/the-psychology-of-emotional-and-cognitive-empathy

25   Parmar, B. (2015, January 8). *Corporate Empathy Is Not an Oxymoron.* Harvard Business Review. https://hbr.org/2015/01/corporate-empathy-is-not-an-oxymoron

26   Kellett, J. B., Humphrey, R. H., & Sleeth, R. G. (2006). Empathy and the emergence of task and relations leaders. *The Leadership Quarterly, 17*(2), 146–162. https://doi.org/10.1016/j.leaqua.2005.12.003

27   Scott, B. A., Colquitt, J. A., Paddock, E. L., & Judge, T. A. (2010). A daily investigation of the role of manager empathy on employee well-being. *Organizational Behavior and Human Decision Processes, 113*(2), 127–140. https://doi.org/10.1016/j.obhdp.2010.08.001

28   Duhigg, C. (2016, February 25). What Google Learned From Its Quest to Build the Perfect Team. *The New York Times.* https://www.nytimes.com/2016/02/28/magazine/what-google-learned-from-its-quest-to-build-the-perfect-team.html?_r=0

29   Thomson, S. (2016, November 18). *10 companies that are great at empathy*. World Economic Forum. https://www.weforum.org/agenda/2016/11/empathy-index-business/

30   *2021 State of Workplace Empathy*. (2021). The Businessolver®. https://www.businessolver.com/resources/state-of-workplace-empathy

31   Mindfulness. (2021, September 1). In *Wikipedia*. https://en.wikipedia.org/wiki/Mindfulness

32   de la Fuente-Anuncibay, R., González-Barbadillo, A., Ortega-Sánchez, D., & Pizarro-Ruiz, J. P. (2020). Mindfulness and Empathy: Mediating Factors and Gender Differences in a Spanish Sample. *Frontiers in Psychology, 11*. https://doi.org/10.3389/fpsyg.2020.01915

33   https://events.economist.com/innovation-work/

34   https://www.howardschultz.com/my-story/#beginnings

35   Heller, C. (Host). (2019, March 25). How Starbucks Built an Empire with Empathy - Howard Schultz. [Audio podcast episode]. In *Don't Keep Your Day Job*. https://www.dontkeepyourdayjob.com/episodes/howard-schultz

36   Henkel, E., & Grant, A. (2018, September 28). *To Get Employees to Empathize with Customers, Make Them Think Like Customers*. Harvard Business Review. https://hbr.org/2018/09/to-get-employees-to-empathize-with-customers-make-them-think-like-customers

37   Ideo. (2015). *Customer-Friendly Utility Bills*. https://www.ideo.com/case-study/customer-friendly-utility-bills

38   Morning Future. (2018, June 18). *Satya Nadella: when empathy is good for business.* https://www.morningfuture.com/en/2018/06/18/microsoft-satya-nadella-empathy-business-management/

39   Empatiapakkaus. (n.d.). *WELCOME TO THE EMPATHY PACKAGE!* Retrieved 6 September, 2021, from https://empatiapakkaus.fi/en/

40   Microsoft. (n.d.). *Empathy in Business. Turning empathy into bottom line value.* https://pulse.microsoft.com/uploads/prod/2020/06/Microsoft-Empathy-in-Business.pdf

41   Hill+Knowlton Strategies Helsinki. (n.d.). *Microsoft: Empathy Package.* https://www.hkstrategies.fi/en/case-study/microsoft-empathy-package/

42   Solis, B., & King, H. (2020, December 4). *Post-Pandemic, Brands Must Find Empathy.* Techonomy. https://techonomy.com/2020/12/post-pandemic-brands-must-find-empathy/

43   Heller, C. (Host). (2019, March 25). How Starbucks Built an Empire with Empathy - Howard Schultz. [Audio podcast episode]. In *Don't Keep Your Day Job.* https://www.dontkeepyourdayjob.com/episodes/howard-schultz

CHAPTER 5

1   Khoury, G., & Crabtree, S. (2019, February 6). *Are Businesses World-wide Suffering From a Trust Crisis?* Gallup. https://www.gallup.com/workplace/246194/businesses-worldwide-suffering-trust-crisis.aspx

2   Botsman, R. (2019, January 19). *DLD Munich Conference 2019* [Conference]. DLD Conference 2019, Munich, Germany. https://www.youtube.com/watch?v=-vbPXbm8eTw

3   Botsman, R. (2019, April 1). *Being More Trustworthy: The Basics.* The
     OECD Forum Network. https://www.oecd-forum.org/posts/47378-
     being-more-trustworthy-the-basics

4   Botsman, R. (2020, January 31). *Why Trust Matters with Rachel Botsman.*
     LinkedIn Learning. https://www.linkedin.com/learning/why-trust-
     matters-with-rachel-botsman/the-importance-of-trust

5   Pavao, K. (2017, December 12). Trust Shift: *How to earn customer confi-
     dence on a swiftly turning planet.* Profit Magazine. Oracle. https://blogs.
     oracle.com/profit/trust-shift

6   Pew Research Center. (2021, May 17). *Public Trust in Government:
     1958-2021.* https://www.pewresearch.org/politics/2021/05/17/public-
     trust-in-government-1958-2021/

7   Gollom, M. (2016, June 26). *Brexit vote part of an anti-establishment
     'wake-up call'.* CBC News. https://www.cbc.ca/news/world/brexit-
     vote-anti-establishment-leave-remain-1.3652059

8   Edelman. (2019, June 18). *Edelman Trust Barometer Special Report: In
     Brands We Trust?* https://www.edelman.com/research/trust-barometer-
     special-report-in-brands-we-trust

9   Reuters. (2020, October 20). *Italian government enlists top influencers
     to promote COVID masks.* https://www.reuters.com/article/uk-health-
     coronavirus-italy-influencers-idUKKBN27525X

10 Vidili, I. (2021). Customer Experience: The New Competitive Advantage for Companies That Want Their Customer at the Center of Their Business. In: J. Pelet (Ed.), Handbook of Research on User Experience in Web 2.0 Technologies and Its Impact on Universities and Businesses (pp. 183–209). IGI Global. https://doi.org/10.4018/978-1-7998-3756-5

11 Morrison, M. (2015, April 24). *No One Trusts Advertising or Media (Except Fox News).* Ad Age. https://adage.com/article/media/marketers-media-trusts/298221

12 Forrester. (2021, May 13). *Forrester: Brand Loyalty Is Up For Grabs As Consumer Trust Wanes In Traditional Institutions.* https://go.forrester.com/press-newsroom/forrester-brand-loyalty-is-up-for-grabs-as-consumer-trust-wanes-in-traditional-institutions/

13 Botsman, R. (2019, January 19). *DLD Munich Conference 2019* [Conference]. DLD Conference 2019, Munich, Germany. https://www.youtube.com/watch?v=-vbPXbm8eTw

14 Conway, J. (2021, February 4). *Global coffee consumption 2012/13-2020/21.* Statista. https://www.statista.com/statistics/292595/global-coffee-consumption/

15 Bunn, C., Läderach, P., Ovalle Rivera, O., & Kirschke, D. (2014). A bitter cup: climate change profile of global production of Arabica and Robusta coffee. *Climatic Change, 129*(1–2), 89–101. https://doi.org/10.1007/s10584-014-1306-x

16 World Coffee Research. (2020, March 13). *Study: All Arabica derived from a single ancestral plant.* https://worldcoffeeresearch.org/work/measuring-genetic-diversity-coffea-arabica/study-confirms-all-arabica-coffee-diversity-available-today-derived-single-ancestral-plant/

17   illycaffè. (2018, September 14). *Presentata la prima sequenza del genoma di Coffea arabica completamente disponibile in Open-Access.* https://www.illy.com/it-it/company/store-eventi/press/comunicati-stampa/sequenza-genoma-coffea-arabica

18   Botsman, R. (2019, January 19). *DLD Munich Conference 2019* [Conference]. DLD Conference 2019, Munich, Germany. https://www.youtube.com/watch?v=-vbPXbm8eTw

19   Rooney, K. (2018, October 11). *After the crisis, a new generation puts its trust in tech over traditional banks.* CNBC. https://www.cnbc.com/2018/09/14/a-new-generation-puts-its-trust-in-tech-over-traditional-banks.html

20   N26. (2021, January 28). *N26 celebrates 7 million customers globally.* https://n26.com/en-us/press/press-release/n26-celebrates-7-million-customers-globally

21   N26. (2020, June 9). *The Big Banking Chat: answering common banking questions.* https://n26.com/en-eu/blog/the-big-banking-chat-answering-common-banking-questions

22   N26. (2021). *Split expenses the easy way with Split the Bill.* https://n26.com/en-eu/split-the-bill

23   N26. (n.d.). *The Big Banking Chat: answering your banking questions.* Retrieved 6 September, 2021, from https://n26.com/en-eu/the-big-banking-chat

24   Thompson, B. (2018, April 12). *Ryanair: Low Prices + Unhappy Customers = CX Success Story?* CustomerThink. https://customerthink.com/ryanair-can-low-prices-plus-unhappy-customers-equal-cx-success-story/

25   Forrester. (2021, May 13). *Forrester: Brand Loyalty Is Up For Grabs As Consumer Trust Wanes In Traditional Institutions.* https://go.forrester.com/press-newsroom/forrester-brand-loyalty-is-up-for-grabs-as-consumer-trust-wanes-in-traditional-institutions/

26   Stolfo, S. (2021, March 1). *Make Room For The Chief Trust Officer In The C-Suite.* Forbes. https://www.forbes.com/sites/forbestech-council/2021/03/02/make-room-for-the-chief-trust-officer-in-the-c-suite/?sh=3d0fd70d1d6a

CHAPTER 6

1   Goodreads. (n.d.). *A quote by Albert Einstein.* https://www.goodreads.com/quotes/44156-the-human-spirit-must-prevail-over-technology

2   Brooke, C. (2009, September 16). 'I was only following satnav orders' is no defence. Driver who ended up teetering on cliff edge convicted of careless driving. *Mail Online.* https://www.dailymail.co.uk/news/article-1213891/Driver-ended-teetering-cliff-edge-guilty-blindly-following-sat-nav-directions.html

3   Blandino, G. (n.d.). *RACHEL BOTSMAN: "The issue of trust does not lie in the technology, it lies in the culture."* Innovatrics. Retrieved 7 September, 2021, from https://trustreport.innovatrics.com/rachel-botsmanthe-issue-of-trust-does-not-lie-in-the-technology-it-lies-in-the-culture/

4   IBM. (2020, June 3). *Artificial Intelligence (AI).* https://www.ibm.com/
    cloud/learn/what-is-artificial-intelligence#:%7E:text=Artificial%20
    intelligence%20leverages%20computers%20and,capabilities%20of%20
    the%20human%20mind.

5   Casey, K. (2020, November 19). *How to explain machine learning in
    plain English.* The Enterprisers Project. https://enterprisersproject.com/
    article/2019/7/machine-learning-explained-plain-english

6   Harvard Business Review Analytic Services. (2018*). Pulse Survey: Scaling
    Human Interaction in Customer Experiences.* https://s3.amazonaws.com/
    media.mediapost.com/uploads/HBRon24.pdf

7   Vidili, I. (2021, February 16). *How to Reduce Tech-Related Stress for
    Customers and Employees.* Entrepreneur. https://www.entrepreneur.com/
    article/364528

8   Parker, B. (2019, May 22). *Find The Human-Technology Balance To
    Champion Your Customers.* Forbes. https://www.forbes.com/sites/forbes-
    financecouncil/2019/05/22/find-the-human-technology-balance-to-
    champion-your-customers/?sh=30b34b2439a6

9   Joyce, C., Fisher, J., Guszcza, J., & Hogan, S. K. (2018, April 16). *Positive
    technology: Designing work environments for digital well-being.* Deloitte
    Insights. https://www2.deloitte.com/us/en/insights/focus/behavioral-
    economics/negative-impact-technology-business.html?id=us:2el:3lk:4di_
    gl:5eng:6di&range=0/3/11/3/1/3/39/26/0:0,0/0/1/3/11/3/1/3/39/26/0:1

10   Business Wire. (2017, September 18). *Information and App Overload Hurts Worker Productivity, Focus and Morale Worldwide, According to New Independent Survey.* https://www.businesswire.com/news/home/20170918005033/en/Information-App-Overload-Hurts-Worker-Productivity-Focus

11   Hamel, G., & Zanini, M. (2020). *Humanocracy: Creating Organizations as Amazing as the People Inside Them.* Harvard Business Review Press.

12   Büchel, B., & Floreano, D. (2018, May 2). *Tesla's problem: overestimating automation, underestimating humans.* The Conversation. https://theconversation.com/teslas-problem-overestimating-automation-underestimating-humans-95388

13   Shastri, A. (2020, August 6). *Preserve Innovation And Empathy As You Automate.* Forbes. https://www.forbes.com/sites/arunshastri/2020/08/06/preserve-innovation-and-empathy-as-you-automate/?sh=5c9638fe6045

14   Wheless, J., & Mithel, N. (n.d.). *Using Advanced Technologies to Deliver an Uncommon Customer Experience Every Day.* Tata Consultancy Services. https://www.tcs.com/perspectives/articles/using-advanced-technologies-to-deliver-an-uncommon-customer-experience-every-day

15   Wilson, J., & Daugherty, P. R. (2018, August). *Collaborative Intelligence: Humans and AI are Joining Forces.* Harvard Business Review. https://hbr.org/2018/07/collaborative-intelligence-humans-and-ai-are-joining-forces

16   Simonite, T. (2018, March 19). *This Call May Be Monitored for Tone and Emotion.* Wired. https://www.wired.com/story/this-call-may-be-monitored-for-tone-and-emotion/

17   Confessore, N. (2018, April 4). Cambridge Analytica and Facebook: The Scandal and the Fallout So Far. *The New York Times*. https://www.nytimes.com/2018/04/04/us/politics/cambridge-analytica-scandal-fallout.html

18   Business & Human Rights Resource Centre. (2020, March 27). *China: Weibo admits to leak of personal data on millions of users*. https://www.business-humanrights.org/en/latest-news/china-weibo-admits-to-leak-of-personal-data-on-millions-of-users/

19   Iyer, B., Getchell, K., & Fleischmann, F. (2018, July 10). *Humanizing Tech May Be the New Competitive Advantage*. MIT Sloan Management Review. https://sloanreview.mit.edu/article/humanizing-tech-may-be-the-new-competitive-advantage/

20   Gallo, A. (2014, October 29). *The Value of Keeping the Right Customers*. Harvard Business Review. https://hbr.org/2014/10/the-value-of-keeping-the-right-customers

21   Reichheld, F. (n.d.). *Prescription for cutting costs*. Bain & Company. https://media.bain.com/Images/BB_Prescription_cutting_costs.pdf

22   Harvard Business Review Analytic Services. (2018). *Pulse Survey: Scaling Human Interaction in Customer Experiences*. https://s3.amazonaws.com/media.mediapost.com/uploads/HBRon24.pdf

23   Kelion, L. (2020, October 5). *Excel: Why using Microsoft's tool caused Covid-19 results to be lost*. BBC News. https://www.bbc.com/news/technology-54423988

24   Landler, M., & Mueller, B. (2020, December 17). In U.K.'s Test and Trace: Now You See 'em, Now You Don't. *The New York Times.* https://www. nytimes.com/2020/10/05/world/europe/uk-testing-johnson-hancock. html

25   Lexology. (2018, January 3). *Is Legacy Technology Affecting your End Customer Experience?* https://www.lexology.com/library/detail. aspx?g=f5d084cc-ab1d-4245-8849-051525cb3ae3

26   Warner, M. R., & Fischer, D. (n.d.). *Detour Act Final.* Scribd. https:// www.scribd.com/document/405606873/Detour-Act-Final

27   Hatmaker, T. (2019, April 9). *Proposed bill would forbid big tech platforms from using dark pattern design.* TechCrunch. https://techcrunch. com/2019/04/09/dark-pattern-bill-senate-warner-detour/?guccounter=1

28   Ma, A., & Canales, K. (2021, May 9). *China's 'social credit' system ranks citizens and punishes them with throttled internet speeds and flight bans if the Communist Party deems them untrustworthy.* Business Insider. https://www.businessinsider.com/china-social-credit-system-punish-ments-and-rewards-explained-2018-4?r=US&IR=T

29   Deepfake. (2021, September 2). In *Wikipedia.* https://en.wikipedia.org/ wiki/Deepfake

30   Lomas, N. (2021, April 21). *Europe lays out plan for risk-based AI rules to boost trust and uptake.* TechCrunch. https://techcrunch. com/2021/04/21/europe-lays-out-plan-for-risk-based-ai-rules-to-boost-trust-and-uptake/

31   MacDonald, D., Shiever, H. R., Rekhelman, N., Raza, R., Gerrard, P., &
      Heacock, D. (2020, July 27). *Human-Centered Design Is More Impor-*
      tant Than Ever. BCG Global. https://www.bcg.com/publications/2020/
      the-importance-of-human-centered-design

32   de Quintanilha, J. [Forrester]. (2021, January 1). *European Predictions*
      2021 Webinar Series [Video]. Forrester. https://go.forrester.com/predic-
      tions/europe-2021-webinar/

33   Berdak, O., Beeson, M., & Deya, L. (2020, November 17). *The European*
      Banking Customer Experience Index, 2020. Forrester. https://www.
      forrester.com/report/The-European-Banking-Customer-Experience-
      Index-2020/RES162655?objectid=RES162655

34   de Quintanilha, J. [Forrester]. (2021, January 1). *European Predictions*
      2021 Webinar Series [Video]. Forrester. https://go.forrester.com/predic-
      tions/europe-2021-webinar/

35   Newman, D. (2018, September 30). *Balancing Customer Experience And*
      Tech: Do You Have Too Much Technology In Your Workplace? Forbes.
      https://www.forbes.com/sites/danielnewman/2018/09/30/balancing-
      customer-experience-and-tech-do-you-have-too-much-technology-in-
      your-workplace/?sh=5859f8a52063

CHAPTER 7

1   Goodreads. (n.d.). *A quote by Pablo Picasso.* https://www.goodreads.com/
     quotes/73121-computers-are-useless-they-can-only-give-you-answers

2   Salesforce. (n.d.). *What Are Customer Expectations, and How Have They*
     Changed? https://www.salesforce.com/resources/articles/customer-
     expectations/?sfdc-redirect=369

3   SmarterHQ. (n.d.). *Millennials: Where they shop, How they shop, Why it matters* [White paper]. Retrieved September 8, 2021, from https://smarterhq.com/millennials-where-they-shop-how-they-shop-why-it-matters

4   Tran, T. (2020, July 21). *The Ultimate Breakdown of Social Video Metrics for Every Platform*. Hootsuite. https://blog.hootsuite.com/social-video-metrics/

5   Zorfas, A., Magids, S., & Leemon, D. (2015, November). *The New Science of Customer Emotions*. Harvard Business Review. https://hbr.org/2015/11/the-new-science-of-customer-emotions

6   Marr, B. (2021, July 2). *How Much Data Is There In the World?* Bernard Marr & Co. https://bernardmarr.com/how-much-data-is-there-in-the-world/

7   Reinsel, D. (2019, November 4). *How You Contribute to Today's Growing DataSphere and Its Enterprise Impact*. IDC. https://blogs.idc.com/2019/11/04/how-you-contribute-to-todays-growing-datasphere-and-its-enterprise-impact/

8   Embee. (n.d.). *6 Industries That Are Most Vulnerable to Digital Disruption*. Retrieved 8 September, 2021, from https://embee.co.in/blog/6-industries-most-vulnerable-to-digital-disruption/

9   Gujral, V., Malik, N., & Taraporevala, Z. (2019, February). *Rewriting the rules: Succeeding in the new retail banking landscape*. McKinsey & Company. https://www.mckinsey.com/~/media/mckinsey/industries/financial%20services/our%20insights/rewriting%20the%20rules%20in%20retail%20banking/rewriting-the-rules-succeeding-in-the-new-retail-banking-landscape.ashx

10   Vidili, I. (2019, June 4). *How much time is left for banks? The lost battle of incumbent Barclays vs agile "neobanks".* The Smarter Crew. https://thesmartercrew.com/customer-experience-in-the-banking-sector/

11   Lauchlan, S. (2021, February 26). *Digital banking - NatWest and HSBC bank on automation and analytics to capitalise on the customer shift online.* Diginomica. https://diginomica.com/digital-banking-natwest-and-hsbc-bank-automation-and-analytics-capitalise-customer-shift-online

12   Salesforce. (n.d.). *What Are Customer Expectations, and How Have They Changed?* https://www.salesforce.com/resources/articles/customer-expectations/?sfdc-redirect=369

13   Matisoff, E. (n.d.). *Why data democratization is crucial to your business.* Business Adobe. Retrieved 8 September, 2021, from https://business.adobe.com/resources/data-democratization-is-crucial-to-your-business.html#:%7E:text=%E2%80%9CData%20democratization%20means%20that%20everybody,the%20gateway%20to%20the%20data.&text=The%20ability%20to%20instantly%20access,translate%20into%20more%20agile%20teams.

14   Parthasarathy, S. (2021, September 16). *What Is Predictive Analytics?* Logi Analytics. https://www.logianalytics.com/predictive-analytics/what-is-predictive-analytics/

15   Edwards, J. (2019, April 11). *7 ways predictive analytics can improve customer experience.* CIO. https://www.cio.com/article/3387640/7-ways-predictive-analytics-can-improve-customer-experience.html

16   Accenture. (2018). *Making it Personal: Why brands must move from communication to conversation for greater personalization.* Pulse Check 2018. https://www.accenture.com/_acnmedia/PDF-77/Accenture-Pulse-Survey.pdf

17   Leviathan, Y., & Matias, Y. (2018, May 8). *Google Duplex: An AI System for Accomplishing Real-World Tasks Over the Phone.* Google AI Blog. https://ai.googleblog.com/2018/05/duplex-ai-system-for-natural-conversation.html

18   Jeff Grubb's Game Mess. (2018, May 8). *Google Duplex: A.I. Assistant Calls Local Businesses To Make Appointments* [Video]. YouTube. https://www.youtube.com/watch?v=D5VN56jQMWM

19   Bergen, M. (2018, May 10). *'Silicon Valley is ethically lost': Google grapples with reaction to its new 'horrifying' and uncanny AI tech.* Financial Post. https://financialpost.com/technology/personal-tech/silicon-valley-is-ethically-lost-google-grapples-with-reaction-to-its-new-horrifying-and-uncanny-ai-tech

20   Feeney, C. (2021, January 28). *What Marketers Should Know About Privacy Regulations: GDPR, CCPA, LGPD, and More.* Modern Marketing Blog. Oracle. https://blogs.oracle.com/marketingcloud/post/what-marketers-should-know-about-privacy-regulations-gdpr-ccpa-lgpd-and-more

21   Blandino, G. (n.d.). *RACHEL BOTSMAN: "The issue of trust does not lie in the technology, it lies in the culture."* Innovatrics. https://trustreport.innovatrics.com/rachel-botsmanthe-issue-of-trust-does-not-lie-in-the-technology-it-lies-in-the-culture/

22   Morey, T., Forbath, T., & Schoop, A. (2015, May). *Customer Data: Designing for Transparency and Trust*. Harvard Business Review. https://hbr.org/2015/05/customer-data-designing-for-transparency-and-trust

23   Kline, K. (2016, September 7). *Here's How Important Brand Transparency Is for Your Business*. Inc. https://www.inc.com/kenny-kline/new-study-reveals-just-how-important-brand-transparency-really-is.html

24   Sirich, S. (2020, March 25). *Data Transparency In The Age Of Privacy Protection*. Forbes. https://www.forbes.com/sites/forbescommunicationscouncil/2020/03/25/data-transparency-in-the-age-of-privacy-protection/?sh=6eb2d6d746b2

25   Marriott, S. (2020, February 18). *How to explain GDPR in plain English*. Plain English Ireland. https://plainenglish.ie/how-to-explain-gdpr-in-plain-english/

26   Lewis, S. (2019, July 9). *Parks Associates: 79% of Consumers are Concerned About Data Security or Privacy Issues*. PR Newswire. https://www.prnewswire.com/news-releases/parks-associates-79-of-consumers-are-concerned-about-data-security-or-privacy-issues-300881440.html

27   Morgan, B. (2020, January 12). *5 Steps To Secure Your Customer Data*. Forbes. https://www.forbes.com/sites/blakemorgan/2020/01/12/5-steps-to-secure-your-customer-data/?sh=3317c5d52df9

28   CoGo. (n.d.). *Built by experts: The CoGo Carbon Footprint tracker*. https://cogo.co/our-carbon-footprint-tracker

29   NatWest. (n.d.). *Love low-carbon living*. https://personal.natwest.com/personal/banking-with-natwest/our-purpose/climate.html

CHAPTER 8

1 Goodreads. *A quote by Leonardo da Vinci.* https://www.goodreads.com/quotes/9010638-simplicity-is-the-ultimate-sophistication-when-once-you-have-tasted

2 Goodwin, T. (2018). *Digital Darwinism: Survival of the Fittest in the Age of Business Disruption (Kogan Page Inspire).* Kogan Page.

3 Van Belleghem, S. (2020). The Offer You Can't Refuse: What If Customers Want More Than Excellent Service? Lannoo Publishers

4 Cambridge English Dictionary. (n.d.). Efficiency. In *cambridge.org. dictionary.* Retrieved 8 September, 2021, from https://dictionary.cambridge.org/dictionary/english/efficiency

5 Van Belleghem, S. (2020). *The Offer You Can't Refuse: What If Customers Want More Than Excellent Service?* Lannoo Publishers.

6 Samuely, A. (n.d.). *Domino's overshadows competition with zero-click mobile ordering, incentivized Instagram game.* Retail Dive. https://www.retaildive.com/ex/mobilecommercedaily/dominos-overshadows-competitors-with-zero-click-mobile-ordering-incentivized-instagram-game

7 Schiffer, J. (2020, January 8). *Customisation is at the centre of L'Oréal's Technology Incubator.* Vogue Business. https://www.voguebusiness.com/beauty/loreals-technology-incubator-customisation

8   Fanderl, H., Matthey, A., Pratsch, S., & Stöber, J. (2019, March 7). *Driving the automotive customer experience toward the age of mobility.* McKinsey & Company. https://www.mckinsey.com/industries/automotive-and-assembly/our-insights/driving-the-automotive-customer-experience-toward-the-age-of-mobility

9   Wired. (2019, December 18). *How Polestar's electric cars are changing an entire industry.* Wired UK. https://www.wired.co.uk/article/bc/polestar-2-volvo

10   Saxena, A. (2020, February 3). *Everything You Need to Know About In-Vehicle Infotainment Systems.* Einfochips. https://www.einfochips.com/blog/everything-you-need-to-know-about-in-vehicle-infotainment-system/

11   Alphabet International. (2020, October 8). *Polestar 2's Android Automotive infotainment system is motoring innovation of the year.* https://www.alphabet.com/en-gb/auto-digest/polestar-2s-android-automotive-infotainment-system-motoring-innovation-year

12   Automotive World. (2021, July 26). *Polestar on course to double market presence and retail footprint in 2021.* https://www.automotiveworld.com/news-releases/polestar-on-course-to-double-market-presence-and-retail-footprint-in-2021/

13   Eliot, L. (2019, August 4). *The Reasons Why Millennials Aren't As Car Crazed As Baby Boomers, And How Self-Driving Cars Fit In.* Forbes. https://www.forbes.com/sites/lanceeliot/2019/08/04/the-reasons-why-millennials-arent-as-car-crazed-as-baby-boomers-and-how-self-driving-cars-fit-in/?sh=43266dea63fc

14   Merchant Savvy. (2020, February). *Global Mobile eCommerce Statistics, Trends & Forecasts (2020)*. https://www.merchantsavvy.co.uk/mobile-ecommerce-statistics/

15   Vu, L. (2021, February 23). *Insights from Trending mCommerce Statistics*. SimiCart. https://www.simicart.com/blog/m-commerce-statistics/

16   Stratta, R. (2021, February). *Ask a researcher: 3 reasons you're losing customers on your mobile site*. Think with Google. https://www.think-withgoogle.com/intl/en-145/marketing-strategies/app-and-mobile/customer-loss-shopping-on-mobile/?utm_medium=social&utm_campaign=thinkwithgoogle&utm_source=linkedin&utm_content=customer-loss-shopping-on-mobile

17   Stratta, R., & Voxlin, D. (2020, September). *5 ways retailers can improve mobile CX and their bottom line*. Think with Google. https://www.think-withgoogle.com/intl/en-cee/marketing-strategies/app-and-mobile/improve-mobile-shopping-cx/

18   Think with Google. (2020, September 17). *Mobile pains & incremental gains*. https://www.thinkwithgoogle.com/_qs/documents/11174/POLAND_REPORT_Mobile_Pains__Incremental_Gains_Retail_2019-2020_Poland_EN.pdf

19   Stratta, R. (2021, February). *Ask a researcher: 3 reasons you're losing customers on your mobile site*. Think with Google. https://www.think-withgoogle.com/intl/en-145/marketing-strategies/app-and-mobile/customer-loss-shopping-on-mobile/?utm_medium=social&utm_campaign=thinkwithgoogle&utm_source=linkedin&utm_content=customer-loss-shopping-on-mobile

20   Monetate. (2018). *The Cross-Device Imperative*. (Monetate Ecommerce Quarterly Report | Q4 2017). Monetate. https://info.monetate.com/rs/092-TQN-434/images/EQ4-2017_The-Cross-Device-Imperative.pdf

21   Council of Europe. (2021, January 28). *Facial recognition: strict regulation is needed to prevent human rights violations.* https://www.coe.int/en/web/human-rights-rule-of-law/-/facial-recognition-strict-regulation-is-needed-to-prevent-human-rights-violations

22   Hotel Technology News. (n.d.). *Vietnamese Hotel Brand Becomes the Latest to Adopt Facial Recognition Technology.* https://hoteltechnologynews.com/2019/04/vietnamese-hotel-brand-becomes-the-latest-to-adopt-facial-recognition-technology/

23   Kaspersky. (n.d.). *What is Facial Recognition – Definition and Explanation.* Retrieved 8 September, 2021, from https://www.kaspersky.com/resource-center/definitions/what-is-facial-recognition

24   Capgemini US. (2020, July 16). *Research: AI in Customer Experience.* https://www.capgemini.com/us-en/news/research-ai-in-customer-experience/

25   Inkbot Design. (2020, April 9). *Zero UI: The End of Screen-based User Interfaces and What it Means For Businesses.* https://inkbotdesign.com/zero-ui/

26   Phillips, T. (2021, January 26). *BNP Paribas to offer biometric payment cards to premier card customers.* NFCW. https://www.nfcw.com/2021/01/26/370345/bnp-paribas-to-offer-biometric-payment-cards-to-premier-card-customers/

27   MacDonald, D., Shiever, H. R., Rekhelman, N., Raza, R., Gerrard, P., &
      Heacock, D. (2020, July 27). *Human-Centered Design Is More Impor-*
      tant Than Ever. BCG Global. https://www.bcg.com/publications/2020/
      the-importance-of-human-centered-design

28   Apple Inc. (n.d.). *Accessibility.* Developer. Retrieved 8 September, 2021,
      from https://developer.apple.com/design/human-interface-guidelines/
      accessibility/overview/introduction/

29   Williams, A. (2021, March 15). *Starbucks to release new large-print*
      and Braille menus this summer amid other accessibility moves. Business
      Insider. https://www.businessinsider.com/starbucks-braille-menus-
      accessibility-retail-coffee-2021-3?IR=T

CHAPTER 9

1   Goodreads. *A quote by Galileo Galilei.* https://www.goodreads.com/
      quotes/64597-all-truths-are-easy-to-understand-once-they-are-discovered

2   Euro-Lifts. (2019, October 21). *The History of the Lift Eleva-*
      tor. https://www.euro-lifts.co.uk/2019/10/21/history-lift-
      elevator/#:%7E:text=The%20earliest%20form%20of%20
      elevators,steel%20lifts%20we%20see%20today.

3   Post, T. (2020, July 26). *What Do Self-Driving Cars and Elevators Have*
      in Common? Medium. https://medium.com/swlh/what-do-self-driving-
      cars-and-elevators-have-in-common-b6816312bdd2

4   Nichols, S. R. (2018). *The Evolution of Elevators: Physical-Human Interface,*
      Digital Interaction, and Megatall Buildings. National Center for Biotechnol-
      ogy Information. https://www.ncbi.nlm.nih.gov/books/NBK481624/

5   Rogers, E. M. (1983). *DIFFUSION OF INNOVATIONS* (3 ed.). The Free Press.

6   Clark, L. (2020, March 26). *Innovation in a Time of Crisis.* Harvard Business Publishing. https://www.harvardbusiness.org/innovation-in-a-time-of-crisis/

7   Halotherapy Solutions. (n.d.). *What is Halotherapy?* Retrieved 8 September, 2021, from https://halotherapysolutions.com/faq/

8   Salesforce UK. (2020, June 30). *What is Customer Journey Mapping & Why is it Important?* https://www.salesforce.com/uk/blog/2016/03/customer-journey-mapping-explained.html#:%7E:text=Customer%20journey%20mapping%20(also%20called,business%20from%20the%20customer's%20perspective.

9   Gupta, S. (2020, October 1). *Are You Really Innovating Around Your Customers' Needs?* Harvard Business Review. https://hbr-org.cdn.ampproject.org/c/s/hbr.org/amp/2020/10/are-you-really-innovating-around-your-customers-needs

10   Roof, K. (2017, August 2). *Booster raises $20 million to fill your car at work.* TechCrunch. https://techcrunch.com/2017/08/01/booster-raises-20-million-to-fill-your-car-at-work/

11   Booster. (n.d.). *We reinvented a cleaner fuel delivery service to bring the energy directly from source to vehicle.* Retrieved 8 September, 2021, from https://boosterusa.com/how-it-works/

12   Tricks, H. (2021, March 11). *The return of one-to-one commerce.* The Economist. https://www.economist.com/special-report/2021/03/11/the-return-of-one-to-one-commerce

13   Walton, C. (2020, August 26). *3 Reasons To Love Nike's Reported Decision To Cut Ties With Wholesalers*. Forbes. https://www.forbes.com/sites/christopherwalton/2020/08/26/3-reasons-to-love-nikes-reported-decision-to-cut-ties-with-wholesalers/?sh=1b0942d55184

14   Wassel, B. (2021, March 29). *Reports: Nike Cutting Ties With Six Retailers, Including DSW and Urban Outfitters*. Retail TouchPoints. https://retailtouchpoints.com/features/news-briefs/reports-nike-cutting-ties-with-six-retailers-including-dsw-and-urban-outfitters

15   Peterson, H. (2020, August 25). *Nike is expected to cut ties with Zappos, Belk, Dillards and 6 other retailers as the footwear giant doubles down on digital*. Business Insider. https://www.businessinsider.com/nike-cuts-ties-with-zappos-belk-dillards-and-others-report-2020-8?IR=T

16   Business of Fashion. (n.d.). *Inside Nike's Radical Direct-to-Consumer Strategy*. Retrieved 8 September, 2021, from https://www.businessoffashion.com/education/courses/case-study-nike-direct-to-consumer-sportswear-mark

17   Tricks, H. (2021, March 11). *The return of one-to-one commerce*. The Economist. https://www.economist.com/special-report/2021/03/11/the-return-of-one-to-one-commerce

18   The Economist. (2021, March 11). *Welcome to democratised retail*. https://www.economist.com/special-report/2021/03/11/welcome-to-democratised-retail

19   Khoury, K. (2020, August 12). *Retailer's social shopping experience blends digital and physical worlds*. Springwise. https://www.springwise.com/innovation/retail/burberry-tencent-wechat-shop

20   Colameo, L. (2020, December 22). *An Inside Look at Digital Innovation at The Estée Lauder Companies.* Perfect Corp. https://www.perfectcorp.com/business/blog/success-story/an-inside-look-at-digital-innovation-at-the-estee-lauder-companies

21   Shacknai, G. (2021, January 11). *A.I. in the beauty industry: How the pandemic finally made consumers care about it.* Fortune. https://fortune.com/2021/01/11/ai-artificial-intelligence-personalized-beauty-cosmetics-brainstorm-reinvent/?cid=other-eml-onp-mip-mck&hlkid=2f107d1623184328a8ffd47159663849&hctky=11340839&hdpid=6d142ecbc63c-4e3f-be6c-11107cc00c61

22   Freitag. (n.d.). *MAKE YOUR OWN F719 MEL AT GRÜNGASSE.* https://www.freitag.ch/en/kyoto

23   Becoming with BDC. (n.d.). *Farfetch launches its "Store of the Future".* Retrieved 8 September, 2021, from https://www.bdc-retail.com/uk/farfetch-store-of-the-future/

24   Segran, E. (2021, April 1). *The exhilarating world of post-pandemic shopping.* Fast Company. https://www.fastcompany.com/90587325/the-exhilarating-world-of-post-pandemic-shopping?cid=other-eml-onp-mip-mck&hlkid=5ca3632cb38d4ae7b43f3b06177f4c9a&hctky=11340839&hdpid=10272f61-68e5-41c3-ae7d-3200eb2355f5

25   The Economist. (2021, March 13). *21st-century consumers will change capitalism for the better.* https://www.economist.com/leaders/2021/03/13/21st-century-consumers-will-change-capitalism-for-the-better

26   Segal, T. (2021, May 31). *Enron Scandal: The Fall of a Wall Street Darling.* Investopedia. https://www.investopedia.com/updates/enron-scandal-summary/

27   Bryant, B. (2011, April 20). *Deepwater Horizon and the Gulf oil spill - the key questions answered*. The Guardian. https://www.theguardian.com/environment/2011/apr/20/deepwater-horizon-key-questions-answered

28   Rapier, R. (2020, June 20). *Fossil Fuels Still Supply 84 Percent Of World Energy — And Other Eye Openers From BP's Annual Review*. Forbes. https://www.forbes.com/sites/rrapier/2020/06/20/bp-review-new-highs-in-global-energy-consumption-and-carbon-emissions-in-2019/?sh=26651b1a66a1

29   Ritchie, H., & Roser, M. (n.d.). *Emissions by sector*. Our World in Data. Retrieved 8 September, 2021, from https://ourworldindata.org/emissions-by-sector#sector-by-sector-where-do-global-greenhouse-gas-emissions-come-from

30   Schenker, J. L. (n.d.). *How Enel Is Powering Change*. Medium. Retrieved 8 September, 2021, from https://innovator.news/how-enel-is-powering-change-a8278c515f0f

31   Ellen MacArthur Foundation. (n.d.). *The Circular Economy In Detail*. Retrieved 8 September, 2021, from https://archive.ellenmacarthurfoundation.org/explore/the-circular-economy-in-detail

32   Ellen MacArthur Foundation. (n.d.). *What is a circular economy?* Retrieved 8 September, 2021, from https://ellenmacarthurfoundation.org/topics/circular-economy-introduction/overview

33   Enel. (n.d.). *Innovation Hubs*. Retrieved 8 September, 2021, from https://startup.enel.com/en/innovation-hub.html

34 Enel X. (2020, January 23). *JuiceAbility, la ricarica a portata di tutti: Enel X presenta al CES 2020 la soluzione per ricaricare sedie a ruote elettriche.* https://www.enelx.com/it/it/news/2020/01/juice-ability-ricarica-sedia-ruote-elettriche

35 https://www.anglat.it/tmpl/3/index.php

36 Enel X. (n.d.). *JuicePass.* Retrieved 8 September, 2021, from https://www.enelx.com/it/it/privati/mobilita-elettrica/juicepass

37 Wylie-Harris, M. (2018, March 13). *Co-creation: The Future For Brands – Part 1.* Research World. https://www.researchworld.com/co-creation-the-future-for-brands-part-1/

38 The Economist. (2020, November 28). *How Enel became Europe's climate centurion.* https://amp.economist.com/business/2020/11/28/how-enel-became-europes-climate-centurion

CHAPTER 10

1 The Catholic Thing. (2017, June 20). *Do not wander far.* https://www.thecatholicthing.org/2017/06/20/do-not-wander-far/

2 Dharma. (2021, September 4). In *Wikipedia.* https://en.wikipedia.org/wiki/Dharma

3 Merriam-Webster. (n.d.). Soul-searching. In *Merriam-Webster.com dictionary.* Retrieved 9 September, 2021, from https://www.merriam-webster.com/dictionary/soul-searching

4   The Editors of Encyclopaedia Britannica. (n.d.). *soul*. Encyclopaedia
    Britannica. Retrieved 9 September, 2021, from https://www.britannica.
    com/topic/soul-religion-and-philosophy

5   Copleston, F. (1950). *A History of Philosophy. Volume II: Medieval Philos-
    ophy, Augustine to Scotus*. Newman Press.

6   Hannegan, OSB, J. (2015, August 9). *How Augustine Made Us More than
    Matter—and Immortal*. Homiletic & Pastoral Review. https://www.hprweb.
    com/2015/08/how-augustine-made-us-more-than-matter-and-immortal/

7   Groysberg, B., Lee, J., Price, J., & Yo-Jud Cheng, J. (2018, January). *The
    Leader's Guide to Corporate Culture*. Harvard Business Review. https://
    hbr.org/2018/01/the-leaders-guide-to-corporate-culture

8   Schinkel, C. (2017, September 25). *Take your Culture Off Cruise Control*.
    CPHR. https://www.cphrmb.ca/news/367293/Take-your-Culture-Off-
    Cruise-Control.htm

9   Explorable. (2010, July 8). *Chameleon Effect*. https://explorable.com/
    chameleon-effect

10 Deloitte University Press. (2016). *Global Human Capital Trends 2016*.
    Deloitte. https://www2.deloitte.com/content/dam/Deloitte/global/
    Documents/HumanCapital/gx-dup-global-human-capital-trends-2016.pdf

11 5W. (n.d.). *Consumer Culture | 5W Public Relations Report* https://
    www.5wpr.com/new/research/consumer-culture-report/

12 Business Wire. (2016, April 7). *Better Quality of Work Life is Worth a
    $7,600 Pay Cut for Millennials*. https://www.businesswire.com/news/
    home/20160407005736/en/Quality-Work-Life-Worth-7600-Pay-Cut

13   Joly, H., & Lambert, C. (2021). *The Heart of Business: Leadership Principles for the Next Era of Capitalism* (pp. 77–78). Harvard Business Review Press.

14   Joly, H., & Lambert, C. (2021). *The Heart of Business: Leadership Principles for the Next Era of Capitalism* (p. 49). Harvard Business Review Press.

15   Joly, H. [Harvard Business Review]. (2021, June 14). *A New Leadership Model for the Future of Business and Work* [Video]. Harvard Business Review. https://hbr.org/webinar/2021/06/a-new-leadership-model-for-the-future-of-business-and-work

16   Joly, H., & Lambert, C. (2021). *The Heart of Business: Leadership Principles for the Next Era of Capitalism* (pp. 140–141). Harvard Business Review Press.

17   https://deniseleeyohn.com/fusion/

18   Disney Institute. (2019, February 19). *Disney Customer Service 101: Why Courtesy Is Not Always Our First Priority*. https://www.disneyinstitute.com/blog/disney-customer-service-101-why-courtesy-is-not-always-our-first-priority/

19   Kramer, M. (2020, May 29). *Creating shared value to tackle climate change*. Enel Group. hhttps://www.enel.com/company/stories/articles/2020/05/creating-shared-value-climate-change

20   Carlisi, C., Hemerling, J., Kilmann, J., Meese, D., & Shipman, D. (2017, May 15). *Purpose with the Power to Transform Your Organization*. BCG Global. https://www.bcg.com/publications/2017/transformation-behavior-culture-purpose-power-transform-organization

21 Enel Group. (n.d.). *Working with United Nations and building a sustainable business model.* Retrieved 9 September, 2021, from https://www.enel.com/company/our-commitment/sdg-onu

22 Enel Green Power Chile. (n.d.). *Cerro Pabellón Geothermal Power Plant.* Retrieved 9 September, 2021, from https://www.enel.cl/en/meet-enel/chiles-energy-is-transforming/cerro-pabellon-geothermal-power-plant.html

23 Blanco, C., Metzner, M., & Stroehle, J. (2021, March). *Pathways to Purposeful Transformation through Shared Value and Innovation: An Economics of Mutuality Case Study.* Saïd Business School. https://www.sbs.ox.ac.uk/sites/default/files/2021-04/Enel-Case-Study.pdf

24 Shared Value Initiative. (n.d.). *Enel: Redefining the Value Chain.* Retrieved 9 September, 2021, from https://www.sharedvalue.org/resource/enel-redefining-the-value-chain/

25 The Economist. (2020, November 28). *How Enel became Europe's climate centurion.* https://amp.economist.com/business/2020/11/28/how-enel-became-europes-climate-centurion

26 Enel Group. (n.d.). *Commitment to the fight against climate change.* Retrieved 9 September, 2021, from https://integratedreporting2020.enel.com/sites/enelar20/files/allegati/dc/eng/sustainability-report_2020.pdf#page=22

27 Schenker, J. L. (n.d.). *How Enel Is Powering Change.* Medium. Retrieved 8 September, 2021, from https://innovator.news/how-enel-is-powering-change-a8278c515f0f

28   Collins, J., & Porras, J. I. (1996, September). *Building Your Company's Vision*. Harvard Business Review. https://hbr.org/1996/09/building-your-companys-vision?utm_medium=email&utm_source=circ_other&utm_campaign=subbenemail_20210523&hideIntromercial=true&tpcc=subbenemail&deliveryName=DM133553

CHAPTER 11

1   Goodreads. (n.d.). *A quote by The Dalai Lama.* https://www.goodreads.com/quotes/1295390-give-the-ones-you-love-wings-to-fly-roots-to

2   Joly, H., & Lambert, C. (2021). The Heart of Business: Leadership Principles for the Next Era of Capitalism (p. 77). Harvard Business Review Press.

3   Fink, L. (n.d.). *Larry Fink's 2019 Letter to CEOs.* BlackRock. Retrieved 9 September, 2021, from https://www.blackrock.com/corporate/investor-relations/2019-larry-fink-ceo-letter

4   Gartenberg, C., & Serafeim, G. (2019, August 20). *181 Top CEOs Have Realized Companies Need a Purpose Beyond Profit.* Harvard Business Review. https://hbr.org/2019/08/181-top-ceos-have-realized-companies-need-a-purpose-beyond-profit

5   Serafeim, G., & Gartenberg, C. (2016, October 21). *The Type of Purpose That Makes Companies More Profitable.* Harvard Business Review. https://hbr.org/2016/10/the-type-of-purpose-that-makes-companies-more-profitable

6   Harvard Business Review Analytic Services. (2020). *A Winning Approach to Employee Success.* Quantum Workplace. https://marketing.quantumworkplace.com/hubfs/A-Winning-Approach-to-Employee-Success-HBRAS-QW.pdf?hsCtaTracking=7d2e3059-bb06-405b-89ef-e519eaa2aa07%7C8efba980-f5de-44a4-a73e-3323920f928e

7   Wigert, B., Agrawal, S., Barry, K., & Maese, E. (2021, March 13). *The Wellbeing-Engagement Paradox of 2020*. Gallup. https://www.gallup.com/workplace/336941/wellbeing-engagement-paradox-2020.aspx

8   Ryba, K. (2021, March 2). *What is Employee Engagement? What, Why, and How to Improve It*. Quantum Workplace. https://www.quantum-workplace.com/future-of-work/what-is-employee-engagement-definition#:%7E:text=Employee%20engagement%20definition,their%20teams%2C%20and%20their%20organization.

9   Gallup. (n.d.). *What Is Employee Engagement and How Do You Improve It?*. Gallup. Retrieved 9 September, 2021, from https://www.gallup.com/workplace/285674/improve-employee-engagement-workplace.aspx

10   McGregor, L., & Doshi, N. (2015, November 25). *How Company Culture Shapes Employee Motivation*. Harvard Business Review. https://hbr.org/2015/11/how-company-culture-shapes-employee-motivation

11   Wharton School. (2011, March 30). *The Problem with Financial Incentives — and What to Do About It*. Knowledge@Wharton. https://knowledge.wharton.upenn.edu/article/the-problem-with-financial-incentives-and-what-to-do-about-it/

12   Sarma, S. (2021, July 28).*5 Factors That Restore The Power Of Intrinsic Motivation In The Workplace*. Vantage Circle. https://blog.vantagecircle.com/intrinsic-motivation-in-the-workplace/

13   O'Hara, D. (2017, December 18). *The intrinsic motivation of Richard Ryan and Edward Deci*. American Psychological Association. https://www.apa.org/members/content/intrinsic-motivation

14   Sutton, J. (2021, August 18). *Intrinsic Motivation in the Workplace: 5 Techniques to Motivate Employees*. Positive Psychology. https://positive-psychology.com/intrinsic-motivation-in-the-workplace/

15   Royal Dutch Airlines. (2019). *KLM Annual Report 2019*. https://img.static-kl.com/m/65c2d45449a35d2e/original/KLM-2019-Annual-Report.pdf

16   KLM. (2015). *Moving Your World: Our KLM story*. https://www.typeset-ter.nl/wp-content/uploads/2017/05/Voorbeeld-zetwerk-Engels.pdf

17   Hunt, V., Layton, D., & Prince, S. (2015, January 1). *Why diversity matters*. McKinsey & Company. https://www.mckinsey.com/business-functions/organization/our-insights/why-diversity-matters

18   KLM. (2019, March 8). *KLM striving for more women in leading positions*. https://news.klm.com/klm-striving-for-more-women-in-leading-positions/

19   Air France-KLM. (n.d.). *DIVERSITY AND INCLUSION*. Retrieved 9 September, 2021, from http://airfranceklm20.wpengine.com/en/english-diversity-and-inclusion/

20   van Rijn, N. (2019, August 15). *Journey of Progress: fifty years after Stonewall*. KLM Blog. https://blog.klm.com/journey-progress-fifty-years-stonewall/

21   KLM. (2019, April 4). *KLM most attractive employer and Travellers' Choice Major Airline*. https://news.klm.com/klm-most-attractive-employer-and-and-travellers-choice-major-airline/#:~:text=KLM%20Royal%20Dutch%20Airlines%20today,annual%20Randstad%20Employer%20Brand%20Research.

22   Brap. (2020, June 15). *Race fluency.* https://www.brap.org.uk/post/race-fluency

23   Wharton School. (2011, March 30). *The Problem with Financial Incentives — and What to Do About It.* Knowledge@Wharton. https://knowledge.wharton.upenn.edu/article/the-problem-with-financial-incentives-and-what-to-do-about-it/

24   Deloitte. (2021). *The Deloitte Global 2021 Millennial and Gen Z Survey.* https://www2.deloitte.com/global/en/pages/about-deloitte/articles/millennialsurvey.html

25   Godin, S. (2020, June 13). *Krulak's law.* Seth's Blog. https://seths.blog/2020/06/krulaks-law/

26   Gallup. (n.d.). *What Is Employee Engagement and How Do You Improve It?* Gallup. Retrieved 9 September, 2021, from https://www.gallup.com/workplace/285674/improve-employee-engagement-workplace.aspx

27   Pink, D. H. (2009). *Drive: The Surprising Truth About What Motivates Us.* Riverhead Books.

28   Ritz-Carlton Leadership Center. (2019, March 19). *The Power of Empowerment.* https://ritzcarltonleadershipcenter.com/2019/03/19/the-power-of-empowerment/

29   Karasek, Jr., R. A. (1979). Job Demands, Job Decision Latitude, and Mental Strain: Implications for Job Redesign. *Administrative Science Quarterly*, 24(2), 285–308. https://doi.org/10.2307/2392498

30   Peek, S. (2021, August 31). *Do Results-Only Workplaces Really Work?* business.com. https://www.business.com/articles/do-results-only-workplaces-really-work/

31   Joly, H., & Lambert, C. (2021). *The Heart of Business: Leadership Principles for the Next Era of Capitalism* (pp. 179). Harvard Business Review Press.

32   Wharton School. (2011, March 30). *The Problem with Financial Incentives — and What to Do About It.* Knowledge@Wharton. https://knowledge.wharton.upenn.edu/article/the-problem-with-financial-incentives-and-what-to-do-about-it/

33   Deloitte. (2015, January 27). *Becoming irresistible: A new model for employee engagement.* Deloitte Insights. https://www2.deloitte.com/us/en/insights/deloitte-review/issue-16/employee-engagement-strategies.html

34   Glassdoor. (n.d.). *Best Places to Work UK.* Retrieved 9 September, 2021, from https://www.glassdoor.co.uk/Award/Best-Places-to-Work-UK-LST_KQ0,22.htm

35   Vidili, I. (2021, February 16). *How to Reduce Tech-Related Stress for Customers and Employees.* Entrepreneur. https://www.entrepreneur.com/article/364528

36   Mendoza, N. F. (2020, October 19). *IBM report: Employees say they have a lack of skills, support, and transparency.* TechRepublic. https://www.techrepublic.com/article/ibm-report-employees-say-they-have-a-lack-of-skills-support-and-transparency/

37   Vidili, I. (2021, February 16). *How to Reduce Tech-Related Stress for Customers and Employees.* Entrepreneur. https://www.entrepreneur.com/article/364528

38   Lee Yohn, D. (2018, October 2). *6 Ways to Build a Customer-Centric Culture.* Harvard Business Review. https://hbr.org/2018/10/6-ways-to-build-a-customer-centric-culture

39   Medallia. (n.d.). *The Business Case for a Customer-Centric Culture.*
Retrieved 9 September, 2021, from https://www.medallia.com/resource/
business-case-customer-centric-culture/

40   Keller, S. (2017, November 24). *Attracting and retaining the right talent.*
McKinsey & Company. https://www.mckinsey.com/business-functions/
organization/our-insights/attracting-and-retaining-the-right-talent

41   Catayst. (2020, April 16). *Turnover and Retention (Quick Take).*
Catalyst. https://www.catalyst.org/research/turnover-and-
retention/#:%7E:text=In%202019%2C%20the%20total%20
quits,%2C%20when%20it%20was%2023.7%25.&text=A%20negative%20
workplace%20culture%20can,responsible%20for%20setting%20the%20
tone.

42   Upwork. (2019, October 3). Sixth annual "Freelancing in America" study
finds that more people than ever see freelancing as a long-term career path.
https://www.upwork.com/press/releases/freelancing-in-america-2019

43   Work Institute. (2019). *2019 Retention Report: Trends, Reasons, & A Call to
Action.* http://info.workinstitute.com/retentionreport2019

44   Edelman. (2020). *Special report: Brand trust in 2020.* 2019 Edelman Trust
Barometer Special Report: In Brands We Trust? https://www.edelman.
com/sites/g/files/aatuss191/files/2020-06/2020%20Edelman%20Trust%20
Barometer%20Specl%20Rept%20Brand%20Trust%20in%202020.pdf

45   Deloitte. (2021a). *A call for accountability and action: The Deloitte Global
2021 Millennial And Gen Z Survey.* https://www2.deloitte.com/content/
dam/Deloitte/global/Documents/2021-deloitte-global-millennial-survey-
report.pdf

CHAPTER 12

1   Goodreads. A quote by Niccolò Machiavelli. https://www.goodreads.com/quotes/9777550-it-should-be-borne-in-mind-that-there-is-nothing

2   Fleming, A. (2020, April 5). *The secret life of plants: how they memorise, communicate, problem solve and socialise.* The Guardian. https://www.theguardian.com/environment/2020/apr/05/smarty-plants-are-our-vegetable-cousins-more-intelligent-than-we-realise

3   Nicola, L. (2020, April 5). *Homo sapiens have to learn from plants | IBSA Foundation.* IBSA Foundation. https://www.ibsafoundation.org/en/blog/homo-sapiens-have-to-learn-from-plants

4   TEDx [TEDx Talks]. (2015, March 4). *Are plants conscious?* [Video]. YouTube. https://www.youtube.com/watch?v=gBGt5OeAQFk

5   Nicola, L. (2019, July 9). *The fascinating secret life of plants | IBSA Foundation.* IBSA Foundation. https://www.ibsafoundation.org/en/blog/the-fascinating-secret-life-of-plants

6   Hamel, G., & Zanini, M. (2020). *Humanocracy: Creating Organizations as Amazing as the People Inside Them.* Harvard Business Review Press.

7   Minnaar, J. (n.d.). *Destroy The Hierarchical Pyramid And Build A Powerful Network of Teams.* Corporate Rebels. Retrieved 10 September, 2021, from https://corporate-rebels.com/rebel-trends-2-network-of-teams/

8   McChrystal, S., Collins, T., Silverman, D., & Fussell, C. (2015). *Team of Teams: New Rules of Engagement for a Complex World.* Portfolio.

9   Lynch, S. (2018, October 19). *Team of Teams. Business lessons from an Army General.* LinkedIn. https://www.linkedin.com/pulse/team-teams-business-lessons-from-army-general-stephen-lynch/

10   BBC. (n.d.). *Dunbar's number: Why we can only maintain 150 relation-ships.* BBC Future. Retrieved 10 September, 2021, from https://www.bbc.com/future/article/20191001-dunbars-number-why-we-can-only-maintain-150-relationships

11   Kniberg, H. [Henrik Kniberg]. (2019, July 30). *Spotify Engineering Culture - Part 1* [Video]. YouTube. https://www.youtube.com/watch?v=Yvfz4HGtoPc

12   Wigert, B., Agrawal, S., Barry, K., & Maese, E. (2021, March 13). *The Wellbeing-Engagement Paradox of 2020.* Gallup. https://www.gallup.com/workplace/336941/wellbeing-engagement-paradox-2020.aspx

13   Giles, S. (2016, March 15). The Most Important Leadership Competencies, According to Leaders Around the World. Harvard Business Review. https://hbr.org/2016/03/the-most-important-leadership-competencies-according-to-leaders-around-the-world

14   Mankins, M., & Garton, E. (2017, February 9). *How Spotify Balances Employee Autonomy and Accountability.* Harvard Business Review. https://hbr.org/2017/02/how-spotify-balances-employee-autonomy-and-accountability

15   Kniberg, H. [Henrik Kniberg]. (2019, July 30). *Spotify Engineering Culture - Part 1* [Video]. YouTube. https://www.youtube.com/watch?v=Yvfz4HGtoPc

16   Stanford Alumni. (2014, October 9). *Developing a Growth Mindset with Carol Dweck* [Video]. YouTube. https://www.youtube.com/watch?v=hiiEeMN7vbQ

17   McKinsey & Company. (2020, February 18). *Have you made it safe to fail?* https://www.mckinsey.com/business-functions/mckinsey-digital/our-insights/fasttimes/have-you-made-it-safe-to-fail

18   Kniberg, H. [Henrik Kniberg]. (2019, July 30). *Spotify Engineering Culture - Part 2* [Video]. YouTube. https://www.youtube.com/watch?v=vOt4BbWLWQw

19   Ibarra, H., & Scoular, S. (2019, November). *The Leader as Coach*. Harvard Business Review. https://hbr.org/2019/11/the-leader-as-coach

20   Ibarra, H., & Rattan, A. (2018). *Microsoft: instilling a growth mindset.* London Business School Review. https://herminiaibarra.com/wp-content/uploads/2019/07/IBARRA_et_al-2018-London_Business_School_Review.pdf

21   Husband, J., & Chong, I. (2011). Behavior Modeling. In: S. Goldstein, J. A. Naglieri (eds) *Encyclopedia of Child Behavior and Development*, 225–226. Springer https://doi.org/10.1007/978-0-387-79061-9_307

22   Ibarra, H., & Scoular, S. (2019, November). *The Leader as Coach*. Harvard Business Review. https://hbr.org/2019/11/the-leader-as-coach

23   Giles, S. (2016, March 15). *The Most Important Leadership Competencies, According to Leaders Around the World*. Harvard Business Review. https://hbr.org/2016/03/the-most-important-leadership-competencies-according-to-leaders-around-the-world

24   Goleman, D. (1996). *Emotional Intelligence: Why it can matter more than IQ*. Bloomsbury.

25   Goleman, D. (2004, January). *What Makes a Leader?* Harvard Business Review. https://hbr.org/2004/01/what-makes-a-leader?referral=00060

26   Goleman, D. (1998). *What Makes a Leader?* Harvard Business Review. http://fs.ncaa.org/Docs/DIII/What%20Makes%20a%20Leader.pdf

27   Goleman, D. (1996). *Emotional Intelligence: Why it can matter more than IQ*. Bloomsbury.

28   Landry, L. (2019, April 3). Why Emotional Intelligence Is Important in Leadership. Harvard Business School Online. https://online.hbs.edu/blog/post/emotional-intelligence-in-leadership

29   Leading Effectively. (2021, August 31). *What Is Psychological Safety at Work?* Center for Creative Leadership. https://www.ccl.org/articles/leading-effectively-articles/what-is-psychological-safety-at-work/

30   Goleman, D. (2004, January). *What Makes a Leader?* Harvard Business Review. https://hbr.org/2004/01/what-makes-a-leader?referral=00060

31   Chouhan, V. S., & Srivastava, S. (2014). Understanding Competencies and Competency Modeling — A Literature Survey. *IOSR Journal of Business and Management, 16*(1), 14–22. https://doi.org/10.9790/487x-16111422

32   Thompson, J. (2012, February 9). *Jens Hofma: Meet the man who wants to sell a slice of Pizza Hut*. The Independent. https://www.independent.co.uk/news/people/profiles/jens-hofma-meet-man-who-wants-sell-slice-pizza-hut-6673546.html

33   Barsh, J. (2014, September 1). *Can women fix capitalism?* McKinsey & Company. https://www.mckinsey.com/featured-insights/leadership/can-women-fix-capitalism

CHAPTER 13

1   IMDb. (n.d.). *Pinocchio (1940)*. Retrieved 10 September, 2021, from https://www.imdb.com/title/tt0032910/characters/nm0892867

2   Le avventure di Pinocchio. Storia di un burattino. (2021, September 6). In *Wikipedia*. https://it.wikipedia.org/wiki/Le_avventure_di_Pinocchio._Storia_di_un_burattino

3   Martin, R. L. (2010, January). *The Age of Customer Capitalism*. Harvard Business Review. https://hbr.org/2010/01/the-age-of-customer-capitalism

4   Markey, R. (2020, January 1). Are You Undervaluing Your Customers? HBR Store. https://store.hbr.org/product/are-you-undervaluing-your-customers/s20011?sku=S20011-PDF-ENG

5   Markey, R. (2020, January 1). *Are You Undervaluing Your Customers?* HBR Store. https://store.hbr.org/product/are-you-undervaluing-your-customers/s20011?sku=S20011-PDF-ENG

6   McCarthy, D., & Fader, P. (2020, January). *How to Value a Company by Analyzing Its Customers*. Harvard Business Review. https://hbr.org/2020/01/how-to-value-a-company-by-analyzing-its-customers

7   McCarthy, D., Fader, P., & Hardie, B. (2015). Valuing Subscription-Based Businesses Using Publicly Disclosed Customer Data. *SSRN Electronic Journal*. Published. https://doi.org/10.2139/ssrn.2701093

8   McCarthy, D., & Fader, P. (2018). Customer-Based Corporate Valuation for Publicly Traded Non-Contractual Firms. *SSRN Electronic Journal.* Published. https://doi.org/10.2139/ssrn.3040422

9   Theta. (n.d.). *Theta Equity Partners. Customer-Based Corporate Valuation: Revolutionizing Finance* Retrieved 10 September, 2021, from https://thetaclv.com/resources/?_sft_category=cbcv

10   Markey, R. (2019, December 10). *December 10, 2019.* FABS. https://www.fasb.org/cs/BlobServer?blobkey=id&blobnocache=true&blobwhere=1175836085893&blobheader=application%2Fpdf&blobheadername e2=Content-Length&blobheadername1=Content-Disposition&blobheadervalue2=664894&blobheadervalue1=filename%3DAR-2019.UNS.027. BAIN_COMPANY_INC._ROB_MARKEY.pdf&blobcol=urldata&blobtable=MungoBlobs

11   McCarthy, D., & Fader, P. S. (2019, December 16). *December 16, 2019.* FABS. https://www.fasb.org/cs/BlobServer?blobkey=id&blobnocache=true&blobwhere=1175836086174&blobheader=application/pdf&blobheadername2=Content-Length&blobheadername1=Content-Disposition&blobheadervalue2=722799&blobheadervalue1=filename%3DAR-2019.UNS.028.PETER_S._FADER_DANIEL_MCCARTHY.pdf&blobcol=urldata&blobtable=MungoBlobs

12   Plender, J. (2021, April 4). *Stakeholder capitalism must find ways to hold management to account.* Financial Times. https://www.ft.com/content/4eeaa803-511c-4227-962e-018ea1dc2883

13   Sundheim, D., & Starr, K. (2020, January 22). *Making Stakeholder Capitalism a Reality.* Harvard Business Review. https://hbr.org/2020/01/making-stakeholder-capitalism-a-reality

Printed in Great Britain
by Amazon

80859612R00169